Mormon Polygamous Families

The University of Utah Press
is pleased to announce a new series,
PUBLICATIONS IN MORMON STUDIES,
intended to encourage creation and submission
of work on Mormon-related topics
that would be of interest to scholars and the general public.
The Press is also pleased to announce that
Linda King Newell, noted author and editor,
has agreed to accept the position of series editor.
The initiation of the series
represents an acknowledgment by the Press and the editor
of the region's rich historical and literary heritage
and of the quality of work being done
in various areas of Mormon studies today.

Mormon Polygamous Families

Life in the Principle

by

Jessie L. Embry

Foreword by Linda King Newell

Volume One
Publications in Mormon Studies

University of Utah Press
Salt Lake City
1987

Volume One
Publications in Mormon Studies
Linda King Newell, Editor

Library of Congress Cataloging-in-Publication Data

Embry, Jessie L.
    Mormon polygamous families.

    (Publications in Mormon studies; v. 1)
    Bibliography: p.
    Includes index.
    1. Polygamy—History.   2. Mormon Church—History.
3. Family—United States. I. Title. II. Series.
HQ994.E52   1987   306.8'423   87-18991
ISBN 0-87480-277-6

This book is dedicated to
The People interviewed by the Charles Redd Center
LDS Polygamy and LDS Family Life Oral History Projects.

Contents

Tables

Illustrations

Foreword

With this book, *Mormon Polygamous Families* by Jessie Embry, the University of Utah Press initiates a new series, PUBLICATIONS IN MORMON STUDIES. Embry's work draws from both sociology and history to examine the workings of polygamous households in late nineteenth- and early twentieth-century Mormonisn. It helps fill the need for a straightforward, scholarly approach to an era of regional history that has too often been relegated to folklore and myth. This volume taps into a growing body of scholarship in the field of Mormon studies that is of interest both to scholars and to the general public.

The University of Utah Press plans to build on Jessie Embry's solid beginning to attract the work of the best writers and researchers in Mormon studies. Although from time to time the Press has published books in this area, the introduction of the series PUBLICATIONS IN MORMON STUDIES represents a commitment by the editors to mine this rich vein of our region's historical and literary heritage.

The University of Utah Press plans to publish up to four titles a year in this series with the expectation of expanding that number when the availability of qualified manuscripts makes this possible. The University Press Faculty Advisory Committee will make the final selections based on independent peer review of the manuscripts. Those chosen for publication will be the result of scholarly research in the traditional disciplines of sociology, history, biography, autobiography, and fiction, and will reflect the high level of excellence being achieved in the various areas of Mormon studies today. As series editor I anticipate with pleasure the task of identifying promising areas of research, working with the authors, and seeing their work brought into print.

Linda King Newell
Series Editor

Introduction

Almost everyone who has heard of the Church of Jesus Christ of Latter-day Saints (LDS Church) knows of its practice of polygamy. When governor of Utah George D. Clyde and his wife visited South America during the 1950s, a guest at a reception inquired, "I would like to know how many wives you have?" The governor replied with a twinkle in his eye, "I just brought the one with me." When Larry Troutman joined the Church in 1984, his mother asked, "What? The one where they have all the different wives?"[1]

Members of the LDS Church have also had difficulty understanding why the Church practiced polygamy. Many new converts, like Larry Troutman, have never had to deal with the problem. Others who have polygamous ancestors look with pride at their faith, but still struggle to understand why the Church members accepted the practice. As Jonathan Cannon explained, "It is strange that I would feel as monogamous as I feel and yet feel all the love and affection and appreciation of my parents who were polygamists."[2]

Fundamentalist groups whose members have been excommunicated from the LDS Church believe that the Church should have continued the practice of plural marriage. Ervil LeBaron, unofficial spokesman for a polygamous group called the Church of the Firstborn, was convicted of complicity in his brother Joel's murder in 1972, of the 1977 murder of Rulon Allred, the leader of a rival polygamous group, and of conspiring to murder another brother, Verlan. Ron and Don Lafferty, who also led a polygamous group, were convicted of murdering their sister-in-law Brenda and her 15-month-old baby, in 1984. Others, like Royston Potter who was fired from his job as a Murray City policeman or the residents of Colorado City, Arizona, continue to live quietly with several wives.[3]

Non-Mormons, Mormons, and fundamentalists all have their views about how polygamy was practiced in the LDS Church during the late nineteenth and early twentieth centuries. None of their views are completely accurate, however. In order to understand how men and women living a Victorian life-style adapted to polygamy, one needs to examine the participants themselves, which is one of the purposes for this study. It is based on interviews conducted during the 1930s, 1970s, and 1980s with the husbands, wives, and children who lived in Mormon polygamous households.

The 1930 interviews were conducted by James Hulett and Kimball Young and were used in writing Hulett's dissertation "The Sociological and Social Psychological Aspects of the Mormon Polygamous Family" and Young's book *Isn't One Wife Enough?*[4] Through the efforts of Dennis Rowley of the Manuscript Division of the Brigham Young University Harold B. Lee Library and grants from the College of Family, Home, and Social Sciences and the Library at Brigham Young University, xeroxed copies of the notes from their interviews, as well as excerpts from journals and autobiographies, were obtained from the Garrett Theological Seminary at Northwestern University. Notes are available from interviews with 13 husbands, 50 wives, 5 husbands and wives interviewed jointly, and 83 children of polygamous families.

Despite clear biases, Kimball Young's book has been the only major study on polygamy. The title suggests a negative view, but Young found that most of the families he studied were "successful." Without the advantages of recording devices, Hulett and Young had to depend on their own note-taking abilities to remember what their informants told them. Sometimes it is difficult to determine where the opinion of the interviewee or the interviewer is being expressed. In order to protect identities, Young used pseudonyms throughout his study and has no footnotes, so scholars have been unable to identify his sources. Perhaps the most serious flaw though is that the examples Young cites are not representative of even his own sources. After reading his book and the sources, it appears he took the most interesting and most dramatic cases and then used them as "typical" examples and drew generalizations from them.

In 1976, Maud Taylor Bentley, the third wife of Joseph C. Bentley, a former bishop and stake president in Colonia Juarez, a Mormon colony in Chihuahua, Mexico, passed away. Members of the board of the Charles Redd Center for Western Studies at Brigham Young University, recognizing the valuable information she could have given in an oral history interview, encouraged the Redd Center to interview others who lived in polygamous families. From 1976 until 1982, the Redd Center interviewed over 250 children of Church-sanctioned polygamous families. Interviewees were selected by a snowball method. Those interviewed suggested brothers and sisters — full and half — and others they knew who had been raised in polygamous families. Because of the sensitive nature of the topic and the LDS Church's policy not to encourage the current practice of polygamy, not all those contacted agreed to be interviewed. At first, almost half the people refused, but as the project progressed, that number dropped to less than 25 percent. The plan was to interview people whose parents were married before 1904 and whose marriages were Church-sanctioned. Two exceptions were made where plural marriages were performed after 1904.

In 1982, the project expanded to interview children from monogamous families who grew up during the same time period, thus forming a comparison group. Approximately 150 were interviewed. In order to assure a more accurate comparison, the parents of those interviewed had to have been married before 1904. Since many of the polygamous children had been born as late as the 1920s, the monogamous children's birthdate was not a deciding factor, only parents' marriage date. Brigham Young University Public Communications issued a press release that was published in many papers in Utah as well as Arizona and California. A large number of people responded to the request, and time, location, and availability determined who was interviewed. Some efforts were made to interview people who grew up in towns where there were polygamists, and an outline for both sets of interviews was developed based on topics Kimball Young discussed.

The Redd Center interviews also have limitations. All of the interviews are adult memories of childhood and might offer more favorable impressions of polygamy, since people usually like to remember and report positive elements of their past. In addition, children only have a limited knowledge of parental activities. Especially in the nineteenth century, they were not told about their parents' sexual activities, and they were probably not aware of all the family's economic and religious activities. In the case of polygamy, they would not have been told all the reasons why their parents chose to marry in polygamy. Despite these limitations, however, the interviews provide valuable data, in some cases the only source of information about how plural families were set up. The children report on their relationships with their parents and their fathers' other wives and how they saw the families operate.

The Redd Center oral history interviews and the Kimball Young Collection at the Brigham Young University Library provided the bulk of information for this study. Diaries, autobiographies, and interviews available in the Archives of the Historical Department of the Church of Jesus Christ of Latter-day Saints and the Brigham Young University Manuscript Collections were also used. Since all the sources did not contain the same information, the totals used in the statistical sections are not always the same. However, the lives of approximately 200 plural husbands and 400 plural wives and 150 monogamous husbands and wives were used.

A different picture of the Mormon polygamous family emerges from the interviews than the stereotypical oppressed plural wife, the first wife who was dropped for a younger bride, or the emancipated woman who could "do her own thing" because she had co-wives to help care for their husband and her children. When carefully examined, most of these stereotypes do not hold true. Rather, Mormon polygamous families were not much different than Mormon monogamous families and other non-Mormon families of the same era. The Mormons simply adapted Victorian ideology to fit their new polygamous life-style. Since polygamy was practiced for such a short time in the LDS Church, these adaptions varied from family to family, making it impossible to describe the typical Mormon polygamous family. Understanding the diverse experiences of individual families is an antidote for oversimplified conclusions and stereotypes.

An examination of the practice of polygamy is essential to fully understand Mormonism historically. To gain a complete insight into the practice, however, one needs to look beyond the revelation and the laws that were passed against polygamy to the motives, beliefs, perceptions, and experiences of those who were part of polygamous families.

Technically, polygamy means the practice of having more than one spouse at the same time. Polyandry refers to having more than one husband; polygyny means having more than one wife. The Mormons, however, used the general term of polygamy to define their practice or other terms such as the principle, plural marriage, or celestial marriage. Therefore, I refer to the Mormon practice in terms they would have used. The Church of Jesus Christ of Latter-day Saints is usually referred to as "the Church" or "the LDS Church" with its members referred to as "Latter-day Saints" or "Mormons."

A number of people made this book possible. The College of Family, Home, and Social Sciences gave the Redd Center research grants to complete the interviews, and Amy Bentley, Tillman Boxell, Rochelle Fairbourn, Leonard Grover, Stevan Martin Hales, Marsha Martin, Chris Nelson, Laurel Schmidt, and Gary Shumway helped in conducting interviews, each bringing their unique personalities to benefit the project. This book is dedicated to the interviewees who spent from one to three hours discussing their experiences in LDS polygamous families. Typists at the Redd Center transcribed and retyped the interviews, spending long hours over typewriters and computers. Natalie Ethington and Kristine Judd Ireland especially helped by organizing the numerous research cards I produced. I would especially like to thank Thomas G. Alexander, the director of the Charles Redd Center, for his support and encouragement of the oral history project and this writing endeavor. My sister, Janet Embry, helped me edit the manuscript. Then with a grant from the Women's Research Institute at Brigham Young University, I was able to hire Lavina Fielding Anderson of Editing, Inc., in Salt Lake City to help in the editing process. Thomas G. Alexander, Kenneth L. Cannon II, Lowell "Ben" Bennion, Martha S. Bradley, and Natalie Ethington also read parts or all the manuscript and offered valuable suggestions.

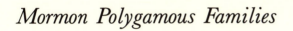

Mormon Polygamous Families

1

The Practice of Polygamy Worldwide and Among the Latter-day Saints

Although polygyny, the marital pattern of one husband and several wives, was a practice peculiar to nineteenth-century Mormons in the United States, it was not their unique invention. Old Testament patriarchs had plural wives, and many societies throughout the world still practice polygyny. Many are not aware that some of the Protestant reformers such as Martin Luther saw polygamy as a possibility and that the Catholic Church considered it an option following the Thirty Years War. This chapter will briefly examine the practice of polygyny throughout the world and then focus on the LDS Church's practice.

Of 862 societies listed in George Peter Murdock's *Ethnographic Atlas*, nearly 84 percent practiced polygyny in some form with only 16 percent strictly monogamous. (Polyandry, a wife married to several husbands, occurred in less than .1 percent.) Over 99 percent of the societies in Africa practiced polygyny. In East-Eurasia, the Insular Pacific, and North and South America, more than 70 percent of the men had more than one wife. These figures support ethnographist Melvin Ember's conclusion: "About 70 percent of the societies known to anthropology permit a man to be married to two or more wives simultaneously." However, in nearly half of the societies listed in Murdock's *Atlas* that permitted polygyny, it was practiced by only a fraction of the men. In 15 percent of the societies in Africa only a small percentage of the people were involved in polygynous families. In East Eurasia, 80 percent of the societies practicing polygyny had only a limited number of men who were actually polygynists.[1]

Old Testament Polygamy

Polygamy was historically an option, but not a requirement, in Old Testament society. For instance, Sarah asked her husband Abraham to marry her handmaiden Hagar when Sarah appeared to be barren. When Sarah had a child, she asked Abraham to send Hagar and her son Ishmael away. After Sarah's death, Abraham married Keturah. Abraham's son Isaac had only one wife, Rebekah. His son Jacob had two legal wives, sisters Rachel and Leah, but the handmaidens of both women also bore him children. These handmaidens, sometimes referred to as concubines in the Old Testament, were legal wives, yet their children could not be heirs to their father's estate. Mosaic law regulated polygyny by requiring a man who "takes him another wife" to provide "her food, her raiment, and her duty of marriage," spelling out inheritance laws, and strongly encouraging a man to marry his brother's widow regardless of his own marital status.[2]

The Old Testament, while giving no specific instructions on who could have plural wives, records other men who had more than one wife. Hannah, mother of the prophet Samuel, was one of Elkanah's two wives. Though the Lord condemned David for committing adultery and arranging the death of Uriah the Hittite so he could marry his wife Bathsheba, David was not punished for marrying more than one wife. Solomon "had seven hundred wives, princesses, and three hundred concubines." He "loved many strange women," marrying wives from many countries, who turned him from worshiping the God of Israel. It was for his lack of devotion, not his many marriages, that the Lord censured him.[3]

Polygamy During the Sixteenth, Seventeenth, and Eighteenth Centuries

John Cairncross, a professor of Romanic languages, based his history *After Polygamy Was Made a Sin* on sources written during the sixteenth, seventeenth, and eighteenth centuries that presented arguments for and against polygamy. According to his sources, polygamy was not seen as violating the Christian tradition until A.D. 600 when the Catholic Church consolidated its power in Rome. He said the Roman Church gradually adopted a pro-celibacy position similar to Paul's letter to the Corinthians.[4]

Later, according to Cairncross, public discussions of polygamy grew out of the Protestant Reformation in Germany in the early 1500s. Protestant theologians replaced the pope's authority with scriptural authority and assigned the Old Testament patriarchs a more prominent role in theology than simply being the forerunners of Christ. Martin Luther attacked the Catholic tradition of celibacy and encouraged marriage. "For the first time in Europe, the text 'increase and multiply' resounded with predictable regularity from the pulpit." Luther wrote to Henry VIII of England, "I would allow the king to take another [wife] given in accordance with the example of the patriarchs of old who had two wives at the time." Other Reformation leaders also discussed polygamy favorably and encouraged rulers to marry more than one wife.[5]

The Catholic Church also apparently encouraged polygamy at one point. In 1650 after the Thirty Years War in Germany, the Regional Council of Catholic Franconians, with the approval of the Catholic archbishops of Bamberg and Würzburg, suggested that laymen marry two wives for a period of ten years as a means of rebuilding the population. There are examples of men who married plural wives during that time.[6]

The last record Cairncross found promoting polygamy was written by Martin Madan during the late eighteenth century in England. After that Cairncross says, "Reformers . . . concentrated on raising women's low status, on improving their education and on reforming the approach to prostitution and vice. They ceased to debate whether the patriarchs practiced polygamy, and campaigned for an attenuation of the patriarchal attitude in general."[7]

Mormon Polygamy

Although some Protestant reformers considered polygamy as an option and discussed it in theory, few if any European or American Christian sects or denominations formally instituted procedures of marrying more than one legally recognized wife until Joseph Smith introduced the concept to members of the Church of Jesus Christ of Latter-day Saints.[8] According to LDS Church doctrine, Joseph Smith's prophetic mission began in New York in 1820 at the age of 14 when he received a visitation from God the Father and Jesus Christ. In answer to his prayer to know which church to join, he was told that Christ's church was not on the earth but that he would be instrumental in restoring it. Ten years after his initial vision, he organized the Church of Jesus Christ of Latter-day Saints.

Latter-day Saints believe this new church was a restoration of truths lost from the Christian churches during the "apostasy," the period between the death of Christ's apostles and the founding of the LDS Church. As part of this restoration, Smith revised the Bible to correct errors and to return, as the Book of Mormon puts it, "plain and most precious" truths which had been removed to "pervert the rights of the Lord [and] blind the eyes and harden the hearts of the children of men."[9] During this period, Smith recorded numerous revelations, often in answer to his questions, which are now included in the Doctrine and Covenants, part of LDS canon. For example, he asked why many of the Old Testament leaders had more than one wife. His recorded response reads: "Prepare thy heart to receive and obey the instructions which I am about to give unto you; for all those who have this law revealed unto them must obey the same. . . . If any man espouse a virgin, and desires to espouse another, and if the first give her consent, and if he espouse the second, and they are virgins, and have vowed to no other man, then is he justified; he cannot commit adultery with that that belongeth to him and to no one else."[10]

This revelation, now Section 132 of the Doctrine and Covenants, was not recorded until 1843, at the request of Smith's brother Hyrum, apparently in an effort to reduce the opposition of Joseph's wife, Emma Hale Smith. Current research suggests that Joseph Smith may have received this revelation as early as the 1830s in Kirtland, Ohio, where the members of the new church moved after a large number of the Disciples of Christ in that area were converted. However, verses 51 through 57 were clearly contemporary to the summer of 1843 and Emma's objection to plural marriage.[11] W. W. Phelps recalled that on 17 July 1831 Joseph Smith told him and others, "It is my will, that in time, ye should take unto you wives of the Lamanites [Indians according to the Book of Mormon]." To Phelps's question about how those who had wives could marry again, he was told, "In the same manner that Abraham took Hagar and Keturah; and Jacob took Rachel, Bilhah and Zilpah, by Revelation." According to some sources, Smith married his first plural wife, Fanny Alger, in 1835.[12]

Although most of the Church membership was probably unaware of the doctrine, rumors circulated and some non-Mormons protested sharply. In response, Phelps, editor of a Mormon newspaper and Smith's secretary, read an "Article on Marriage" at a general Church assembly in Kirtland on 17 August 1835, which said in part: "Inasmuch as this church of Christ has been reproached with the crime of fornication, and polygamy, we declare that we believe that one man should have one wife, and one woman but one husband, except in time of death, when either is at liberty to marry again." Since Smith was in Michigan at the time, historian B. H. Roberts asserted during the 1930s that Phelps's doctrine was adopted by the assembly without Smith's permission. Other studies suggest, however, that Phelps presented the document at Smith's request. This statement was canonized as scripture in the Doctrine and Covenants as Section 101 until it was deleted in 1876.[13]

After the Saints settled in Nauvoo, Illinois, in 1839, Joseph Smith explained the doctrine of plural marriage to some of his closest associates and the Church leadership. Many of these Church leaders found polygamy difficult to accept. Brigham Young, for example, later reported, "Some of these brethren know what my feelings were at the time Joseph revealed the doctrine; I was not desirous of shrinking from any duty, nor of failing in the lack to do as I was commanded, but it was the first time in my life that I desired the grave, and I could hardly get over it for a long time." John Taylor explained, "I had always entertained strict ideas of virtue, and I felt as a married man that this was to me . . . an appalling thing to do."[14] Yet despite their misgivings, Brigham Young, John Taylor, Joseph Smith's brother Hyrum, and many of the other leaders eventually married additional wives.

During the 1840s, only selected leaders knew about the practice of polygamy and married plural wives. They used code words in an attempt to conceal the practice from the enemies of the Church and most Church members and issued public statements denying that they were practicing polygamy. However, polygamy surfaced and was part of the reason why John Cook Bennett, at one time mayor of Nauvoo, and William Law, a member of the First Presidency (consisting of the President of the Church and two counselors), and his brother Wilson not only left the Church but also published statements against it. The Laws, along with other dissidents, organized a separate church and published the *Nauvoo Expositor* whose primary theme was opposition to polygamy. Joseph Smith and the Nauvoo City Council's decision to destroy that press led to Smith's arrest and later martyrdom in Carthage, Illinois, in 1844.[15]

With Smith's death and reduced persecution after the move to Utah, Brigham Young felt that it was no longer necessary to conceal the practice of plural marriage. In 1852 Orson Pratt, an apostle who had left the Church for a short time when Joseph Smith proposed marriage to Pratt's wife, made a public speech defending polygamy as a tenet of the Church. Hosea Stout recalled that conference. "Orson Pratt preached today on the subject of polygamy or plurality of wives as believed and practiced by the Latter Day Saints. In the afternoon the Revelation on the subject given to Joseph Smith . . . was publicly read for the first time to the great joy of the saints who have looked forward . . . for the time to come when we could publickly declare the . . . greatest principles of our holy religion."[16]

From 1852 until 1890 Church leaders preached and encouraged Church members, especially those in leadership positions, to marry additional wives. For example, in the 1850s Brigham Young reported, "If any of you deny the plurality of wives and continue to do so, I promise that you will be damned." Heber C. Kimball, who had 43 wives and 65 children, explained, "I have noticed that a man who has but one wife and is inclined to that doctrine, soon begins to wither and dry up, while a man who goes into plurality looks fresh, young, and sprightly." In 1880 John Taylor, who became President of the Church after Brigham Young, asked at a General Conference, "Has God given us a law? Yes! We won't forsake our god and all those willing to abide by the law of god signify by raising the right hand." The voting was unanimous. His successor, Wilford Woodruff, wrote in his journal in 1889, "The word of the Lord was for us not to yield one particle of that which he had revealed and established."[17]

Opposition to Polygamy

The reactions from outside of the Church to Pratt's 1852 announcement and subsequent statements about polygamy were immediate and negative. In 1854 the Republican party termed polygamy and slavery the "twin relics of barbarism." Opponents petitioned Congress to pass laws, and in 1862, the Morrill Act, introduced by Representative Justin S. Morrill of Vermont, prohibited plural marriage in the territories, disincorporated the Church, and restricted the Church's ownership of property to $50,000. Although Abraham Lincoln signed the bill, the nation was in the midst of the Civil War and he reportedly said, "You tell Brigham Young if he will leave me alone, I'll leave him alone."[18]

In 1867 the Utah Territorial Legislature asked Congress to repeal the Morrill Act. Some federal officers saw this as an attempt by the Mormons to legalize polygamy, and the House Judiciary Committee asked why the law was not being enforced. The Cullom Bill, introduced by Illinois Representative Shelby M. Cullom in 1870 and calling for greater federal control in Utah Territory, attempted to strengthen the Morrill Act.[19] Three thousand women immediately signed a petition protesting the bill. The women, who had just been granted the right to vote, objected that they were not oppressed, as non-Mormons commonly believed, and that the Cullom Bill was unjust. According to one historian, "The Cullom Bill passed the House of Representatives on March 23, 1870, but lobbying by the transcontinental railroad's financial interests succeeded in keeping it off the Senate floor. The prevailing sentiments, supported by many Utah non-Mormon liberals, was that the railroad would in time introduce 'civilizing elements' that would take care of the 'Mormon problem.' " Although the Cullom Bill did not pass, most of its provisions later became law. Out of a number of other bills introduced during the 1870s against polygamy, only the Poland Act passed in 1874. Introduced by Vermont's Lake P. Poland, it gave district courts all civil and criminal jurisdiction and limited the probate courts to matters of estate settlement, guardianship, and divorce.[20]

The Mormons continued to practice polygamy despite these laws since they believed they were protected by the freedom of religion clause in the Bill of Rights. In order to test the constitutionality of the laws, George Reynolds, Brigham Young's private secretary, agreed to be tried. The case eventually reached the Supreme Court, which in 1879 upheld the Morrill Act. According to the court's opinion, "Laws are made for the government of actions, and while they cannot interfere with mere religious belief and opinion, they may with practices." John Taylor responded to the Reynolds ruling, "We are between the hands of God and the hands of the Government of the United States. God has . . . commanded us to enter into these covenants with each other. . . . I know they are true, . . . and all the edicts and laws of Congress and legislators and decisions of courts could not change my opinion."[21]

Three U.S. Presidents, Rutherford B. Hayes in 1880 and James A. Garfield and Chester A. Arthur in 1881, spoke against the "barbarous system" of polygamy. In addition, petitions against the LDS practice flooded Congress during 1881 and 1882. In response, Congress passed the Edmunds Act in 1882, which was actually a series of amendments to the Morrill Act. George F. Edmunds, a Vermont Republican, introduced the bill, restating that polygamy was a felony punishable by five years of imprisonment and a $500 fine. Unlawful cohabitation, which was easier to establish since the prosecution only had to prove the couple had lived together rather than that a secret ceremony had taken place, remained a misdemeanor punishable by six months imprisonment and a $300 fine. Polygamists were disenfranchised and ineligible to hold political office. Those who practiced polygamy were disqualified from jury service, and those who professed a belief in it could not serve in a polygamy case. All registration and election officers in Utah Territory were dismissed and a board of five commissioners was appointed to direct elections. The Utah Commission selected election officers and required male voters to take an oath: "I solemnly swear (affirm) that . . . I do not live or cohabit with more than one woman in the marriage relation." In 1885 the U.S. Supreme Court upheld the disenfranchisement of polygamists but declared the test oath "null and void." The commission replaced the oath by a new one that left out the terms "marriage relationship."[22]

Because the Edmunds Act was unsuccessful in controlling polygamy in Utah, in 1884 Congress debated legislation to plug the loopholes. Finally in 1887 the "hodge-podge Edmunds-Tucker Bill," as one historian called it, was passed. It required plural wives to testify against their husbands, dissolved the Perpetual Emigrating Fund (a loaning institution to help members of the Church come to Utah from Europe), abolished the Nauvoo Legion, and provided a mechanism for acquiring the property of the Church already disincorporated by the Morrill Act. The Cullom-Struble Bill with even stricter measures was debated in 1889, but the Church helped to prevent its passage by promising to do away with polygamy.[23]

Adaptation to Antipolygamy Laws

All of these pressures impacted on the Church, even though they did not compel the Latter-day Saints to abolish polygamy. John Taylor and Wilford Woodruff publicly affirmed the continual practice of polygamy. Church leaders as well as many of the members of the Church went into hiding, on the "underground" as it was called, to either avoid arrest or to avoid having to testify. John Taylor, who had argued he was not violating the law because he had not married a plural wife since before the Morrill Act was passed in 1862, operated the Church in hiding. According to fundamentalist belief, President Taylor received a revelation that the practice of polygamy would continue. He married an eighth wife, Josephine Roueche, in 1886, before dying the following year.[24]

Wilford Woodruff, his successor, initially supported the continued practice of polygamy. However, as pressures increased, he began questioning

In 1890, Wilford Woodruff issued a press release, the Manifesto, that ended "any marriages forbidden by the law of the land." Seated here with Woodruff is his second wife, Emma. Utah State Historical Society.

whether the Church should maintain the system. On 20 October 1889 in the *Salt Lake Tribune* and on 27 October 1889 in the *Salt Lake Herald*, he was quoted that the Church meant to obey the law. "I have refused to give any recommendations for the performance of plural marriages since I have been President."[25]

The next year he went beyond not simply giving recommendations. Woodruff's journal entry for 25 September 1890 stated, "I have arrived at a point in the history of the Church of Jesus Christ of Latter-day Saints where I am under the necessity of acting for the temporal salvation of the Church." The next day he issued a press release, the Manifesto, which read, "I publicly declare that my advice to the Latter-day Saints is to refrain from contracting any marriages forbidden by the law of the land." Because federal officials would not accept the declaration as binding without a sustaining vote by the Church membership, the Manifesto was approved at the General Conference of the Church on 6 October 1890.[26] Andrew Jonus Hansen, expressing his feelings about the Manifesto, stated, "Fortunes have been spent, and some lives had been lost, all in defending what this people believed to be their right and to be the will of God and all this has been upheld by the Court of Last Resort and nothing more could be done. It was quite apparent that no good could be accomplished by continuing the unequal struggle. The Government of the United States had assumed the responsibility for saying what was the 'will of God.' . . . And so it was that the Lord inspired his servant, the Prophet, the Seer, and the Revelator."[27]

Reaction to the Manifesto was mixed although most accepted it as revelation. Hansen went on to explain, "To most people in this church this came like a Thunderbolt out of the clear sky because no one thought the practice would be discontinued. With me individually, the trial was of short duration, but none the less bitterly severe while it lasted."[28] Annie Gardner explained, "I was there in the Tabernacle the day of the Manifesto and I tell you it was an awful feeling. There President Woodruff read the Manifesto that made me no longer a wife and might make me homeless. I sat there by my mother and she looked at me and said, 'How can you stand this?' But I voted for it because it was the only thing to do. I raised my hand and voted a thing that would make me a unlawful wife."[29]

Rather than resolving the polygamy question, according to one historian, "For both the hierarchy and the general membership of the LDS Church, the Manifesto inaugurated an ambiguous era in the practice of plural marriage rivaled only by the status of polygamy during the lifetime of Joseph Smith."[30] On 7 October 1890, the day after the sustaining conference, at a meeting of the First Presidency, the Quorum of the Twelve Apostles, and all stake presidents, "President Woodruff drew the attention of the brethren to the fact that the Manifesto did not affect our present family relations but it simply stated that all plural marriages had ceased." Woodruff's counselor George Q. Cannon stated, "A man who will act the coward and shield himself behind the Manifesto by deserting his plural wives should be damned."[31] In June 1891, the *Deseret News*, the Church-owned newspaper, published in three editions an interview with Woodruff and Cannon in which they were asked whether they or any officer of the Church would authorize a polygamous marriage or countenance unlawful cohabitation. Their reply was, "Again, we have to say we can only speak for ourselves, and say that we would not authorize any said marriage or any practice violative of the law."[32]

In October 1891, when Woodruff appeared before Judge Charles F. Loofbourow, appointed to decide the fate of Church property, he asked Woodruff if the Manifesto covered "living or associating in plural marriage by those already in the status." Woodruff replied, "I intended the proclamation to cover the ground, to keep the law — to obey the law myself and expect the people to obey the law." On 12 November 1891 Woodruff told the First Presidency and the Twelve that "he was placed in such a position on the witness stand that he could not answer other than he did. Yet any man who deserts and neglects his wives or children because of the Manifesto, should be handled [tried] on his [membership]."[33]

Andrew Jonus Hansen expressed confusion about the Manifesto and the General Authorities' statements. "But there was much speculation and doubt as to how it was going to work out. The Instrument was very brief, and few would venture to pass an opinion as to what was really meant. We did not know if it was intended for such as had plural families to abandon their plural wives or what was meant and we could not get the 'Brethren' to ask for a definition of its meaning, for they would not commit themselves."[34]

A few couples separated as a result of the Manifesto. According to John Brown's daughters, "At the time of the Manifesto Father deeded the two homes to the wives. The Church recommended that. Men were supposed to give up their wives (plural) but they were supposed to support them and for safety the Church asked the men to deed the property equally to the wives."[35] Elizabeth Ann Schurtz McDonald said her husband, William, deeded his property to her, the second wife, and provided for her as he had before but did not live with her until after the first wife had died and he had married her as a legal wife. She explained, "He would have lived with both women, but he had an old country respect for law and his first wife determined that he give the second one up."[36]

Others interpreted the Manifesto as applying only to new marriages. All polygamous General Authorities (Church leaders including the First Presidency, Council of the Twelve Apostles, Church patriarch, First Council of Seventy, and Presiding Bishopric) continued to cohabit with their wives, and based on impressionistic evidence in family histories and genealogical records, "most" polygamists followed the General Authorities' example.[37] Conover Wright, the son of Amos Russell and his second wife Martha Loella Weaver Wright, said, "After many years of practicing polygamy, it was unreasonable to expect the thing to cease immediately after the Manifesto. Of course, it was never intended that plural wives should stop having children but only that no more marriages should be contracted."[38] A few children reported that their fathers had specific sanction from Church leaders to continue plural relationships. Lorin "Dutch" Leavitt noted, "My dad was a very good friend and grew up . . . with Anthony W. Ivins [who became a member of the Church's First Presidency after he was the stake president in Mexico]. . . . It was just after the Manifesto had gone into real effect and things were really beginning to take over. My dad asked him, . . . 'Now, Tony, you know I have the two families and two wives. What am I going to do? Am I going to give one of them up?' . . . He said, 'No, I don't think the Lord intended you to give them up. But I can promise you that if you do keep them and take care of them the Lord will bless you for it.' "[39]

Nor did all new plural marriages end in 1890. In an interview George Q. Cannon gave to the *New York Herald* on 5 February 1899, he explained if a man's wife was barren, "a man might go to Canada and marry another wife. He would not be violating our laws, and would not be in danger of prosecution unless the first wife should follow him there from Utah and prefer a charge of bigamy against him. He might go to Mexico and have a religious ceremony uniting him to another that would not violate our law."[40] There were more cases than simply having a barren wife that led General Authorities to authorize plural marriages in Mexico and Canada and polygamy was against the law in both of the U.S. neighbors. In Canada, the law was strictly enforced so that husbands lived with only one wife in that country, essentially having one legal wife in the United States and one in Canada. The law was not enforced in Mexico, so plural families lived openly together.[41] Apostles also performed marriages in the United States, as Matthias Cowley explained at his Church trial before the First Presidency and Council of the Twelve Apostles where he was disfellowshipped for performing plural marriages after 1904. "I was never instructed to go to a foreign land to perform those marriages. President Cannon told me to do these things or I would have never had done it."[42]

In a Senate investigation in 1904 concerning the seating of Reed Smoot, a monogamist but a member of the Quorum of the Twelve Apostles, in the United States Senate, Joseph F. Smith, then President of the Church, testified before the Senate Committee on Privileges and Election, admitting his own continued cohabitation and explaining he preferred "to meet the consequences of the law rather than abandon my children and their mothers, and have cohabited with my wives, not openly, that is not in a manner that I thought would be offensive to my neighbors — but I have acknowledged them; I have visited them."[43]

After meeting with the Quorum of the Twelve Apostles, Smith presented what historians have called the "Second Manifesto" on 7 April 1904. This states, "Inasmuch as there are numerous reports in circulation that plural marriages have been entered into contrary to the official declaration of President Wilford Woodruff, . . . I . . . do hereby affirm and declare that no such marriages have been solemnized with the sanction, consent, or knowledge of the Church of Jesus Christ of Latter-day Saints." He then added a punishment for those who disobeyed the Manifesto. "If any officer or member of the church shall assume to solemnize or enter into any such marriage he will be deemed in transgression against the church and will be liable to be dealt with according to the rules and regulations thereof and excommunicated therefrom."[44]

Matthias Cowley and John W. Taylor, two apostles, continued to be involved in plural marriages after 1904, and as a result, Cowley was disfellowshipped and Taylor excommunicated from the Church. In 1909 a committee of apostles including Francis M. Lyman, John Henry Smith, Heber J. Grant, and George F. Richards met to investigate post-Manifesto polygamy. By 1910, Church leaders had a new policy for dealing with polygamists. Those married after 1904 were excommunicated, and those married between 1890 and 1904 were not to have Church callings where the members would have to sustain them.[45]

Although the Church officially prohibited new plural marriages after 1904, many plural husbands and wives continued to cohabit until their deaths in the 1940s and 1950s. Some plural wives were still living during the 1970s. But just as polygamy had not been an easy practice to accept, it was difficult to stop — especially when children were involved. Rather than discipline those who had married with Church sanction, ecclesiastical officials simply allowed the practice to die out and sanctioned no new marriages.

Polygamy, although not a practice unique to the LDS Church, was unusual to Euro-American traditions. When Joseph Smith announced the revelation, both Mormons and non-Mormons reacted negatively to the idea, but Latter-day Saints accepted it as a commandment of God and non-Mormons fought it by passing legislation. The interplay between the two groups helped to determine the practice of polygamy in the LDS Church. At first, Mormons responded by obeying the law of God and ignoring the laws of the United States. Wilford Woodruff's Manifesto in 1890 eliminated "marriages forbidden by the laws of the land." Yet many saw the Manifesto as only a political move and others felt that it applied to only new marriages. With differing public and private statements by Church leaders, some husbands stopped living with their plural wives, many continued to cohabit, and a few even married other wives in polygamy. Joseph F. Smith's Second Manifesto which spelled out disciplinary methods and the Lyman committee which investigated post-1890 marriages finally brought an official halt to Church-sanctioned polygamy.

2

The Impact of the Antipolygamy Laws

As the previous chapter pointed out, non-Mormon reaction influenced the LDS Church's practice of polygamy. Only between 1852 and 1862 was polygamy a publicly declared practice of the Church with no attempt by the U.S. government to control it. The laws passed against polygamy not only affected the Church as a whole but changed the lives of individual Latter-day Saints. The Manifesto and the Second Manifesto also influenced LDS polygamous family life. Having given a general overview of the history of polygamy, this chapter will show how these policies impacted members of the Church.

The Underground

With the passage of the Edmunds Act in 1882, many Mormons reacted with statements as did Jane Synder Richards. "What a sin it would be not only to deprive wives of what they considered their lawful husbands, but to brand their children as illegitimate, many of these children now grown with families of their own. The Government has no right to deprive our women and children of their husbands and fathers. And yet there hangs over their heads the threatened fine and imprisonment of all men who have more than one wife." Joel Hills Johnson expressed the same sentiment. "Another Christian crusade against the Saints is on hand. Petitions into Congress from all sides to enact laws to prescribe the Saints in their rights of Citizenship by disenfranchising all who believe in Celestial marriage."[1]

Given the feelings that the laws were unjust and that they were denied religious freedom, men and women tried a variety of ways to avoid arrest. Since "going on the underground" could be anything from hiding in a room or a ditch for a few hours to moving to Mexico or Canada, it is impossible to determine how many polygamists were involved. There was always the fear that men would be arrested and imprisoned and women forced to testify against their husbands and possibly imprisoned for contempt of court if they refused.

Sometimes men hid near or within their own homes. Torrey Austin's father, Edwin Nelson, built a secret room in the duplex his families shared. "He had a little false room built in the attic right up above those two windows. It was just high enough for a man to stand in. He had a false partition put in that was just like the outer wall as near as he could make it." He went on to explain that although a marshal could find the trap door, he would not know that the false partition was not the wall. On 17 June 1889 George W. Terry and a Brother Rapilee were out cutting willows when they were alarmed seeing several buggies go by. "Bro. Rapilee and I ran for the brush. I crept down by the side of the river holding to roots and rose bushes, up to my knees in mud, getting my hands filled with thorns." It turned out that the men in the buggy were Mormon polygamists and not U.S. marshals though.[2]

In some of the smaller Mormon communities warning systems notified polygamists when the marshals were coming. William James Frazier McAllister hid in a ditch by his house when someone signaled that a stranger who might be a marshal had arrived in town. The residents of Fairview, Utah, would alert Eli A. Day when the marshals arrived in town so he could get away.[3] Torrey Austin described a local resident of his hometown, John Synder, as a "rather recluse. He was a man that never married, who was inclined to be a toper, heavy drinker. He used to haul block wood from our sawmill [near Bear Lake, Idaho] to Montpelier and Paris [Idaho], and sell it for firewood. Somehow or other he always was able to find out when the marshals were coming over through that part of the valley. He never failed in coming back. He might be so drunk he didn't know where he was going and his lines were dragging on the ground. But he'd always make one holler, 'The marshals are coming.' These four or five polygamists would hurry up and get into the room" in the Austin's home.[4]

Although polygamy was against the law in most states, the Morrill, Edmunds, and Edmunds-Tucker acts only specifically applied to territories. The federal marshals assigned to Utah did not have jurisdiction in the surrounding states and could not arrest polygamists residing in or visiting Idaho, Wyoming, Colorado, or Arizona. Truman Call said that his father, John Holbrook, settled in Star Valley, Wyoming, because "they were polygamists. They came to Afton because the Wyoming governor said he wanted some good citizens in this end of the state. There were a lot of polygamists that came to Afton, Star Valley, about that time."[5] Christopher Layton recorded, "Finally my wives and children agreed that, although they disliked very much to do without my presence, yet they would rather know that I was at liberty than to have me dodging the hounds of the laws, and under these conditions I accepted a call to preside over, and make a home for, Saints in Southern Arizona." Specific laws were passed against polygamy and men tried for cohabitation, however, in states as well, and some plural husbands served time in prison for practicing polygamy.[6]

Wives could be subpoenaed to testify against their husbands, and a relative few were jailed for contempt of court when they refused. They often went into hiding to avoid having to appear in court. Ann Amelia Chamberlain Esplin said, "They'd take the women as evidence. . . . Mother said she never wanted to testify against her husband." On one occasion "when they hadn't had any deputies for awhile" the wives decided to get together. Her mother saw "a man step across the ditch and she said, 'Girls, here's the deps.' That was just like saying the house is on fire. Aunt Chastie was ironing, and so she pulled her bonnet . . . down over her face and stuck her head down there and looked so busy ironing. [Mother] started up to the outside toilet with her baby in her arms. She said she looked around and there he was right behind her. He said, 'Stop lady, stop. . . . I won't hurt you.' . . . But she just kept going and got there and slammed the door in his face."[7]

Wives moved more often than the husbands while on the underground. A husband could not be jailed without his wives or children or someone else who knew the family to testify that he was cohabiting with more than one wife. Since the man's occupation would require him to be on his farm or at his place of business, quite often the wives moved to avoid the marshals. Emma Westerman, the second wife of William Booth Ashworth, complained, "Not long after we were married the officers got after me and I never was able to stay anywhere more than a few weeks at a time. I never had a place to lay my head that I could call my own." Amanda Bailey, the second wife of William A. Murray, went to western Utah, and William's freighting business made occasional visits possible.[8] Torrey Austin's mother, Emma Wood, had to leave her home near Bear Lake in Idaho and spent up to a year at a time in Logan, Utah. "She would leave part of her children with the first wife and take maybe one or two of the youngest children with her. . . . Then as things kind of cooled off and there was not very much that the government was doing to force the law, she could go back up home."[9]

The danger of the marshals determining that a man was cohabiting was greater when a plural wife was pregnant or had children. Emma Hoth McNeil posed as the first wife's housekeeper until her first child was born. Then she was constantly on the move. In one year, she moved seven times. "I would pity a dog when he had to move around so much," she said.[10] Annie Gardner, the second wife of John, tells about hiding in a granary when one of her children was small and trying to persuade it to nurse to prevent it from crying. When the ward teachers came (men assigned by the bishop to visit the homes of the families in the ward), she had to lie in her room and stifle her baby's cries. "There was no one you could trust in those days."[11] Georgina Bollette Critchlow Bickmore remembers being on the underground with her mother when she was three years old and the second child, a son, died at eight months. "There she was all by herself. Father could not come see her. I guess it was pretty hard. I can never remember as a little child seeing my mother when she wasn't in tears." She corrected herself, "She wasn't always in tears, but she was sober." Christopher Layton explained after he moved to Arizona, "My women folks became quite lonesome, discouraged, and homesick at times, although they tried to be cheerful and I consoled them by telling them of our blessings and showing them that our heavenly Father was very kind and merciful to us because things might have been a great deal worse."[12]

Being on the underground had adverse effects not only on the women but also on their newborn children. Sometimes these were only folk beliefs that were not actually caused by the traumatic experience. One night Betsey Leavitt Wyatt "saw a man outside of her window and it frightened her. She always thought that . . . was when she marked her son with his birthmark. . . . She just didn't know it wasn't possible."[13] Other ill effects were directly related to the mother's confinement and lack of exercise. Lula Roskelley Mortensen said that her oldest brother Leonard was born in

Smithfield "while Mother was living on 'the underground.' She was 'in hiding' and was never seen by anyone nor was she ever out of the room until after dark. She said that when Leonard was born on September 16, 1888 he looked just like a little shriveled up old man."[14]

Like their husbands, some wives left Utah and moved to surrounding states. Georgina Bickmore explained, "I don't remember very many things as a child. Mother and I moved from place to place and lived in different places under different names until I was almost four years old. At that time there was a settlement in Wyoming called Afton, Star Valley where quite a number of the polygamous families had gathered. . . . We lived there for six years." Nevada Watson Driggs received her unusual name because "I was born in Panaca, Nevada, April 28, 1891. The reason I was born in Nevada was because my father who had another wife was being so harassed by the marshals that Mother had to be taken out of . . . Utah in order to have serenity when I was born."[15] Pipe Springs, Arizona, was just a few miles over the state line from Utah. "The authorities came down and if they had an order to arrest a Utah man and he was in Arizona, why it was no good," explained Ann Amelia Chamberlain Esplin. "So when women would get pregnant, they'd take them to Pipe Springs. . . . They finally dubbed it as the lambing ground for the polygamists, and Joseph Chamberlain and my brother Edwin . . . were both born out there."[16]

Despite the hardships, the wives accepted the necessity of hiding. Alma Elizabeth Mineer, the second wife of Joseph H. Felt, said, "I made up my mind that I should do my part. She was the first wife, and my part was to keep Brother Felt from jail. I made up my mind that nothing in polygamy would ever embitter me, and I never allowed myself to feel hurt or imposed upon. But it was a long time. I used to think, 'Will this never end?' " Manomus Lovinia Gibson, the second wife of James Andrus, agreed. "I always said that if one of us had to suffer, I wanted to be the one because I was the second wife and I don't think any one should interfere with the rights of the first wife. I went to Idaho for about two years and lived there so there wasn't any trouble. I was in a comfortable place and had plenty so I got along all right. I never suffered."[17]

For both men and women, the lack of the comforts of home proved difficult. Morgan Hinman who arrived in Cardston, Alberta, in 1889, recorded in his journal on 30 June, "Rhoda Harrod played the organ, and it is the first one I have heard since I was forced to leave my home. I have not heard one since the last Sunday in August 1886."[18] Jonathan Layne wrote, "Arrest meant conviction, cost of suit and from six months to two years in the penitentiary with the worst of criminals and when the time was out they would be liable to arrest again if they went to visit their wives and children even though the latter might be sick. Each visit of a man to his plural family was considered a crime. I suffered great anxiety and discomfort during those times, but by the blessings of the Lord, managed to be away from home at certain critical times." On 1 July 1897 Levi Savage and his plural wife Adelaide went to Milford and then on to Salt Lake City. "Here we bedded together for the first time in 8 years as the law forbid us acknowledging ourselves to be husband and wife."[19] Having to send a wife on the underground was also hard on the husband. Georgina Bickmore said, "I think it grieved [my father] a great deal. I don't think he expected . . . her [to] go through all she did. . . . I have some letters he wrote to her. I can tell from those letters home he worried about her and how grieved he was about those things."[20]

Children were also instructed to protect their parents during the underground period. After her first sons were born, Agnes Wildman Roskelley "had to teach them that they didn't know what their name was; they didn't know where they lived; they didn't know who their dad or mother was. The deputy marshals would corner the kids and get them to tell them who their dad and mother were and where they lived . . . in order to track down the polygamists." Reuben, the fourth child of George and Elizabeth Hill, said, "Even after the family moved to Springville the younger children were not allowed to talk to strangers for fear of the answers they might give when asked who their father was."[21]

Someone asked William McNeil at the temple if his second wife's daughter Emma was the one he went to jail for. Emma, only a little girl, felt very responsible and also felt that the first family blamed her for sending their father to jail. Georgina Bickmore said her mother's unhappiness "had its impression on me. . . . Father felt like it did." Her sister Lottie "had a very lively disposition. I would have been a little more lively if I had had a little more encouragement, but . . . my mother was always either in tears or sad. I was alone with her."[22]

Mormon Polygamy in Mexico and Canada

For many, life underground was only a temporary relocation or a move to another state. Others attempting to get completely away from the

Some plural wives were on the underground with their children in Mexico. Their husbands, some of whom were General Authorities of the LDS Church, remained in the United States. LDS Church Archives.

U.S. laws and marshals moved to Mexico and Canada. In 1884 President John Taylor wrote Christopher Layton, who was by then established in Arizona, "Our counsel has been and is to obtain a place of refuge under a foreign government to which our people can flee when menaced in this land. [It is] better for parts of families to remove and go where they can live in peace than to be hauled to jail."[23] In 1885 Taylor, his counselors in the First Presidency, Layton, and some other members of the Church explored the states of Sonora and Chihuahua in Mexico. They chose a place near Casa Grande in Chihuahua and made arrangements to purchase land. Then "by mail or by messengers, it was grapevined to remotest hamlets in the Region. In St. Johns, Snowflake, Sunset, Luna, Smithville in Arizona, in Savoy, Socorro and other locations in New Mexico and even in many towns in Southern Utah troubled men heard the message and were moved to go in search of the promised land."[24] By May 1885 about four hundred prospective colonists were waiting near the Mexican border for the land deal to be completed. Eventually the Mormons established six communities in Chihuahua: Colonia Diaz about 50 miles from the U.S.

border, Colonia Dublan and Colonia Juarez between 150 and 200 miles from the border and Colonia Pacheco, Chuichupa, and Garcia in the mountains, and two communities in Sonora: Colonia Oaxaco and Colonia Morelos.

In 1886 Charles Card, the stake president in Cache Valley, planned to move to these new colonies in Mexico to escape arrest. Before leaving, however, he talked with President John Taylor who advised him to go to Canada, explaining, "I have always found justice under the British flag." Following Taylor's advice, Card first went to British Columbia. He recorded in his journal on 29 September 1886 when he crossed the Canadian border "at 25 minutes to 10, . . . I took off my hat, swung it around and shouted, 'In Columbia we are free.' "[25] When Card could not find any land in British Columbia, he selected property in the Northwest Territory (the area was later included in the province of Alberta). The Mormons eventually established a number of small communities in southern Alberta including Cardston and Raymond.

Mormons settled in both Mexico and Canada to escape what they felt were unjust laws. In an article entitled "Polygamy in Mexico" in the Anthony W. Ivins papers, an unknown author explained that land was purchased there "with the thought of providing a refuge where men who had obeyed the law of plural marriage might find a place where they could live with their wives and children without being regarded as lawbreakers." Card expressed the same type of feeling about his move to Canada. "My fate seems to be an exile and driven or compelled for freedom's sake to seek a foreign land."[26]

Initially Mormon leaders approached the Mexican and Canadian governments to let Mormon men live with their plural wives in those countries. Charles W. Kindrick, the U.S. consul in Ciudad Juarez in 1899, explained, "They asked for non-interference with their institutions, believing that their creed justified the practice of polygamy and made the marriage tie with the second and third wife as sacred . . . as the law of the land held the marriage tie with the first wife."[27] At first, the sudden influx of a large number of Americans frightened some Mexican officials; they feared another Texas. On 9 April 1885, shortly after the Mormons started arriving in Chihuahua, the acting governor issued an order requiring the Americans to leave within 15 days. When Mormon leaders were unable to convince him they should be allowed to stay, Apostles Moses Thatcher and Erastus Snow went to Mexico City to see if the order would be reversed. As part of President Porfirio Diaz's plan to encourage foreigners to settle in the northern states, Secretary of Public Works Carlos Pacheco agreed to let the Mormons, who were known to be good farmers, stay and bring their plural families. Although polygamy was against the law in Mexico and apparently Diaz did not give the Mormons permission to live it, Mormon plural families lived together and new marriages were performed without discipline by the Mexican government.[28]

When the Mormons first arrived in Alberta, they were not sure if the Canadian government would allow them to bring their plural families, so at first husbands came with only one wife. In the fall of 1888 Apostles Francis M. Lyman and John W. Taylor along with Charles Card traveled to Ottawa to ask for special land, water, and immigrant privileges and to determine the political situation in respect to polygamy. In a letter to Canadian Prime Minister John A. Macdonald, these men explained they were not asking Canada to legalize polygamy or to sanction plural marriage but simply to accept existing families. They offered some reasons why Mormons practiced polygamy, argued only 5 percent of the Church practiced polygamy, and then pointed out that it was practiced in other areas of the British Commonwealth. "The comparatively few who need to seek rest and peace in Canada," they argued, "would not be a drop in the bucket compared with the millions of people who are protected in their faith and practice plural marriage under the Government of Great Britain."[29]

The Mexican and Canadian governments made completely different responses to the request. Although polygamy was technically against the Mexican law, Diaz did not enforce statutes criminalizing its practice. He was, as some historians have explained, "quite willing to subordinate whatever reservations [he] felt about Mormon domestic manners to the more important goal of allowing industrious settlers to colonize vacant lands along the border." In Canada, however, MacDonald denied the request and informed the Mormon leaders that their people would be allowed to settle only if they agreed to live with just one wife. In April 1890 the Canadian government emphasized that polygamy was against the law by amending the criminal law requiring those practicing polygamy to be imprisoned for five years instead of two.[30]

Because of this policy, Eunice Stewart Harris, the wife of Dennison Emer Harris, said that they went to Mexico because "it seemed there were only two courses for us to choose and be safe. One was to go to Mexico where all the family could go, or go to Canada where a man could take

only one wife. We chose Mexico where we could all go and live in peace."
Jonathan Ellis Layne, however, chose Canada. "I had made up my mind . . .
that I would go south and see the country. . . . But after thinking the situation all over and the character of the people in Canada and the government
and character of the Spanish in Mexico, I decided that the English government was the more likely to give the men their rights before the laws, so
I decided to go to Canada."[31]

The government policies also made life very different in Mexico and
Canada. In Mexico, husbands brought all their wives and continued to
marry in polygamy until 1904. Church officials sent couples to be married
there. Polygamy was well accepted. According to a contemporary account,
the practice of polygamy was "almost universal" and "close to 100 percent
of the people than living in the Juarez Stake were so attached to this order
that it was the very woof and warp of their domestic life and also the
theme and central ideal of community worship."[32] The Eyring family is an
example of polygamists who went to Mexico. Henry Eyring recorded in
his journal on 27 January 1887 that he was advised to go to there by
Erastus Snow. "Rather than see you hunted by marshals and imprisoned,
I would like you to come to this good country to help us, where you will do
better for yourself than you have ever done in St. George." In 1889 he
invited his son Edward Christian Eyring to come to Mexico to help him
with his store and cattle business. Edward married his first wife, Caroline
Romney, in 1893. Then "I decided to try and enter the holy order of plural marriage, so with the help of my wife, I was able to woo my wife's
sister Emma and after considerable persuasion married her in November
1903." Edward described his life in Mexico, noting, "At that time the colonies were in their best days. . . . I feel now that the twenty-five years of
my life that I spent in Mexico were wonderful indeed."[33]

According to John Taylor, however, Canada was to be "a place of
refuge where we [can] raise one family and wait till the clouds . . . disperse."
Men usually took only one wife to Canada. Some visited other wives in the
United States twice each year at General Conference time while others
never returned.[34] Sam Smith Newton, for example, married his second
wife, Amy Susan Johnson, in 1900 in the Logan Temple. At first the two
families lived in Salt Lake City, but in 1904 Sam moved his second family
to Alberta "in order to avoid the law." A year later Lizzie, his first wife,
died in Utah, and their three youngest children came to Canada to live
with the second family.[35] Heber Allen went to Canada with his polyga-

mous father and there married his first wife, Amy Leonard, who also was from a polygamous family. In 1903, Matthias Cowley, John W. Taylor, Joseph F. Smith, Anthon Lund, and Reed Smoot came to Cardston to divide the stake. Allen, then president of the Alberta Stake, was asked to move to Raymond to preside over the new Taylor Stake, named for John W. Taylor. At that time, either Cowley or Taylor convinced Allen and the new president of the stake in Cardston, Edward James Wood, to marry plural wives. Allen's second wife, Elizabeth Hardy, lived in Salt Lake City and he visited her twice each year.[36]

The laws against polygamy, the Manifesto in 1890, and the Second Manifesto in 1904 had a profound impact on the Latter-day Saint practice of polygamy. Although they did not completely end polygamous families living together, they forced Mormons to analyze their life-style. In response to the laws against polygamy, plural wives and husbands practiced a form of civil disobedience. Since they felt the laws were unjust, they chose to ignore them and even went into hiding to avoid being arrested. Going on the underground could mean anything from simply hiding in a secret room at home, extensive traveling, or moving all or part of the family to a nearby community or another state. Both husbands and wives were involved in hiding, the husbands to avoid jail terms and the wives to prevent having to testify against them and the possibility of going to jail for contempt of court. Some who found no safety anywhere in the United States moved to Mexico and Canada. Though polygamy was against the law in both countries, decisions by Mexican officials not to enforce the law and by Canadian leaders to strengthen it led to different experiences in the two countries.

3

Demographic Characteristics of Mormon Polygamous Families

Mormon polygamy raises a lot of questions about demography. Since polygamy was practiced for such a short period of time and no known official records were kept of plural marriages, questions such as how many wives each husband had, how old the wives were when they married, how many children they had, and just where in Mormon country polygamists lived are difficult to answer. Many of the popular stereotypes about polygamy are in response to these frequently asked questions. Using data collected for this study and other studies, this chapter looks at the practice of polygamy from a statistical point of view.

Studies on Mormon Polygamy

Scholars have explored Mormon polygamy from a variety of perceptions. James Hulett, a sociologist, conducted interviews with plural husbands and wives and children raised in those families for his doctoral dissertation. Kimball Young, also a sociologist, used Hulett's interviews in his *Isn't One Wife Enough?* and concluded that most polygamous families were successful. Stanley S. Ivins's historical article on the number of Mormons who practiced polygamy has been a standard for many years. Vicky Burgess-Olson used many of Hulett's interviews in her doctoral dissertation comparing monogamous and polygamous families.[1] And historians, geographers, and social scientists have written on the practice of polygamy in St. George and the Washington County area, Kanab, the colonies in Mexico, and the settlements in Alberta, Canada, Cache Valley, Springville, and parts of Davis County. Lowell "Ben" Bennion, a professor of geography at Humboldt State, is currently working on a study to determine the numbers of polygamous families based on the 1880 census.

Although not the final word on the demographics of polygamy, this chapter provides a statistical overview based on family group sheets, listing husbands, wives, and children submitted to the LDS Genealogical Department by descendants of the families included in this study. The total number of plural wives and husbands varied with each category since family group sheets were not available for all wives and some of the information was not listed on all the sheets. Since the interviews cited in this study were mainly conducted in the 1930s (Hulett) and between 1976 and 1984 (Redd Center), it deals with a later period of polygamy. Had it been done a generation earlier, it would have been possible to capture the memories of those who lived between 1852 and 1880 before opposition became formal and intense. As it is, these reminiscences reflect the problems encountered by those who lived "the principle" during the last sanctioned days.

Characteristics of Sampled Polygamous Families

Over 60 percent of the men, nearly 75 percent of the first wives, and over 80 percent of the other wives were born after 1847 when the Mormons settled Utah. (See Table 1.) These husbands and wives married into polygamy during the underground period of 1881 to 1890 and between 1891 and 1904, between the First and Second Manifestos. (See Table 2.) Most of the marriages, especially to the first wife, were performed in the Endowment House in Salt Lake City, Utah. The next most frequent sites were St. George where the first temple was completed in 1876, Logan where the second temple was finished in 1885, and Mexico, where polygamists fled to escape the U.S. marshals in 1885 and where plural marriages were performed after 1890 by Stake President Anthony W. Ivins and various General Authorities who determined that these marriages were not, in the phrase of the Manifesto, "contrary to the laws of the land." (See Table 3.)

The sampling also shows that the majority of the plural wives lived in Utah for most of their childbearing years. First wives were more likely to have their children in Utah because they were not vulnerable to arrest as were subsequent plural wives. The largest percentage of children were

Table 1

Birthdate of Husbands and Wives

Sample includes 169 husbands, 150 first wives, 143 second wives, 60 third wives, and 21 fourth wives.

Date of Birth	Husbands	1st Wife	2nd Wife	3rd Wife	4th Wife
Pre–1847	38.3%	28.0%	11.9%	13.3%	9.5%
1847–60	40.0	36.0	30.0	21.7	33.4
1861–70	17.7	24.7	37.1	33.3	23.8
1871–80	4.0	9.3	14.7	21.6	14.3
1881–90	0.0	2.0	6.3	10.1	19.0
Total	100.0	100.0	100.0	100.0	100.0

Table 2

Date of Marriage

Sample includes 171 husbands, 171 first wives, 162 second wives, 54 third wives.

Date of Marriage	1st Marriage	2nd Marriage	3rd Marriage
Pre–1860	17.0%	4.9%	5.6%
1861–70	21.6	10.5	16.6
1871–80	32.8	21.6	18.4
1881–90	18.7	37.7	27.7
1891–1904	9.9	25.3	31.7
Total	100.0	100.0	100.0

Table 3

Place of Marriage

Sample includes 158 first marriages, 136 second marriages, 42 third marriages, and 19 fourth marriages.

Place of Marriage	1st Marriage	2nd Marriage	3rd Marriage	4th Marriage
Salt Lake City	51.3%	40.4%	35.7%	42.1%
Logan	4.4	17.6	14.3	15.8
Manti	1.0	2.9	0.0	0.0
St. George	13.3	15.4	16.7	10.5
Mexico	2.0	14.7	13.0	21.0
Canada	5.0	3.7	3.0	5.3
Other	23.0	5.3	17.3	5.3
Total	100.0	100.0	100.0	100.0

born in Salt Lake and Cache counties. For those areas outside of Utah, the greatest number of children were born in Mexico. (See Table 4.) Many of the husbands and wives maintained continuous residence in Utah or returned to the state before their deaths. The Mormon colonies were abandoned in 1912 during the Mexican revolution, and many of the colonists did not return. Therefore, less than 10 percent of the husbands and wives died in Mexico. Arizona, where many of the colonists settled after they left Mexico, rather than Mexico itself, was the second deathplace listed after Utah. (See Table 5.)

Between 40 and 50 percent of the husbands and wives were born in Mormon country, including Utah and southern Idaho. Less than one-third were born outside the United States. (See Table 6.) Other studies show that these figures were true not only of polygamous but also of other families in Utah at that time. Dean May's demographic portrait of Cache Valley shows that in 1860, 67 percent of the population there was U.S. born; in 1870, 62 percent; and in 1880 roughly the same. Gene Pace's study of nineteenth-century LDS bishops also shows that 60 of the bishops and two-thirds of their wives were born in the United States.[2]

These figures do not match Nels Anderson's conclusion, however. He found that only 2 of 71 polygamous husbands and 15 of 150 polygamous wives in Washington County in 1880 had been born in Utah. He concluded that the immigrant women were older and "anxious to obtain husbands but could not compete with the younger Mormon women for the younger men."[3] Pace also found that immigrants were more likely to marry in polygamy. Of the 835 wives of bishops who served between 1847 and 1900, 69 percent of the immigrants were married in polygamy and 53 percent of the U.S. born were plural wives. He found, however, that "the combination of spouses which most consistently produced polygamous marriages were those involving women, immigrants or Americans, who married immigrant men."[4] These differences show that a final word is not available on the relationship between immigrants and polygamy and that it may have varied in location and social status. Though the sampling for this study shows a slightly higher percentage of foreign-born third wives, the stereotype of the single Danish girl beginning to work as a maid at a home and then marrying the husband as a plural wife does not appear to be the norm.

There are also disagreements on the ages of plural wives. Anderson explained that there were more foreign-born plural wives because they

Table 4

Location of Families by Birthplace of Children

Sample includes birthplaces of children of 157 first wives, 147 second wives, 53 third wives, and 18 fourth wives.

Birthplace	1st Wife	2nd Wife	3rd Wife	4th Wife
Utah	66.7%	51.0%	52.8%	55.6%
Idaho	8.3	8.2	1.9	0.0
Mexico	14.1	23.8	32.0	38.9
Others	10.9	17.0	13.3	5.5
Total	100.0	100.0	100.0	100.0

Table 5

Location of Families by Deathplace of Husbands and Wives

Sample includes deathplace of 179 husbands, 140 first wives, 136 second wives, 45 third wives, and 22 fourth wives.

Deathplace	Husband	1st Wife	2nd Wife	3rd Wife	4th Wife
Utah	55.3%	61.4%	58.8%	66.7%	77.3%
Arizona	7.8	10.0	11.0	6.7	4.5
Idaho	5.6	8.8	9.6	0.0	0.0
Mexico	7.8	6.4	4.4	8.8	9.0
Canada	18.4	8.6	11.0	15.6	4.5
Others	5.1	4.8	5.2	2.2	4.7
Total	100.0	100.0	100.0	100.0	100.0

Table 6

Birthplace of Husbands and Wives

Sample includes 182 husbands, 163 first wives, 148 second wives, 57 third wives, and 21 fourth wives.

Birthplace	Husbands	1st Wife	2nd Wife	3rd Wife	4th Wife
Utah/Idaho	46.2%	57.7%	67.6%	56.1%	52.4%
United States	24.8	17.1	8.1	10.5	14.3
Europe/England	28.0	22.1	23.6	31.6	33.3
Others	1.0	3.1	0.7	1.8	0.0
Total	100.0	100.0	100.0	100.0	100.0

came to Utah as "older women, many of them ranging between 25 and 35 years of age. . . . Polygamy was a boon for them."[5] Another popular view has often been the opposite of Anderson's: there were so few eligible women that men were marrying girls who were 14 years old. Although there are examples of both older women and young girls marrying in polygamy, statistical studies show neither pattern was the norm. The husband was usually in his early twenties when he married his first wife and she in her late teens. (See Tables 7 and 8.) Almost 60 percent of the polygamous husbands married a second wife six to fifteen years later. (See Table 9.) At the time of this marriage, the husband was between the ages of twenty-six and forty, but usually in his early thirties. His second wife was between seventeen and nineteen years of age.[6]

Mormon men did not collect harems. About 60 percent of the men married only one plural wife. Approximately 20 percent had three wives, the last wedding occurring two to five years later in just under one-third of the cases, six to ten in about one-quarter of the sample, and eleven to fifteen in just over one-fifth of the cases. The husband was usually in his late thirties; the third wife's average age was nineteen. Ten percent of the husbands married a fourth wife, and he was usually between thirty-six and forty-five. The fourth wife's age still averaged nineteen. Just under 40 percent of the marriages took place between two and five years after the third marriage, and the same percentage took place between six and ten years.[7]

To put these figures another way, men chose women for their second, third, or fourth wives who were approximately the age of his first wife at the time of their marriage even though he was from ten to thirty years older. (See Table 10.) Husbands selected a first wife within five years of their age, but less than one-fifth were within five years of their second wife's age. Most of the second wives were between six and twenty years younger than their husbands. For third wives, most were between eleven and twenty years younger. More than a quarter were over twenty-one years younger than their husbands. One possible reason is that men were attracted to younger women. Another is that the revelation on plural marriage — "if any man espouse a virgin, and desire to espouse another" — suggested that the plural wife should not have been married before.[8] Furthermore, a woman sealed to a previous husband could be married only for time, not eternity, making widows less desirable. If a man wanted more children (highly valued in Mormon society), the wife's age would have been a factor as well. Marrying younger second wives was not unique

Table 7

Husband's Age at Marriage

Sample includes 157 husbands with first wives, 150 husbands with second wives, 58 husbands with third wives, and 22 husbands with fourth wives.

Husband's Age	1st Wife	2nd Wife	3rd Wife	4th Wife
15–20	28.0%	1.3%	0.0%	0.0%
21–25	59.2	18.0	3.5	0.0
26–30	11.5	29.3	12.1	4.6
31–35	1.3	27.3	22.4	18.2
36–40	0.0	12.7	27.5	31.8
41–45	0.0	4.7	15.5	22.7
46–50	0.0	5.3	12.1	13.6
51–55	0.0	0.7	6.9	0.0
56–60	0.0	0.7	0.0	9.1
Total	100.0	100.0	100.0	100.0

Table 8

Wife's Age at Marriage

Sample includes 152 first wives, 145 second wives, 56 third wives, and 23 fourth wives.

Wife's Age	1st Wife	2nd Wife	3rd Wife	4th Wife
15–20	74.3%	56.5%	58.9%	65.2%
21–25	25.0	28.3	25.0	17.4
26–30	0.7	7.6	3.6	4.4
31–35	0.0	4.1	10.7	8.7
36–40	0.0	2.1	0.0	8.7
41–45	0.0	1.4	1.8	0.0
Total	100.0	100.0	100.0	100.0

to polygamy either. Pace found that of the monogamous bishops he studied who married a second time — usually after the death of the first wife — the second wife was on the average sixteen years younger.[9]

It is not clear whether plural marriage actually increased the Mormon population since plural wives had fewer children than their monogamous counterparts. (See Table 11.) Although plural marriage seems to have reduced the number of births per wife, some of the plural wives may not have married if polygamy had not been an option and would not have had

Table 9

Length of Time between Marriages

Sample includes 137 examples between first and second marriages, 46 between second and third marriages, and 18 between third and fourth marriages.

	1st–2nd	2nd–3rd	3rd–4th
0–1 yrs.	2.9%	8.8%	11.1%
2–5 yrs.	23.3	30.4	38.9
6–10 yrs.	35.8	26.2	38.9
11–15 yrs.	23.4	21.5	11.1
16–20 yrs.	7.3	4.4	0.0
21 +	7.3	8.7	0.0
Total	100.0	100.0	100.0

Table 10

Age Difference between Husband and Wife

Sample includes 151 first wives, 151 second wives, 59 third wives, and 18 fourth wives.

	1st Wife	2nd Wife	3rd Wife	4th Wife
Wife Older				
0–5 yrs.	7.9%	3.3%	0.0%	5.5%
Husband Older				
0–5 yrs.	71.5	19.9	6.8	0.0
6–10 yrs.	15.9	27.8	8.5	11.1
11–15 yrs.	4.0	27.2	23.7	16.7
16–20 yrs.	0.7	16.6	35.6	33.3
21–25 yrs.	0.0	2.6	10.1	16.7
26–30 yrs.	0.0	2.6	13.6	16.7
31–35 yrs.	0.0	0.0	1.7	0.0
Total	100.0	100.0	100.0	100.0

any children at all. The number of children per husband definitely increased with polygamy.[10] (See Table 12.)

A common justification for polygamy was that a first wife was childless. Determining the prevalence of this particular pattern is difficult. If a wife had no children, quite often no family group sheet would be submitted to the LDS Genealogical Department. This study found that first wives had more children than other wives. Pace also found that first wives

Table 11

Number of Children per Wife

Sample includes 168 first wives, 160 second wives, 50 third wives, and 27 fourth wives.

Children	1st Wife	2nd Wife	3rd Wife	4th Wife
0	1.9%	0.0%	0.0%	0.0%
1–5	9.0	25.6	32.0	22.3
6–10	46.0	52.5	56.0	55.5
11–15	43.0	21.9	12.0	18.5
16–20	0.1	0.0	0.0	3.7
Total	100.0	100.0	100.0	100.0

Table 12

Number of Children per Husband

Sample includes 144 husbands.

Children	
1–5	0.0%
6–10	5.0
11–15	23.6
16–20	27.8
21–25	22.9
26–30	13.2
31–35	5.5
36+	2.0
Total	100.0

had more children than the other wives. Monogamous bishops' second wives also had fewer children than the first wife.[11]

The intervals between births were under three years for nearly all of the wives.[12] Children interviewed sometimes claimed the wives seemed to be pregnant at the same time and that there was almost a competition between them to have babies, though that was not the norm. James Wyatt recalled a "friendly" rivalry. The two wives of his father, John Horsecroft Wyatt, of Wellsville, Utah, Julia Ann and Betsey Leavitt, who were also full sisters, had fourteen children between 1891 and 1905. Julia had six children and Betsey had eight. Five of them were born within five months of each other. For example, Wyatt had a half sister Hazel born just a month before him.[13] Georgiana Stowell Lillywhite remembered that her mother, Mary Olive Bybee, the first wife, and her sister Rhoda Maria, the second wife (also full sisters), had parallel pregnancies. "They had to get one just because we did," Georgiana said. Olive had six and Rhoda had eight children between 1888 and 1905, and only three of them were within two months of each other.[14] A careful examination of the family group sheets reflects that the Stowell example rather than the Wyatt's was typical. While some children were born at the same time, it was apparently not a competition between the wives to get pregnant.

Geographical Variations

Although such figures give a general view of polygamy, recent studies indicate variations in individual communities. "Ben" Bennion's current study based on the 1880 census in Washington County shows, for example, the figures varied from almost 40 percent in St. George to only just over 11 percent in Harrisburg/Leeds. In Kane County, the figures ranged from 10 percent in Rockville to 67 percent in Orderville. In northern Utah's Davis County, only 5 percent practiced polygamy in South Weber while nearly 30 percent of the families in Bountiful did. His study of Springville (Utah County) showed 15 percent were polygamous families. Larry Logue, a research assistant at the University of Southern California, found that nearly 30 percent of the men in St. George were polygamists in 1870 — a figure that rose to 33 percent in 1880. Chris Nelson determined 63 percent of the Mormon men in Mexico were polygamists.[15] Why did communities vary to such an extent? The relative safety from judicial prosecution drew many polygamists to Mexico, particularly after the 1890 Manifesto. Bennion hypothesized that the higher percentage of polygamists in St. George reflected greater religious commitment in general since many accepted calls from Church leaders to settle there.[16]

Another unanswered question is whether Mormon polygamy was primarily a rural or urban phenomenon. If polygamy was rural, would it have died out with urban development as it did in some African societies? And was Utah a rural or an urban society? Given that the U.S. census lists a community over 2,500 as urban, Utah had six urban areas in 1890 (Logan, Ogden, Provo, Springville, Salt Lake City, and Park City), and twelve in 1900 (the addition of American Fork, Brigham City, Eureka,

Lehi, Payson, and Spanish Fork). However, population alone cannot determine what is urban. Even in these communities, many of the residents were involved in agriculture in some way, usually a characteristic of rural life. Joseph F. Smith, the President of the Church near the turn of the century, lived in Salt Lake City, but his families (he had five wives) had gardens and farm animals on their property. Thomas G. Alexander and James B. Allen used Max Weber's definition of an *Ackerburgerstadt* (best translated as a garden plot city) to define Salt Lake City since although it had a commercial character, the residents grew much of their own foodstuff.[17] Elements of rural life persisted throughout urban Utah into the twentieth century. And according to Pace, the Mormons "foster urban growth by creating settlements which offered the advantages of both urban and rural life. Gathering together in towns and cities, they derived the social and economic benefits of community living, yet still engaged in major agricultural pursuits beyond the principal residential areas. Although numerous small towns lacked the population to qualify as cities, they possessed a number of urban characteristics."[18]

This explanation does not lend clarity to the problem at all. Given Pace's definition, St. George would qualify as an urban area as opposed to some of the smaller communities in Washington County. St. George had a higher percentage of polygamists than some other areas in the county, so it would seem polygamy was urban. However, Springville, a city by the census definition, was only 15 percent polygamist.

What then was the deciding factor? Was it the stake president who refused to advance men in the priesthood or call them to positions of leadership if they did not marry an additional wife? Did some General Authorities preach polygamy more often in some communities? Were more obedient members likely to settle in a particular area? No records exist to answer these questions. Pockets of polygamy developed, especially after the underground period in Mexico and in some communities just outside of Utah in Arizona, Wyoming, and Idaho. A number of men in Davis County apparently married in polygamy because Stake President Frank W. Taylor was a polygamist. Such larger questions may be answered in part by the painstaking sifting of data drawn from the experiences of individual families.

This chapter has shown that this painstaking sifting provides some valuable information about polygamy that can disprove or support the existing stereotypes. Although based on men and women who married into polygamy during the last days of Church sanctioning, the data eliminate many of the popular beliefs. Most of these plural wives and husbands were born after 1847 in Mormon settlements in Utah, Idaho, and other areas of the West. They lived most of their lives in the western United States, although this study reflects a number who moved to Mexico where polygamy was practiced for a longer period of time. Rather than a harem of wives, most plural husbands had only one additional wife. Instead of marrying the very old women to provide for them economically or the very young women because of a shortage of available brides, most husbands married young women in their late teens. As in monogamous families where a husband remarried after the death of a first wife, most first wives in polygamy had more children than subsequent wives. Husbands definitely had more offspring than they would have had with only one wife. Children were spaced about the same in monogamous and polygamous families, and there was no competition between wives for having children. Finally, polygamists were not concentrated in urban or rural areas. Without more data, it is impossible to determine why there were more polygamists in some communities than others. Apparently it had more to do with the families and the Church leaders than with the size or nature of the community. Most importantly, this chapter shows that why and how people practiced polygamy are not easy questions to answer and require a great deal more research.

4

Motivations for Practicing Polygamy

Members of the Church of Jesus Christ of Latter-day Saints came from a Euro-American monogamous background, and the practice of polygamy was very foreign to them. Defending the practice to themselves and to non-Mormons was very important. When Orson Pratt publicly announced the Mormons were practicing polygamy in 1852, he used several arguments to justify the practice, and his reasons were expanded by members of the Church. Pratt argued that polygamy was a revelation received by Joseph Smith, and members of the Church could not receive their highest exaltation in the post-earth life unless they obeyed the commandment of plural marriage. Polygamy helped to fulfill Adam and Eve's commandment to multiply and replenish the earth and to raise the children in religious homes. Monogamy, Pratt also argued, was unnatural when compared with other world societies, and polygamy helped control immorality. Over the years the members also suggested other reasons why polygamy was practiced including a shortage of men because of wars and because there were not enough good male members of the Church for righteous women to marry. They also used the argument that more women than men joined the Church. All of these justifications prove incorrect when compared with history and demographic studies, but they are still given as reasons why the Mormons practiced polygamy. Some children even saw prestige, power, and economics, common reasons for marrying in polygamy in other societies, as reasons why a young girl would want to marry a man established and well accepted by the community rather than a young

41

man her own age just starting out. Few children raised in polygamous homes saw possible sexual motivations, but as children they were not aware of all their parents' actions. However, public justifications for polygamy rarely included the sexual reasons that non-Mormons seemed convinced were the explanation. While other private sexual motivations might have existed, they were out of character with the Victorian ideal to which the Mormons subscribed.

Religious Motivations

For Pratt and most of the Saints, the compelling argument was that plural marriage had been commanded by God through Joseph Smith. Pratt described the Prophet as the "one man in all the world . . . who can hold the keys" to receive "new revelation." Pratt explained that obedience to the principle of plural marriage was necessary so couples could "attain their exaltation" and "be counted worthy to hold the scepter of power over a numerous progeny."[1]

Other members of the Church also argued that in order to reach the highest degree of the celestial kingdom — life in the presence of God where they would be able to create worlds, continue to produce spirit progeny to people them, and become like God — would be withheld from those who did not participate in plural marriage. In 1935 Ross S. Bean, a son of a polygamous marriage, wrote to one of Kimball Young's research assistants that his father "would go the grave without attempting any justification beyond the fact that it was given to our people as a divine principle and that to gain the highest glory in life hereafter we must conform to it."[2] As Orson Welcome Huntsman explained during the Utah Historical Records Survey, "Celestial marriage is one of the most sacred and essential principles of the gospel, for without it neither we nor our forefathers can claim our wives or our wives claim us and enter upon our exaltation in the eternal worlds."[3] Annie Richardson Johnson of the Mormon colonies in Mexico and Arizona, also the child of a polygamous family, summarized the same doctrinal position: "Like Joseph Smith, polygamists had sealed their testimony, not only with their blood but with the power of acceptance when the principle of Plural Marriage was revealed. . . . This extreme test was possible only because they knew that theirs was the revealed Church of Jesus Christ directed by his priesthood and by revelation, and that its blessings came through daily obedience to its principles."[4]

In 1852, Orson Pratt publicly announced that the LDS Church was practicing polygamy.
Utah State Historical Society.

Pratt's second argument was that polygamy would fulfill God's commandment to Adam and Eve to "multiply and replenish the earth." He rhetorically asked, "Does it say continue to multiply for a few years, and then the marriage contract must cease? . . . No. . . . When male and female are restored from the fall, by virtue of the everlasting and eternal covenant of marriage, they will continue to increase and multiply to all ages of eternity." Like other societies where offspring was one of the major motivations for practicing polygamy, the Latter-day Saints believed having large families was a blessing. However, rather than only the economic and prestige factors considered by other groups, in the LDS Church the desire for children had theological overtones.[5] Believing that God had literally fathered spirit children who needed bodies to come to the earth, Mormons saw having children as a way of providing "earthly tabernacles." By husbands marrying more than one wife, the men had more children than they would have had otherwise. Although the women did not have more children, the Mormons argued that some women who may not have had the chance to marry would now have the opportunity to bear children. George W. Brimhall, president of the Brigham Young Academy, recalled attending a meeting on 18 January 1852 where the revelation on celestial marriage was read. The speaker explained polygamy was introduced "for the purpose of peopling this desert land as speedily as possible, for as a rule, the migration from the South and East passed through to better lands." Price Nelson told a young woman he was courting, "I believed in polygamy . . . to have a big family. I love children and I always prayed I would have two wives and go on a mission."[6] As demonstrated earlier, although plural wives did not have more children than their monogamous counterparts, plural husbands did and the Latter-day Saints argued that there probably were more children born because of polygamy than there would have been without it.

Given the theological framework, childlessness in mortality was particularly devastating to Latter-day Saint couples. Although most first wives were not childless, some, like Sarah in the Old Testament, accepted polygamy so their husbands could have offspring. Reuben Hill's father, George, married his mother after twelve childless years of marriage to his first wife. Childless Wealthy Clark of Bountiful, Utah, gave her husband Edward Barrett permission to remarry after a mysterious male visitor promised her children if she allowed a second marriage. She gave permission for a second marriage and had six children in the next fifteen years.[7]

Simply having more children to populate the world was not the only issue, though; children needed to be raised in homes where they could be taught the gospel of Christ, and having more wives enabled members of the Church to have more children who would be raised in righteous homes. The Mormons felt that through polygamy not only more women would have the opportunity to marry, but also they would have the chance to marry men who were active members of the Church. With both parents actively obeying what they saw as God's commandments, proponents argued, there was a better chance that they would be raised in God-fearing homes. Just one righteous parent was incapable of providing the proper home environment.

Children were also "foreordained" to come to certain homes. As Orson Pratt explained in 1852, "Abraham and many others of the great and noble ones in the family of spirits, were chosen before they were born, for certain purposes, to bring about certain works, to have the privilege of coming upon the stage of action among the host of men, in favorable circumstances."[8] According to LDS doctrine, the members of the Church are the descendants of Abraham and heirs to the "promises made to Abraham, Isaac, and Jacob." The Lord commanded Abraham to "lift up your eyes and behold the stars; so thy seed shall be, as numberless as the stars." Pratt told the Saints, "Why not look upon Abraham's blessings as your own, for the Lord blessed him with a promise of seed as numerous as the sand upon the seashore, so will you be blessed, or else you will not inherit the blessing of Abraham." When asked if Abraham was "to accomplish it all through one wife," he replied, "We read . . . of a plurality of wives and concubines, which he had, from whom he raised up many sons."[9]

Mormons often pointed to the illustrious records of polygamous families to show that like Abraham, plural marriage had helped them raise a righteous generation. Orson Rega Card, who grew up in the Mormon settlements of Alberta, Canada, claimed in 1981 to have heard that 90 percent of the present-day bishops were descendants of polygamous families. Joseph Donal Earl, whose family lived in Bunkerville, Utah, speculated, "The controlling factor in the Lord's establishing the principle of polygamy at that time [was] in order to get additional spirits here and to get them through certain family lines." Dorris Dale Hyer said, "Most of the families that went in the mission field came from these very few polygamous families." Linnie Fillerup Monteirth from Mexico added, "A lot of the Authorities of the Church have come through polygamous families."[10] Of course, after several generations of descendants of polygamous families intermarrying with those from monogamous families, a much larger number of people seem to have been descended from plural families. If these same people had been asked if they were descended from monogamous families, that would also be the case. Those using this argument, however, did not go through that logic. The Mormons were attempting to prove the value of polygamy so they looked at it only from that viewpoint.

In a letter from J. E. Hickman, a teacher at the Murdock Academy in Beaver, Utah, to C. M. Haynes of Chicago, dated 18 December 1907, Hickman pointed out what he saw as some of the other virtues of polygamous children. He said that they were superior in weight and height to monogamous children. More of the polygamous children survived childhood and fewer had birth defects such as being tongue-tied or cross-eyed. A greater percentage of polygamous boys (248 of 2,416) than monogamous boys (555 of 19,916) served missions. He concluded, "Again I find a difference which indicates that the boy of the class P has something inherent in him which gives a superiority over the boy of class M."[11]

Finally Pratt argued in 1852 that monogamy was unnatural. He explained, "Only about one-fifth of the population of the globe . . . believe in the one-wife system; the other four-fifths believe in the doctrine of a plurality of wives, . . . and are not so narrow and contracted in their minds as some of the nations of Europe and America, who have done away with the promises." Monogamy, according to Pratt, invited immorality. He erroneously pointed out "haunts of prostitution, degradation, and misery" were not found in ancient Israel, nor in societies practicing polygamy. He went on to explain, "Whoredom, adultery, and fornication have cursed the nations of the earth for many generations; . . . but they must be entirely done away with from those who call themselves the people of God." Prostitution could be "prevented in the way the Lord devised in ancient times; that is, by giving to his faithful servants a plurality of wives by which a numerous and faithful posterity can be raised up, and taught in the principles of righteousness and truth."[12]

Mormon women who met in January 1870 to protest the Cullom Bill wrote, "Resolved: That we acknowledge the institutions of the Church of Jesus Christ of Latter-day Saints as the only reliable safeguard of female virtue and innocence; and that the only sure protection against the fearful sin of prostitution and its attendant evils, now prevalent abroad." Using the same type of argument but with no specific cases to back it up, Ida Stewart Pacey, of Provo, claimed that polygamy would cure the "social evil" of prostitution and argued that if some men had not married several wives, they might not have been faithful husbands.[13]

Folk Justifications

Despite the theological reasons for maintaining polygamy, the Saints frequently buttressed their defense with other reasons, since a logical question would be why the Lord gave the commandment in the first place. Most of these arguments were certainly not unique. Many societies, including nineteenth-century America, viewed marriage as an advantage for women, pitying those who did not marry and assigning them an inferior social and economic status. Yet male mortality often unbalanced the population, particularly in times of war. Anthropologist Melvin Ember argued that polygyny developed in societies where women outnumbered the men. In 1869, a Christian philanthropist advanced the same argument after the Civil War. Since male mortality was higher than female and also since many men refuse to marry, monogamy was "a cruel and oppressive system." He maintained, "Polygamy would even out both excesses—giving the surplus woman a husband and the men more vigorous wives."[14]

Ellen P. (Nellie) Moffett Done, a plural wife in the Mormon colonies of Chihuahua, reported a folk version of this belief. "In the colonies it was very much like the early days of Utah. When they were coming to Utah, you remember the United States grabbed a lot of the men for the Spanish-American War and took them. A lot of them got killed and that left a lot of women in Utah. Brigham Young told the men, 'Take more than one wife.' "[15] Actually the Mormon Battalion was called by the U.S. government in response to the LDS Church's request for help in moving west. When the government suggested in 1846 that Mormon men could help fight in the Mexican-American War, Brigham Young agreed. The Battalion marched south from Nebraska to New Mexico and then on to California. Young promised the men as they were leaving that they would not be involved in the fighting and they were not.[16]

Bernitta Bartley, the child of monogamous parents, also thought that polygamy resulted from war, but she claimed it was the Black Hawk War that "cleared out the men. . . . They had to repopulate in a hurry."[17] The Black Hawk War, a series of skirmishes between 1865 and 1868, involved

Mormon settlers and Ute, Paiute, and Navaho Indians, and few Mormons were actually killed.

Variations of the demographic argument were that there were not enough "good" men (excluding bachelors and nonmembers) in the Utah Territory to provide a husband for each "good" woman. As Sarah Hendricks of Cove, Utah, explained in an interview, "There were so many women that were good women in the Church. There were many more than there were men. A lot of them would have never had the privilege of becoming mothers and wives if they hadn't had polygamy. It was a blessing for them in that day." Charles Smith Merrill of Salt Lake City ventured, "There are probably a third more women who are righteous than there are men. What are these women going to do? If they can't have a husband, they can't have the joy of family life."[18] Linnie Fillerup Monteirth added, "The authorities counseled a girl that was not married when she was quite old to take a husband and be a second wife to him. They would select some man that they thought would make a good husband for her. It would give her a chance to raise a family." Her own father, Charles Richard Fillerup, had complied when the stake president asked him to take Mary Johnson, an "older woman," as his second wife. Linnie explained, "It was almost like being called on a mission." "Older woman" was obviously a relative term in this case. Examination of family group sheets reveals that Mary was only 18 years old when she married Charles.[19]

Carrie C. Smith, a resident of Cardston, Alberta, felt that the population imbalance still prevailed after the Manifesto of 1890. With many young men "partaking of the habits of the world," she queried rhetorically, "what were the pure daughters of Israel going to do for good LDS husbands?" Mercy Weston Gibbons, a plural wife, used a similar defense in a 1938 interview. "They were all preaching to the men to marry the girls and I guess it was very useful. You look around you nowadays and see plenty of unmarried young girls and old maids but not in those days." Jesse Barney of Arizona averred in 1982 he felt certain polygamy would again be practiced in the Church at least partly because of this perceived demographic imbalance, and quoted Brigham Young as saying, "There would be seven women hanging onto one man's coattail," actually found in Isaiah 4:1.[20]

The demographic argument probably reveals more about the need to defend polygamy than it does about the actual male-female ratios in the Church. For example, in Cache County in 1860 there were slightly more males than females (males 1,317, females 1,288). By 1870 there were a few more females (males 4,071, females 4,158), and by 1880, there were about equal numbers (male 6,286, female 6,291).[21] In areas where plural marriages were practiced extensively, there may have been actual shortages of women. Luke William Gallup wrote his sister in September 1865, "Women are scarce or I should have had another [wife] long before this, but it's all right as it is, my intention is good when one comes along for me."[22] William eventually married twice more, and although all of his wives eventually left him, he implied there was something wrong with them. Unfortunately, it is impossible to tell whether he was a difficult person to live with or if he showed poor judgment in selecting wives.

From an anthropological viewpoint, it is unfortunate that plural marriage flourished without judicial harassment only between the 1850s and 1880s, because responses from second- and third-generation polygamists might have reflected a different perspective. The second generation gave hints of that. Rhoda Ann Knell Cannon, the third wife of David Henry Cannon, the St. George Temple president, explained, "I didn't think a thing about [polygamy]. We just accepted it." Another believer who grew up in a polygamous home and later married two wives himself described his belief. "I believed in polygamy because it had always been taught me and we lived it at home. I always wanted to marry in polygamy, and I'm glad I did."[23]

Prestige, power, and economics also played a role in later polygamous marriages. Vicky Burgess-Olson, studying a sample of eighty-two wives married between 1847 and 1885, found that most of the first and second wives accepted polygamy because of their belief and "dedication to the principle." For more than a quarter of the youngest wives the main motivation was status. Ursula Rich Cole, the daughter of William Lyman Rich and his first wife, Eliza Amelia Pomeroy, explained, "I guess Mira was surprised when father asked her, but she believed in the Principle. And besides father was a good provider and by that time had accumulated property. Any girl would have taken a successful bishop in preference to a single man with nothing."[24]

Sexual Motivations

In some societies sexual motivations were given for marrying in polygamy. When cultural mores prohibited sexual intercourse during pregnancy and lactation, additional wives allowed men to satisfy their sexual neeeds.

Although sexual factors were rarely given in Mormon society, some of the children of polygamous unions were not always convinced of the purity of their fathers' motives. Loraine Farrell Ralph, the daughter of George H. Farrell and his first wife Amanda Adaline Steele, commented, "I don't think for a minute those men married for religious reasons. Yes, I believe it was a divine revelation and there weren't many people and it served its purpose at that time. The men may have kidded themselves that they were marrying for the Principle, but I don't think they did."[25]

E. W. Wright, the eighth son of Amos Russell Wright's first wife Catharine Roberts, said his father believed strongly in the principle and undoubtedly married for religious reasons. Yet knowing he could marry younger women made his first wife less attractive and he did not treat her as well.[26] J. W. Wilson, a monogamist on the high council in the Juarez Mexico Stake, wrote, "Polygamy is a true principle . . . but men did not live it as they should have done. . . . I talked to a man who had married a number of wives. I asked him why he did it and he said . . . that all of his marriages were due to inspiration. . . . I asked him that now as he grew older and his desires were dying if he had inspirations to marry and he said no, that he had no more inspirations. That was the reason polygamy could not be lived, men believed it because of their lustful desires."[27]

Although some children quoted the motives of their fathers for marrying plural wives, very few mentioned sexual motivations — either positive or negative. In interviews conducted during the 1930s, James Hulett asked some questions about sexual relations in polygamy and was told sexual intercourse was practiced only for procreation. On the whole, he did not receive any answers to his inquiries about sex. Of course, one of the reasons for that simply might be that the children were unaware of their parents' sexual activities. Rarely, especially in Victorian America and even today, would parents discuss their sexual behavior with their children. Children were told the religious motivations not only for polygamy but also for sexuality. Although religious motivations may not have been the only reason why Mormons practiced polygamy, there is no way to determine other factors. Certainly they would not have even considered the possibility of plural marriage if they had not been instructed to do so.

Downplaying sexuality in a society trying to cement itself together is another possible reason for polygamy. In *Religion and Sexuality*, Lawrence Foster compared the marriage patterns of Shaker celibacy, Oneida Community complex marriage, and Mormon polygamy. He concluded that additional sexual opportunity was not the reason why Mormons practiced polygamy. Instead, "by partially breaking down exclusive bonds between husband and wife and by undercutting intense emotional involvement in family affairs in favor of Church business, polygamy may well have contributed significantly both to the success of the long-range centralized plans set in motion at this time and to the rapid and efficient establishment of religious and communal order."[28] However, the sources in this study do not support such a conclusion. There was intense love between husbands and wives; while the love had to be shared, plural husbands and wives did have romantic attachments. Even if the "exclusive bonds between husband and wife" were broken by the practice, it was never given as one of the reasons why Mormons upheld polygamy. At best it might be a desired result of the practice, and even that is questionable.

Eunice Stewart Harris, a first wife, expressed the opinion of most polygamous husbands and wives and their children about why they accepted polygamy:

> My husband and I both believed in this principle and both desired to practice it. We both felt within our very souls that the time had come when it was our duty to obey that principle no matter what results might follow. The call had come and we had to obey it. I am thankful I felt it as strongly as he did, otherwise, when the test came, I might have faltered. July 28, 1886, my husband married Annie Jane Wride, a plural wife in the Logan Temple. I want to bear testimony to my children, my grandchildren, and my great grandchildren, that I know to the very depth of my being that this order of marriage is true and that it was revealed from God, and I thank my Heavenly Father for my testimony. Let me say to you as my mother said to her children, "Never say you do not believe it nor tear it down. Rather say you do not understand it."[29]

Most men, women, and children involved in polygamy echoed Harris's feelings. As Kimball Young concluded:

> While we examine the wide range of motives which appear in our records of polygamous families, we note that there is nearly always the basic faith in the principle of plurality of wives. While individuals must have variety in the intensity of their belief in this matter, on the whole the system has become deeply embedded in Mormon culture. It was thought to have divine sanction and to promise rewards here and in the hereafter. . . . Secondary motives . . . emerged, but since the

deeper motives are hidden below the surface of our daily habits, it is not expected that writers of personal documents or informants in interviews would be able to expose their deeper desires in these matters.[30]

Orson Pratt's public announcement of the practice of polygamy set forth the major reasons why the Mormons engaged in plural marriage. The key reason was that, according to LDS Church doctrine, God had revealed his will to Joseph Smith. Pratt's other reasons were a partial explanation of why the Lord gave that commandment. Pratt used biblical examples — the command to Adam and Eve to populate the world and to Abraham that his seed would be as numerous as the sands of the sea, practical examples — children should be born in righteous homes, and plural marriages would help control immorality, and historical examples — polygamy was practiced by most of the societies of the world. Over the years Mormons suggested other reasons for the practice to help explain to themselves and non-Mormons why God would have given such a commandment. None of their motivations were the sexual ones most non-Mormons suggested, and given the Victorian life-style Mormons subscribed to, lascivious desires probably were not a consideration. Whatever the reasons given to justify the practice, most likely none of the Mormon polygamists would have ever considered marrying another wife without the religious motivation, the command from God. The desire to live their religion and follow their prophet has to be seen as the major argument why they accepted the principle.

5

Entering Plural Marriage

Descendants of plural marriages tend to agree that a husband had to obtain the consent of the first wife before he could marry again and had to be asked by, or at least have the permission of, Church officials as well. However, no records are known of a set procedure for obtaining that permission. Assuming plural marriages were performed in the Endowment House, in a temple, or by someone having the "sealing power" to perform them, an interview held, and a recommend issued, there was at least some type of approval by Church officials. But descendants disagree on who could give permission. According to some, this approval had to come from the President of the Church; others felt that it needed to come only from the bishop or the stake president. Also, since quite often the plural wives lived close together, it might be assumed that the first wife had some say in the decision. Although the revelation stated that if the first wife did not give her consent "she then becomes the transgressor," none of the descendants referred to that clause.[1]

These decisions, however, were not made in a uniform way. Sometimes the first wife freely gave her consent or even initiated the decision to practice polygamy. Other wives felt pressured into accepting their husbands' choices for fear of what might happen in the next life, while a few were not even informed of the marriages. Women who accepted a proposal of plural marriage also had a difficult decision to make. Accepting plural marriage was not only a woman's decision; men also had to ponder the choices. Although some men were specifically called to marry in polygamy, others simply felt they were obeying a general commandment of the Church that applied to all members. Most, however, did not marry in polygamy, thus avoiding the decision altogether. For those who did accept the principle, their courtships were the same as monogamous ones during the nineteenth century. Marriages came about not because of romantic physical attraction but because of a desire to work for common goals. The marriages of Joseph C. Bentley, Charles Edmund Richardson, and John Theodore Brandley illustrate some of the variations.[2]

Case Studies

Joseph C. Bentley of St. George helped train his first wife Margaret (Maggie) Ivins at a telegraph office. They married in 1886 when Joseph was 27 and Maggie was 18. Joseph later explained, "When I asked Maggie to marry me I told her that I wanted her to know how I might someday take a plural wife and she said, 'I wouldn't think much of you if you didn't.' " After their marriage, Maggie felt that her cousin, Gladys Woodsmansee of Salt Lake City, a young poet active in Church programs, would be a good choice for her husband's second wife. Gladys, involved in her literary activities, was not really interested in marriage, but she accepted Maggie's invitation to visit her in St. George. Joseph courted her during the visit and later when he came to Salt Lake City for the semiannual General Conferences. Eventually he proposed to Gladys, and after some thought about living polygamy and giving up her career, she accepted.

The First Manifesto had been issued by this time, and few new plural marriages were being performed. According to Bentley family tradition, Joseph approached Church leaders several times about marrying Gladys because he knew that other marriages were being approved, particularly for engagements contracted before the Manifesto. He was finally told to talk to George Q. Cannon, a counselor in the First Presidency, who advised him to move to the colonies in Mexico. Joseph and Maggie moved in 1894, Gladys came to visit, and the marriage finally was performed. Joseph was then 35 and Gladys was 29. Both families continued to live in Mexico, five of Maggie's nine children and all five of Gladys's children being born there.

Joseph became a prominent figure in Colonia Juarez, serving as bishop, businessman, and part owner of a store. One of his partners, Ernest Leander Taylor, had a daughter, Maud, who was known for her red hair and her running ability. Joseph was attracted to Maud while she was still in her teens. Her father was anxious to have Joseph as a son-in-law and encouraged his attentions. When Maud noticed that the bishop was attracted to her, she was embarrassed and upset. She wrote in her autobiography, "No matter what time I went to school I would meet him at the corner of the shoe shop. . . . The first time he met me on the corner after school and asked if he could walk home with me, I was scared to death. . . . When he began to pay too much attention to me, the kids my age would tease me." She also recalled his courting visits on Wednesdays. "One evening I had my hair all in rags for curlers. Brother Bentley came and mother came in to tell me to come out. I said I wouldn't come out. She said that I didn't realize what a wonderful man he was. I said, 'I don't care. Let him go home to his own folks. I don't want him.' " When Joseph asked her to be his third wife, she hesitated but finally accepted. They were married in 1901 when Joseph was 42 and Maud 16, and eventually they had eight children. According to one of the other wives' children, Maud probably did not love Joseph when she married him, but she learned to love him and appreciate her marriage.

Sarah Louise (Sadie) Adams was 14 when she married 24-year-old Charles Edmund Richardson in the St. George Temple in 1882. Several years later while they were living in Wilford, Arizona, Sadie heard a sermon by a General Authority about plural marriage and felt deeply convinced of it. About the same time, Sarah Matilda Rogers, a young woman in the Richardsons' ward, told the bishop that she wanted to marry Edmund. When the bishop approached Edmund with Sarah's request, he was confused. He had no plans to marry again and did not love Sarah, yet he didn't feel he could refuse her outright. He reportedly paced the floor, trying to make a decision. Sadie, however, did not share his confusion. "You know that you should be entering into this principle," she told Edmund, "and you have no right to deprive that good woman of having a family." Edmund finally agreed to marry Sarah, the ceremony taking place in the St. George Temple in 1887 when Edmund was 29 and Sarah 31.

One of Edmund's children observed that he did not experience the same difficulty in marrying a third wife, though again Sadie supplied an important impetus. Caroline Rebecca (Becky) Jacobson, a Danish immigrant, worked in Sadie's home. Sadie was impressed with her and suggested Edmund marry her. He proposed, but Becky refused. Then while Edmund was serving a mission to the Indians in Arizona, he wrote back that he had met several Indian women who might be good candidates for a third wife. Sadie wrote Edmund that he could have all the Indian women that he wanted, but she felt that he should marry Becky. When he returned approximately two years later, he proposed to Becky again, and this time she accepted. The Edmunds-Tucker Act had been passed and U.S. marshals were arresting polygamists, so Edmund, Sadie, Becky, and later Sarah moved to Mexico where he married Becky in Colonia Juarez in 1889. Edmund was then 31 and Becky 14 years younger.

In Mexico, Edmund became a lawyer and acquired a ranch in Colonia Diaz. His legal practice required him to be closer to the government headquarters in Nuevo Casa Grande, so he moved Sadie to Colonia Juarez and his other two wives stayed in Colonia Diaz to take care of the ranch. He traveled back and forth between the two homes. In Colonia Juarez he met Daisie Stout. The comparatively common practice of polygamy in the colonies meant that marriageable girls considered all men, married or single, as possible husbands. Daisie's father, David Fisk Stout, had four wives, and she believed in plural marriage. Edmund, a well-to-do man, she felt would provide the support she wanted for her children.

Edmund was taken aback by the request and expressed doubts about their comparative ages. However, while he considered her proposal, Stake President Anthony W. Ivins warned Edmund that if he didn't marry Daisie soon he would lose the chance since Church President Joseph F. Smith planned to outlaw all plural marriages. Edmund, 46, married Daisie, 20, in March 1904, one month before the Second Manifesto. He did not have time to tell his wives in Colonia Diaz about the marriage, and both Sarah and Becky were shocked and somewhat displeased.

John Theodore Brandley of Richfield, Utah, met his first wife, Marie Elizabeth Naegeli, while serving a mission in Switzerland. After he returned to Utah, she and her mother came to the United States. Theodore and Marie married soon after her arrival in 1872 when Theodore was 21 and Marie was 18. Louis, a son of the second wife, described Marie as Theodore's "first love" and their relationship as a "true and sweet romance."

Ten years later, in 1882, Theodore married 18-year-old Margaret Keeler, Louis's mother. Louis explained that "in Utah polygamy was in flower. The leaders of the Church advised — even urged — the faithful elders to take plural wives as a sacred duty, to hasten, I think the building of Zion. Love and romance were strangely lacking, seemed unnecessary. It was an arrangement designed to fulfill a sacred obligation with the 'highest

order of the celestial kingdom' as its goal and 'eternal increase' its reward."
Louis noted that his mother simply recorded in her journal on the wedding
day, "Today I married Theodore Brandley." Louis said that she saw the
marriage both as a "business arrangement" and as a biblically ordained
model where second wives "always took second place to the chosen wives
and actually became their handmaids." She expressed neither romantic
love for his father nor dismay at the differences in their ages but simply
considered him a faithful Latter-day Saint, worthy to have plural wives.

Theodore served a second mission to Switzerland from 1876 to 1878
where he met Rosina Elizabeth (Eliza) Zaugg and Emma Biefer. Eliza was
from Columbier, Switzerland, and both women were young converts. Louis
said that his father's diary records show him asking the mission president's
permission to take Eliza and a friend on a picnic, and Aunt Eliza later
confirmed to Louis that the romance had begun then.

Theodore's first wife, Marie, died in 1892, just after they had completed a new home and bakery in Richfield. He first asked Maggie to care
for Marie's children, and Maggie moved into the new home. Poor health
left her unable to care for her children and Marie's eight, so she moved
back to her own home. Theodore hired housekeepers, including Eliza and
Emma, who had immigrated to the United States and whom he brought to
Richfield. Later he moved to Canada with Eliza and married her there.
When Emma came to visit, she also married him. Some records indicate
these marriages were performed as early as 1891 and 1893; others set
them at the more likely dates of 1901 and 1903, Eliza having her first child
in 1902 in Canada. Emma returned to live in Salt Lake City. Theodore
visited her twice annually when attending General Conference, and she
had twins in 1909. Maggie continued to live in Richfield until her death in
1910, seeing her husband only when he returned to Utah for conference.
According to Louis, Theodore apparently had two wives successively occu-
pying the prime place in his affections. The other two were "in the same
matrimonial class, not handmaids to the chosen wives, but rather . . . Isaiah's
class of women," Isaiah 4:1 reading, "In that day seven women shall take
hold of one man, saying, We will eat our own bread, and wear our own
apparel; only let us be called by thy name, to take away our reproach."

These stories demonstrate the various roles of wives and Church officials in the decision to marry in polygamy. Though there were some common threads, no set courtship procedure was established. Each relationship developed in its own way.

The First Wife's Consent

As these cases demonstrate, the first wife's involvement could vary from active encouragement — even selecting a second wife as Maggie Bentley did — to having the decision simply announced to her. This range of practice indicates a certain amount of functional ambiguity about whether the first wife's consent was actually necessary. According to the revelation Joseph Smith received, recorded in Section 132 of the Doctrine and Covenants, the first wife was to give her consent. However, she was not always consulted. Joseph Smith apparently did not tell his first wife, Emma, about all of his marriages. Polygamy was practiced openly without opposition from the government for a relatively short time. There were few public announcements and definitely no handbook on the procedure for selecting and marrying a second wife.

Without formal guidance and direction, Latter-day Saint men and women had to rely on the scriptures, a few statements by Church leaders, and their own judgment, all of which contributed to the diversity. Burgess-Olson found only 22 cases where she could determine whether the first wife gave her consent. Of these, over 90 percent agreed to the plural marriage. Alma Elizabeth Mineer, the second wife of Joseph Felt, reported, "When a man married he must have the consent of the Church authorities and of his first wife. He must obtain this consent freely and fully before he married her, and he must be a man worthy to live in polygamy." Agatha Walker, the second wife of Joseph McAllister, also said that the first wife was supposed to give her consent in theory, but sometimes the husbands got it because the wives knew they would have to consent to polygamy and other times the men married without consent anyway.[3]

Andrew Jonus Hansen wrote in his autobiography, "In those days great stress was laid on the importance of Celestial Marriage, including a plurality of wives." He quoted from a 9 October 1875 talk given by Wilford Woodruff, then one of the Twelve Apostles, that many bishops and elders had only one wife because their wives would not let them marry again. According to Woodruff, no man should let a wife prevent him from marrying again. When John Jacob Walser returned to Payson, Utah, from a mission, "I married my second wife. No, my first wife did not like the idea at first. She was upset but she got used to it."[4] Ann Elizabeth Riter Young protested to George Q. Cannon, the First Counselor in the First Presidency, that she could not give her consent for her husband, Seymour, to marry a plural wife because one of their children had cerebral palsy and they had other illness in the family. Hortense Young Hammond described her mother's reaction. "She knew who it was that Papa was courting, and of course, that broke her heart. Papa knew she didn't want it, but Papa was between the devil and the great deep blue sea" because he felt that he had been commanded by revelation to marry another wife.[5] She was referring to a revelation given to John Taylor in 1882 in which Seymour was called to the First Council of Seventy provided "he will conform to my law." In spite of the revelation, he put off taking a plural wife for another 18 months. During April conference in 1884, John Taylor "commanded" Seymour to enter polygamy "immediately." As a result, he married Abbie Corilla Wells on 28 April.[6]

Although some husbands simply did not ask for consent, they were probably the minority. Mae Douglas, the child of Margaret McFarland and P. P. Bingham, said, "Mother just cried her heart out when she found out about it. No, he probably never did consult Mother about the marriage to Isabel, and the marriage just finished her." Her mother, after the first shock, regained a cheerful demeanor and "always put the bright side outside. I think lots of her jovial behavior was just to hide her real feelings." E. W. Wright said of his mother, Catherine Roberts, the first wife of Amos Russell Wright, "I'm pretty sure Mother was resentful of the whole thing. But in such a situation a woman doesn't dare stand in her husband's way, because she'd blame herself for whatever happened to him afterwards."[7] Harriet Snarr Hutchings said that when her father, Daniel Hammer Snarr, was encouraged to marry in polygamy, "My mother [Alice Thompson, the first wife] accepted it; she lived it graciously, but it was always a heartbreak." Harriet, her mother's youngest daughter, said she could not cry when her father died because he had hurt her mother so much, even though her mother "let me know she really loved him."[8]

The children and husbands reported a variety of reasons the first wives allowed or encouraged polygamy. When Brigham Young asked David Henry Cannon, who later became the St. George Temple president, to marry a second wife, he told his first wife, Welhimina Logan Mousley, that he did not want to. According to Douglas, a son of David's third wife, Rhoda Ann Knell, Welhimina said, "You've never questioned him. I can't see any reason why you should start now to question the Prophet."[9] LaVetta Cluff Lunt Taylor, who grew up in the Mormon colonies in Mexico and Arizona, said she knew that her mother, Sarah Ann Weech Cluff, the first wife of Heber Manasseh, had faith for two reasons: his marriage to Susan Carolyn Sims in 1898 after she had seven children, and her encouragement for him to go on a mission when she was pregnant with their tenth child.[10] Gottlieb Ence in his life sketch explained, "My dear wife Elizabeth being a good Latter Day Saint wished to obey all the Principles the Lord has revealed unto Man. . . . She was willing to sacrifice her own feelings in order to be able to inherit a place in his Celestial Kingdom. She then consented and let me have her sister Caroline for my second wife, this she did in full faith that it was a commandment of God, and that she would be rewarded for doing so."[11]

Mary Elizabeth Woolley Chamberlain of Kanab, Utah, wrote an interesting story about how she agreed to marry her husband if he won the consent of his five previous wives. "During the weekend he made the rounds and returned Monday morning with a favorable report. I don't know how much pressure he had to bring to bear but he told me that one wife was more than willing to give her consent when she learned that I was his choice, as she had feared it was to be one whom she disliked very much." Similarly, Dorris Dale Hyer's father, Andrew Larse, at first proposed to a second wife to whom his first wife, Ellen Gilbert, objected. She agreed to a second marriage when he suggested Dorris's mother, Elizabeth Helen Telford, who had been working in the household.[12]

Edna Clark Ericksen of Wyoming said her father, Hyrum Don Carlos Clark, talked to her mother, Ann Eliza Porter, about polygamy before they were married in 1880, explaining, "His family was polygamous minded and that he was too. He said, 'So it might well be that some day I'll want to get another wife.'" Edna's mother talked to her father, Alma Porter, who was also her bishop, because she felt polygamy was "terrible." Her father told her that her future husband's desire to live polygamy was "noble and unselfish. If he wants another wife, you must be equal to it. That is my advice to you. Accept it as nobly as he does."[13]

Ida Walser Skousen, the wife of James, of Salt Lake City, explained, "At conference time we had so many visitors and Emma Mortenson was one. That started it. She and Jim were married several months after it. He talked it over with me. I knew all about it and every time he went to see her and all that happened. One day I was combing his hair and I said to him, 'Would you marry Emma if I refused consent?' He said that he wouldn't, but the responsibility would be on my head. Now I'd be willing to take [the responsibility of him not marrying in polygamy], but I wasn't then."[14]

Deciding to Be a Plural Wife

Just as polygamy could be hard for the first wife to accept, a second wife sometimes struggled in accepting the principle. Some had spiritual manifestations to aid their decision. Julia Ann Angell was not sure she wanted to marry in polygamy when Matthias Knudson asked her to be his second wife, not until she dreamed her deceased niece came and gave her a letter from Eliza R. Snow. The letter read, "If you will live it as it should be lived, you will be blessed." Rosalia Tenney Payne of Colonia Diaz, who became the third wife of Edward in 1903, said she used to make fun of polygamy until she read Section 132 of the Doctrine and Covenants and realized it was a divine principle. When she was asked to be a plural wife, her family was against it and she had doubts that she was making the right decision. "But I finally felt that I was doing the right thing and that assurance has never left me."[15]

In one case, the absence of spiritual manifestation prevented a plural marriage. Annabell Wheeler Hart said her mother's first husband left her when she joined the Church. "In 1887, she went to Utah with some missionaries that were on their way home. . . . They said that she could come and live with them and their families in Southern Utah. Later on, one missionary [who was already married] said, 'What would you say, Sister Doty, if I told you that it had been revealed to me that you should marry me?' . . . My mother had a great spirit. She said, 'He would have to reveal it to me, too.' " Annabell explained, "That ended that because she did not get any response from her asking the Lord about what she should do."[16]

Other family members often played crucial roles in decisions to enter plural marriage. One man married his wife's sister partially because their mother "wanted my dad to marry [her] because she loved my dad too. She wanted my dad to marry these two sisters so that they would keep him in the family."[17] Emma Romney's parents did not approve of the young man who was courting her and were pleased when her sister's husband, Edward Christian Eyring, asked Emma to marry him. Their approval was an important element in her decision. Edward's daughter-in-law, Mildred Bennion Eyring, speculated, "I suspect that when Grandfather Romney found how competent his son-in-law . . . was he at least helped to bring about the second alliance." Matilda Peterson said that she was only allowed to go to dances with old married men because "our father and mother felt we could not be saved unless we went into polygamy." Once she went home with a young single man instead of a twice married man that her father approved of and "paid for it" the next day.[18]

Mary Elizabeth Woolley Chamberlain, who grew up in a polygamous home and had required her husband-to-be to get the consent of his five wives, firmly believed in polygamy. Years before her marriage, she wrote a poem describing the struggles of the Saints to live polygamy in which she asked rhetorically:

> Will the daughters of Zion be fearing
> To choose for the right and for God?
> With fines and imprisonment threatening
> Will they hold fast the Iron Rod?

Her answer was:

> Better marry a man who'd be constant
> Though wives he may have more than you.
> If he is faithful to God and his covenants
> Be onward he'll be faithful to you.
> Though of Babylon's proud wealth he can boast not,
> Don't fear if his heart's only true,
> The riches of earth can compare not
> With affection eternal for you.[19]

Church Encouragement and Approval for Polygamous Marriages

An equally wide variation existed in the second traditional checkpoint in plural marriage: official instruction or permission. Of the approximately 200 men used in this study, 78 of the men or their descendants identified a Church official who asked them to marry in polygamy or who approved the marriage. Over 80 percent of these 78 reportedly received a direct request to marry a plural wife.

George Lake said that President Brigham Young asked him to come to Salt Lake City in 1861 and receive special ordinances in the Endowment House. Lake accepted the invitation and simultaneously had his wife sealed to her first husband, Lake's brother. When Young asked Lake how he was doing, he replied he regretted that his wife had been sealed to another man. Young told him, "You have done your duty my boy and your reward shall be greater. . . . Go to now, and in two weeks be here with two more for yourself." Lake wrote, "I pleaded for a little more time as I wished to make a wise choice, so as not to have trouble with him for a divorce. This he thought would be a good plan but said not to delay."[20]

Arthur E. Snow, a son of Erastus and his third wife, Elizabeth Ashby, told how Brigham Young encouraged his father to marry for a fourth time. Although Erastus was living in a log house with three wives, he obeyed. Arthur added, "During this time Brigham was putting considerable pressure on the men to marry the excess women, generally indicating a likely place to find a wife. Erastus married his fourth wife under these circumstances, and there was no love in this match, although the wife fit well enough into the picture."[21]

Both John Taylor and Wilford Woodruff encouraged all men in official Church positions to marry in polygamy. President Taylor said, "If we do not embrace that principle soon, the keys will be turned against us. If we do not keep the same law that our Heavenly Father has kept, we cannot go with Him. A man obeying a lower law is not qualified to preside over those who keep a higher law."[22] Taylor also said that polygamy "was applicable to High Councillors, Bishops, and their counselors and all who preside in Zion and if these officers should not obey this law, their places should be filled with men, who have obeyed the law."[23] Wilford Woodruff also observed, "The reason why the Church and Kingdom of God cannot advance without the Patriarchal Order of Marriage is that it belongs to this dispensation just as baptism for the dead does, or any law or ordinance that belong to this dispensation. Without it the Church cannot progress. The leading men of Israel who are presiding over stakes will have to obey the law of Abraham, or they will have to resign."[24]

David John recorded in his journal that in 1884 John Taylor, George Q. Cannon, and Joseph F. Smith discussed "Celestial Marriage saying it was binding on all the Latter-day Saints and no man was entitled to the right of Presiding without abiding this law." After explaining that Joseph Smith said that no coward could enter the order the speaker pointed out, "If Bro. Wm. W. Cluff and Abraham [sic] Hatch and other leading men had gone into this order 18 months or more ago Zion would today have been upon a higher place than now." According to William Forman, a bishop and tithing agent in Heber City, Utah, his stake president, Abram Hatch, said at a subsequent local priesthood meeting that it took Wilford Woodruff 40 years to obey the Word of Wisdom and it may take him that long to live polygamy. Forman recorded in his journal on 11 March 1884 that Hatch "feels quite important and says he is not going to resign."[25]

Abram Hatch, the stake president in Wasatch County from 1877 to 1901, was a monogamist and reportedly refused to marry a plural wife. Utah State Historical Society.

Other General Authorities also encouraged men to marry in polygamy and may sometimes have put pressure on them. According to the children of Andrew Larse Hyer, Apostle Marriner W. Merrill "from Richmond, came over and wanted Father to head the seventy's quorum" in Lewiston, Utah, and requested him to take another wife. Hyer agonized, calling it "the hardest decision he ever had to make in his life." After Merrill's third visit, however, he finally talked it over with his first wife, Ellen Gilbert, subsequently married Elizabeth Helen Telford in 1885 in the Logan Temple, and fathered 11 children by her.[26]

Stake presidents and bishops also gave authorization counsel. Laura Andersen Watkins said that the stake president told her father, James Michael, who also lived in Lewiston, that he was well enough off to marry again and suggested Susan Eliza Stephensen, a 22-year-old "good looking" woman not currently courting. "Father just took that for granted what he should do," commented Laura. "I think he accepted it just the same as Mother [Margaret Maria White] did." Mary Diantha Cox Sherratt said that Anthony W. Ivins, president of the Juarez Stake, asked her father, Amos, to marry again since he had no children. He married Mary's mother, and she and Amos had eight children. Torrey L. Austin reported his father, Edwin Nelson, a surveyor who lived in the Bear Lake area of Idaho and who married Alnora Naomi Chase Lane in 1863 and Emma Wood in 1872, did so because "it was a call, an individual call, for each individual to go into that relationship."[27]

Still others, though without specific instructions, felt that additional marriages were in harmony with Church policy. John C. Larsen, interviewed in 1938, said that he just followed general Church counsel and married three wives. Arabelle Parkinson Daines, the daughter of Samuel Rose and his third wife, Maria Smart, said her father was not given specific counsel but that all "worthwhile men" considered polygamy at that time. Lucy Fryer Vance, who was raised by her grandparents Hyrum Smith and Sarah Clarinda Bingham Phelps in Mesa, Arizona, said that her grandfather heard Brigham Young speak in Montpelier, Idaho, encouraging the men to marry in polygamy. Her grandfather thought, "If I am worthy and I am sure I can take care of two, I will take the counsel of the Church Authorities."[28] He married his first wife's sister, Mary Elizabeth Bingham, in Salt Lake City in 1873, seven years after his first marriage.

Courtship

After the decision to enter plural marriage, the problem of pursuing another wife remained. Plural marriages resulted from courtships that were not that much different from other romantic involvements in the nineteenth century. The modern perception of men and women marrying for love was rarely mentioned in marriage manuals. According to them, love should not be a "guiding star" in marriage plans. "A married couple should feel love for each other, but the love should grow out of the relationship rather than being the cause of it." Instead, men and women were to consider religion, character, and physical traits rather than romantic love.[29]

Plural husbands also seemed to have these same feelings about love. When Ida Stewart Pacey asked her father, Andrew, how he could love two women, he simply answered just as she could love two children. Marital love was not seen as something held exclusively for one person. Learning to work together for common goals including the ultimate reward, eternal life, was more important than physical attraction. After telling of his love for each of his three wives as long as they were faithful to him, Joel Hills Johnson's "poem" concluded:

> Should each prove True
> Their work to do
> Like truth and faithful wives
> Then all shall share
> My love and care
> With crown of endless lives.[30]

With this attitude about love, nineteenth-century "dating" in monogamous and polygamous marriages was much different from today. As one historian explained, "Of course, there were courtships. . . . After dances [and] church meetings, . . . young men would . . . ask young women, 'May I carry you home?' When the relationship had progressed to the stage where the suitor had a call on the young woman's family, the couple was said to be 'sparkin'.' These courtships were very short and by our standards quite formal."[31]

Mormon polygamous husbands varied in what they wrote about their marriage plans. While some men described their marriage interests with their first wives in great detail, many were very brief. Walter John Winsor explained his first marriage, "When I was twenty-one, nearly twenty-two,

I got married. . . . We had to make our own entertainment and there wasn't much time for courting."[32] Descriptions of second and third romances also varied in length and courtship was not emphasized in the men's writings. For example, Christopher Layton wrote in his autobiography, "On April 12, 1856, Caroline Cooper and I were married in Salt Lake City. President Brigham Young officiating," and "On August 12, 1862 Rosa Ana Hudson and I were married in Salt Lake City, Daniel H. Wells officiating." He made no mention of these women earlier in his autobiography. Warren Foote recorded in his autobiography that on 18 February 1856 he went to Provo to visit Eliza Maria. On 2 March 1856 he added, "Eliza Maria Ivie was sealed to me by Pres. B. Young in his office at SLC."[33]

Mary E. Croshaw, the fourth wife of George H. Farrell, agreed with this perception of brief courtships. "Married men didn't do any courting of their plural wives. Why, we would have thought it was dishonorable for a mature married man to go sparking like a young man. They just came and asked us, and if we wanted them, we agreed."[34] Laura Moffet, the second wife of W. F. Jones, remembered she was tending her brothers and sisters in her parents' absence when she saw him coming. "He had not paid any attention to me before, nor had I thought of him, but just as soon as I saw him coming across the lot I knew what he wanted. In those days no married man paid attention to a girl unless he wanted to marry her. He did not say much but asked me if there was any reason why I could not marry in polygamy. I knew then we were engaged."[35] Mary Elizabeth Woolley Chamberlain said that she had contact with her husband-to-be before he proposed but it had been all business. "When months later he proposed marriage to me it came like thunder from a clear sky and was such a shock that I resented it very emphatically. I had never dreamed of such a thing." Lydia Naegle Romney, the daughter of John Conrad Naegle and his sixth wife, said her father "always had his eye open" for prospective wives but he courted "in a reserved way."[36]

A few men were apparently more open in their search for plural wives. Murlyn Lamar Brown said that his mother, who had grown up in the Mexican colonies, chose monogamy because she was repelled by what she perceived as impersonal systematization. "There were some brethren in Colonia Juarez and Colonia Dublan that felt it was their duty to make sure that every young lady in the country had an opportunity to go into polygamy. . . . They made a mockery out of it by going around and asking all the girls that they ran into to marry them."[37]

Other families preserve no record of anything but brisk efficiency. Claude E. Hawkes, the son of the first wife of Joshua, explained the bishop advised his father to marry a second wife so he asked the daughter of a neighboring farmer. Claude said that the second marriage was more a "business arrangement" and second wife Sarah saw it as a "chance for a good match." There was "no special love" between them. Anderson P. Anderson, a son of Christian and his third wife, Anna Christiansen, said his father's first wife, Christine, was the first and only love. He married the second wife, Rasmine, because he felt sorry for her, his third, Anna, because the principle was being preached, and his fourth, Hannah, because Anna recommended it.[38]

Although the stereotype of immigrant women being funneled into polygamy is not supported statistically, anecdotal evidence shows some men married immigrants out of duty, simultaneously solving the dual problems of economic support and assimilation. When his wife advised him to marry again, Priddy Meeks of Parowan, Utah, decided upon a "handcart girl," preferably an immigrant without any relatives or money. After several inquiries, he learned of a girl who had just arrived in Salt Lake City and had no relatives. When he approached her, she was not interested. Disappointed, he turned to 16-year-old Mary Jane who had dreamed Meeks, nearly 60, would be her husband. Meeks wrote, "People may say what they want about mismated in age in marriage, but the Lord knows best about these matters. And if ever there was a match consummated by the providences of God this was one." Lawrence Leavitt told how his father, Thomas Dudley, of Bunkerville, Nevada, selected his second wife, Ada Ann Waite: "I think in Dad's case it was a case of she was just a young girl. She had just come from England and didn't know anyone, only just who she met there. . . . They were preaching polygamy. . . . I guess it just fell in line."[39]

In many cases, marriage developed as a logical conclusion to a relationship which may have remained only business or social. Emma Goddard was living with her sister and her husband Benjamin and teaching at the same school Benjamin was. After a year, "we fell in love with each other and we accepted polygamy when we joined the Church. He did not love Allie the less for loving me, but he loved us as much for what we were and he continued to love us both." In this case, marriage "seemed a natural thing to do."[40]

Thirty-three-year-old Melvina Clay Greer, the wife of Daniel Skousen of Colonia Juarez, suffered from lameness after the birth of twins, her fifth and sixth children. A member of the ward, Alma Spilsbury, offered the services of his 17-year-old daughter Sarah. Sarah, who wanted to finish high school, protested, but her father convinced her that the Skousens needed her. She worked for several months, enjoyed the family, and liked the daughters who were slightly older than she was. "She just loved [Daniel's] smile and his happy congenial spirit, his personality, his friendliness to her and appreciation for her work." Sarah was keeping company with a young local man, George C. McClellan, but when Daniel, who was in the Mutual Improvement Association presidency, the Church's organization for young men and women, slipped Sarah a note in Mutual asking her to walk with him instead of George, she did. They were married in 1901. Hannah Skousen Call, one of Melvina's daughters, said that she didn't know why her father married Sarah Spilsbury, but he used to say, apparently in jest, that he married her so that he would not have to pay her wages.[41]

The role of the first wife varied in subsequent courtships. Mary Lucile Clark Ellis said, "My mother told me once that Father was very considerate of her while he was courting Alice Randall. He would always tell her where he was going. When he came home, he would tell her what they did and where they went. She said, 'I would sit home and read the Book of Mormon.'" In other cases the first wife actually participated in courting. George Albert Wilcox noted that he and his first wife visited his choice, Susan G. Crabtree, and the first wife was the spokesperson. They courted for two years although George called it "a case of love at first sight." He then rather ingeniously added a couple of "girls" to his list and asked his wife which she preferred. She selected Susan.[42]

Mercy Weston Gibbons of Laketown, Idaho, accepted two Swiss girls in her home as boarders after a widowed Mr. Irwin brought them from Paris, Idaho. When both her husband and Irwin began courting them, Mercy assumed that the marriage was only a matter of time. Exasperated by sleeplessness, she borrowed 50 dollars from her mother and sent her husband off with the one he was courting to be married. "I guess I only just hurried along the marriage."[43]

Alma Elizabeth Mineer Felt remembered the role the first wife played in her courtship and marriage. "I was still very young when Louie Felt (Louie Ma) [the first wife] fell in love with me. She had no children and she wanted her husband to marry a girl who would give him children. I had done work for her and she liked me so she asked me if I would consider marrying her husband. I laughed at it at first, but later thought more about it." Rudgar H. Daines, the son of William Moroni and his third wife, Chloe Hatch, described a similar situation. "When Mother was sixteen, Aunt Elizabeth noticed how beautiful she was. I guess she went and helped Aunt Lizzie once in a while. . . . The romance developed. Aunt Lizzie told her mother and her father that she wanted Chloe for William's second wife."[44]

At the other end of the spectrum, wives were excluded from the selection of a plural wife. Mary Jane Rigby, the third wife of Samuel Roskelley, said that the whole family knew when Samuel was courting his fifth wife, Sarah Maud Burton, and he made no secret about his intention to marry her. Mary Jane said that the fifth marriage was difficult for all the wives to accept and she could not even describe her feelings. She felt it was probably harder for the first wife. Marva Little said her mother, resentful of her father's courtship of a prospective wife, once locked him out of the house, but her father married the woman nevertheless.[45] Betsy Lowe Allen of Cove, Utah, was still in bed recovering from the birth of her first child when she saw her husband "out spooning" with her sister Nellie who had come to help. As Betsy's son Clarence tells it, "He was holding Nellie in his arms and kissing her. She cried until her milk dried up. When they came and told her that they were in love and wanted to get married, she asked what could she do about it."[46]

Contemporary images of plural marriage are inevitably shaped by reactions read into the past. Assumptions of raging jealousy, supersaintly sweetness, kindly father figures, or lecherously roving eyes are all sufficiently common human behaviors to have occurred. At the very least, plural marriage through the selection of a second wife represented a rite of passage for the first marriage—no matter whether it came as the confirmation of an earlier decision, as a joint effort, or as a resented intrusion. All of these experiences occurred, and none can explain the situation completely. Although the first wife's consent was required by scripture, occasionally it was not sought nor freely given. Church leaders did encourage some men to marry in polygamy, but that did not always happen. Courtships depended on the individuals and could be initiated by the husband, the first wife, or the new wife. However, like all courtships in the nineteenth century, they were usually brief, and romantic love was not the prime reason for marriage. In Mormondòm, the motivation was religious.

6

Living Arrangements and Visiting Patterns

As in all aspects of Mormon polygamy, no set patterns developed as to where wives lived and how often husbands visited. As Kimball Young observed, "After all the plural family was really but an appendage to the basic patriarchal monogamous family. In matters such as the location of the families — whether under the same roof all together or in separate households in the same community or in different localities — there were no definite rules."[1] Although there were no set patterns, some common threads occurred in living arrangements and visiting patterns that were similar to other polygamous societies. Often the wives shared a home just after the second marriage, but as soon as it was financially possible, the husband provided a separate one for each wife. Most often the wives lived in the same community, but schooling arrangements, economic considerations, and personal preference sometimes determined where the wives lived. As children were born, grew, and then left home, living arrangements changed. Since most plural wives lived separately, husbands developed visiting schedules so they could spend time with each family. Living with one wife for a week or a night at a time was a common procedure. There were unique situations when the wives did not live in the same community and the husband visited only on the weekend, at harvest time, or at General Conference time twice yearly. In rare cases, the husband chose to live with only one wife either because of his interpretation of the Manifesto or differences in personalities between himself and a wife. Husbands also developed schedules for attending church and social occasions with their wives.

73

Whatever the arrangements, in some families there was a sense of expectation when the husband and father would live with them, and sometimes a sense of relief when he was gone.

Living Arrangements and Visiting Patterns in Other Polygamous Societies

Mormon living patterns, though not influenced by other polygamous societies, showed parallels to them. In other societies, each wife usually had her own household where she exercised direct supervision over her children and her home operation. Although this arrangement probably prevented intimate bonding among the wives, it almost certainly helped prevent jealousies and personality clashes. Of the polygamous societies in Murdock's *Ethnographic Atlas*, almost 60 percent of the wives lived in separate homes. In Africa the percentage rose to 88. Anthropologist Beatrice B. Whiting reported in Kenya that "each wife had her own house and hearth" and was responsible for her home, children, and animals. Pamela Blakely, an anthropologist who lived with and studied the Bahemba in eastern Zaire, found that plural wives had separate homes with front doors that faced each other so they could visit while working. In one case where the wives did not get along, the doors faced in opposite directions. A third wife's home was usually built so the doorways created a courtyard where they could work together.[2]

In such societies, whether the wives shared a home or had separate dwellings, a husband was expected to divide his time equally between families and to establish some pattern of visiting each home. According to anthropologist Ester Boserup, "Often in African families . . . each wife has her own hut and cooks independently, while the husband in regular succession will live and eat with each of his wives." The Bahemban husband divides his sleeping time equally among his wives although sometimes he has a separate home where he can live independently of all of them.[3] Today on the Comoro Islands off the southeast coast of Africa, Shirazi men alternate among wives by days, weeks, or months depending upon their occupations and locations of the families. A farmer having two wives in the same town might alternate days between them. If he has a wife on a farm and another in town where he has a minor governmental post, then he might change homes every week. Finally, a man with a high governmental position might separate his families between towns many miles apart and stay several months with each.[4]

Mormon Household Patterns

Mormon plural families usually lived in separate homes with the husbands visiting each wife at regular intervals when possible. Examining the families in this study shows that living arrangements occasionally changed during the marriage. Quite often just after a husband married a plural wife, all the wives shared a home. Later in the marriage after families were established, he might build a separate home or a family might move so that children could attend school or a wife could avoid the U.S. marshals. As the children left home and the husbands and wives grew older, living arrangements might be adjusted again. Information on all these stages of married life was unavailable for all families, so totals vary according to the stage of marriage under consideration.

Of 150 families (husband and wives counted as one family) giving information on early married life, 47 percent of the wives shared homes for a while after the husband married an additional wife. Caroline and Emma Romney, two sisters married to Edward Christian Eyring, lived in the same home for a year until he could build a new home for Emma. Severin N. Lee married Emma Ensign in 1874. A year and a half later, he married Olive Forsgen, all three living together while he built Olive a home.[5]

Nearly one-quarter of the wives lived in separate homes in the same town. Isaac B. Nash, for example, set up a blacksmith shop at his home in Franklin, Idaho, where his first wife Hester Elvira Poole, lived and then built a log cabin for his new bride, Eliza Norris, three blocks from the shop. When he married a third wife, Martha Howland, he built her a home on the same lot as the shop.[6] James Galloway Lowe of Preston, Idaho, married a plural wife, Elizabeth Kingsford, in 1885. A daughter of first wife Anna Eliza Doney recalled what she had been told about the living arrangements after the second marriage. "For a while he kept his second wife about three miles distance from our home. . . . In a few years he built her a home. It wasn't a block from our home."[7]

Thus, immediately after marriage, most of the wives lived in the same house or at least the same community despite the attempts by U.S. marshals to arrest those practicing polygamy after 1880. Wives lived in separate towns just after marriage in only 19 percent of the cases, and then it was usually because U.S. marshals forced the new wife on the underground immediately after the marriage was performed. James Amasa Little took third wife Mary Elizabeth Tullidge to Eagle Valley, Nevada, after their marriage in 1865. Later he moved her and his first wife, Mary Jane Lytle, to Kanab, Utah. His second wife, Annie Matilda Baldwin, lived 200 miles away in Payson. James moved to Salt Lake City later and then to Mexico in 1891 where he lived with his wife Ann for 15 years. Mary Elizabeth, who remained in Kanab, did not see her husband until 1906 when he returned to live with her after Ann died. She cared for him until his death in 1908.[8]

Brigham Pond's second wife, Catherine Whittle, also lived in a different community after her marriage. She had worked for his first wife, Aroetta, her sister, in Lewiston, Utah, before her 1885 marriage in the Logan Temple. After the ceremony, they returned to her parents' home in Richmond, Utah, as her son remembered the story. "Dad pulled up to the front gate of my grandmother Whittle's and let Mother out. Then he came home and stayed with his first wife. . . . My mother didn't see him for two weeks. In those days they had to do a lot of things to avoid trouble with the law. Dad took my mother to Oakley, Idaho, where she lived until after her first son was born."[9]

A small fraction of the wives continued to share homes once they started having children. At that time 55 percent lived in separate homes in the same town. The raids against the polygamists were not the prime consideration in determining where wives lived, since only 16 percent of the wives resided in separate communities and most were married after 1880.

Isaiah Coombs could not afford separate homes immediately for both wives when he married Charlotte Augusta Hardy in 1875, so Fanny McLean Coombs, his first wife of 17 years, arranged to give room in her home. Fanny tried to make Charlotte a partner in her home, but she insisted on a separate place.[10] Laura Jones, the daughter of Joseph Ammon Moffett and his second wife, Annie Maria Johnson, reported that her father's two wives lived together in Mexico. First wife Olive Catherine Emmett wanted Annie to stay with her because she was a better housekeeper, but Annie finally got a separate home, when, as her daughter explained, she "got backbone enough to demand a place for herself. She told Father that when a woman's hearthstone was taken away, everything was gone."[11]

Caroline Pederson Hansen shared a two-room home with her husband's first wife, Bengta, after her marriage on 25 July 1878. Although she told no one of her desire, Caroline prayed for a separate home. After her husband returned from a seven-month mission, her father gave her some land, and her husband built her a small adobe house. She later wrote, "I shall never forget how happy I was, and as soon as we were moved in and I was alone, I bowed down before the Lord and poured out my soul in prayer and gratitude for having a house of my own."[12]

Sometimes there were two homes because the families needed more room. John Brown's first two wives shared a common living area as well as the loom house and outbuildings, each wife having her own bedroom. Eventually the wives had so many children that John built two homes a few rods apart.[13] Ella Saunders, the first wife of Louis Cardon, described how she and the second wife, Edith Jamina Done, shared a home in Mexico after the second marriage in 1901. When Louis married Mary Irene Pratt in 1903, she lived with Ella and Edith. Later, when the children needed more room, Louis moved his second and third wives to separate homes, but eventually Edith returned to live with Ella.[14]

James Carson Allen had separate houses for his wives, Betsy and Ellen, in Cove, Utah, until the children were old enough to go to the high school — the Brigham Young College in Logan about fifteen miles away. Then Betsy moved to Logan to keep house for the students while Nellie stayed in Cove with the younger children. "At Thanksgiving and Christmas holidays, I would get to go to Logan," recalls a son, Clarence, "and the older kids would come home and do the chores."[15] George S. Pond described a similar situation: "When the boys got old enough for college, Dad moved Aunt Ettie," the first wife, to Logan. "Dad would rent a house down there and have a stable or something where we could keep that cow. All the college age sons and daughters of the two families would live with Aunt Ettie and go to school at Utah Agricultural College. My mother would stay home and take Aunt Ettie's kids that weren't in college and keep them. We would all live together."[16]

Evan B. Murray, the son of William Archibald and his second wife, Amanda Bailey, of Wellsville, Utah, says both the children's needs and economics determined where his father's wives Amanda and Sarah Jane Park lived. "One house was on the farm where most of the boys from both families lived, and one house was in town which served as a place for children to live who were working or going to school."[17] Mary Ann Stowell, the second wife of Joseph Jackson (he and first wife Prudence Phillips were divorced), said, "People used to say to me, 'Why don't you go out to the mill and take your rightful place?' " Since Mary Ann Jones, the third wife, married Joseph in 1903 when Mary Ann Stowell already had seven of her eleven children, her reply was, "I never wanted to do that. Daddy had married and the children were younger. Mine were growing up and could help me and I knew we could get along."[18] Fourteen percent of the families established living arrangements where one wife lived in town and another wife lived on a farm, usually several miles away.

Nathaniel Hodges's families provide another good example of an evolving living situation. For 10 years after Nathaniel married his second wife, Anna Weston, the sister of his first wife, Louisa, they lived in a four-room house in Laketown, Utah, except for a short time when the house was overcrowded. After his third marriage, to Charlotte Hancock, Nathaniel's wives lived in separate towns, both to avoid the marshals and to help with his businesses. Louisa lived at a mill and cooked for the workers; Anna lived on a farm and cooked for the help there. Charlotte lived first at Fish Haven while hiding from the marshals, then took charge of one of Nathaniel's sheep camps, and finally lived in Randolph, Utah, where she ran a way station for a freighting operation between Laketown and Evanston, Wyoming.

Eventually the wives and children felt Nathaniel's operations were too scattered and asked him to combine his efforts. All three wives and children moved to the Utah shore of the Bear Lake where Nathaniel operated a farm and ranch. As in 8 percent of the cases studied, two wives, Louisa and Anna, lived together on the ranch while Charlotte lived about a mile away. The sisters were in charge of the farming operations, and Charlotte's children quite often lived with them.[19]

Conflicting personalities also influenced living arrangements. Sometimes the wives did not get along with each other, so it was best to have them separated. According to one family history, William Adams's two wives lived together at first but they got along "cooly." After two or three months, William moved the first wife to Parowan, Utah, and the second wife four miles away to his farm, the first wife visiting occasionally to help make cheese. Four years later William moved the second wife back to Parowan near the first wife. According to family tradition, the wives still did not get along. Descendants of the second wife (who wrote the history) claimed that she tried but the first wife was unreasonable or perhaps emotionally disturbed. In another family, a daughter explained, "My father was smart enough to keep one family in Ogden and one in Hyrum," approximately fifty miles apart. "I think they got along better that way."[20]

Sometimes wives chose where they wanted to live according to individual preference. Ruth May, the first wife of Jesse Fox Jr., claimed that

Rosemary Johnson, his second wife, enjoyed the farm work while she did not like doing outside chores. After his families left Mexico, William Moroni Daines's work in a mercantile business and on a ranch took him to Preston, Idaho. Elizabeth Ann Hatch, his first wife, lived in Logan with her married children because "she just didn't want to live in Preston." She joined him in Preston, however, four or five years before he died in 1939.[21]

As the children left home and the wives and the husbands aged, living arrangements sometimes changed again. Of 75 families giving information about living arrangements in later life, 53 percent lived in separate towns while 33 percent still lived in separate homes in the same town. Only 9 percent shared a home. Some wives who had lived close together now lived separately because economic conditions had worsened or their children had moved to a new community. These 75 families represent a large portion of those who came out of Mexico in 1912. They had to abandon everything they owned and quite often the families had to separate to survive.

James Douglas Harvey, for example, married girlhood friends, Sarah Elizabeth Kellett and Nancy Anderson, on 1 August 1888 in Moroni, Utah. Both families moved to Mexico in 1891 and settled in Colonia Diaz. Sarah lived in town so her children could attend school, while Nancy, a former schoolteacher, lived on the farm for a while where she taught her children. James was one of the few Mormons killed by the Mexican revolutionaries, so his wives were left to care for themselves. Sarah and her younger children were visiting relatives in the United States in July 1912, so Nancy brought Sarah's older children with her when the Saints left. Both wives returned to Moroni, but since they had practically nothing, each went to her own relatives for support, Nancy eventually moving to San Juan County in the far southeastern corner of Utah and Sarah going with some of her sons to Duchesne County in the extreme northeastern corner of the state.[22]

A few families separated not only for economic reasons but because they felt that they could not live polygamy in the United States. Another family from the colonies was that of Charles Richard Fillerup and his two wives. In Mexico his second wife, Mary Evelyn Johnson, lived in a back room in first wife Moneta Johnson's home. (The two women were not related.) When the families came to the United States, Charles and Moneta moved to Arizona where he attended college, then went to work for the state extension agency. Mary went to Blanding to live with her parents.

Wilma Turley, Moneta's daughter, said that the exodus "broke up our own family . . . because Aunt Mary decided to go with her father and mother. . . . There were eight children with my mother, no home, didn't know how or where we were going or what to do." Mary brought her daughter from Mexico and she gave birth to a son a month later. Wilma's children disagree whether Charles kept in contact with Mary or whether Mary wanted to communicate with him, but twins born to Moneta in 1922 did not even know their father had a second wife until a stranger told them when they were 18 years old.[23]

Still other families succeeded in transplanting their Mexican pattern. Heber Erastus Farr married Amanda Elizabeth Williams and Romemilda Ranghilda Bluth in Mexico in 1904. After the exodus, the families moved to Binghampton, Arizona, now part of Tucson, where they shared a duplex. Though an interior door connected the two units, the children were taught to use the outside doors. When the families moved to Utah in the late 1920s, Mercelle, a daughter of Amanda Elizabeth, recalled, "We lived on one end of Orem, and Auntie lived on the other end of Orem. Then when we moved to Pleasant Grove, we each had separate homes." Later both families lived on Farr Avenue in Provo, a street named for the family.[24]

Visiting Schedules

Just as there was no standard living arrangement in plural homes, there was no plan for how much time the husband spent with each wife, although he was expected to establish some pattern of visiting each family. Kimball Young examined 50 families and found that about one-fourth alternated days with their wives, another fourth spent a week with each wife, one-fourth had an irregular schedule, and another fourth set up two-day, three-day, fortnight, or monthly schedules.[25] The 156 families on which this study has information show similar conclusions: 27 percent of the husbands changed homes nightly, 21 percent moved every week, only 8 percent had no routine, and 21 percent stayed primarily with one wife. The rest visited either once every three days or rotated monthly. Many of the children interviewed may have been remembering life after the Manifesto, which might have affected the schedule; however, only 16 percent reported dramatically changed life-styles because of the Manifesto or a move from Mexico to the United States.

Almost half of the husbands in this study then had a regular daily or weekly schedule. Karl Skousen reported his father stayed with first wife Ida Walser, and his mother, Emma Fredrika Mortensen, every other day. "I think that he was a little bit wiser in this than some others I'm acquainted with in that he did not make his absence too long. He changed homes every evening." Even some who stayed at each home for more than a day such as Anson B. Call visited each home "every morning." Marva Whipple Cram Little suggested her father's schedule was "a week about. I think that is the way they were told to do it." Her memory, however, may have been influenced by Maureen Whipple's novel about polygamy, *The Giant Joshua*: "The men in there were told to spend one week with one and one week with another, no more, no less."[26]

Husbands who alternated by day or week were usually very faithful in keeping their schedules. Douglas Cannon's father, David Henry, "used to be at our home every third day, regular as clockwork. He stayed at one house one night, the next house another night, and our house the third night. He was in the temple full time, but he was home at one or the other of these three homes every night." Cannon also explained, "Dad always shaved with a razor, and he had a little shaving kit. For years it was my responsibility for that shaving kit to be at the house where he was going to shave the next morning." Esther Whatcott of Mesa, Arizona, said that her father Hyrum Smith Phelps's schedule was "just like clockwork. . . . Father had a regular schedule to be over to Mother's every [scheduled] night to have supper and the breakfast the next morning. He would stay for dinner. Then he would go back to Aunt Clarinda," the first wife, an older sister.[27]

Edward Christian Eyring had a weekly schedule. LeRoy, a son of Emma Romney Eyring, the second wife, says that polygamy "was then so natural to me that I did not notice particularly his weekly packing of his leather valise to move over to 'Aunt Caroline's' for the week, or his return the following Saturday with his things put away in the leather container. It also seemed perfectly natural that he should leave our house a little before bedtime to go over to say goodnight to 'Auntie' when it was our week, or for his coming just before bedtime to kiss us goodnight when it was his week over there."[28]

Sometimes a visiting pattern was imperceptible. Glenn Whetten, a son of John Amasa and first wife Ida Elizabeth Jasperson, who lived in Mexico, could not remember his father's schedule. "Sometimes of a necessity he would be at one place and then the other. At least he would be staying nights at one place and then the other. I would imagine it was pretty well divided."[29] Divorced from his first wife, Edward William Payne, of Mexico, stayed with his second wife, Lucy Alice Farr, or his third wife, Rosalia Tenney, depending on where he was needed. "He wasn't stringent on it. But his wives didn't demand it that way either. They had an understanding; they knew that he was trying to make everything as nearly equal as he could. . . . It wasn't a hard and fast rule like some people like to make you think as long as it was fair,"[30]

When wives did not live in the same community, the husband would often visit one family only on the weekend, at harvest time, or at conference time. Benjamin Chamberlain Critchlow would visit his second wife, Elizabeth, in Hyrum, Utah, every 10 days when they had a water turn and then go back to Ogden for 10 days to be there for stake high council meetings.[31] Charles Rich Clark moved his first wife, Mary Emma Woolley, from Morgan, Utah, to a homestead in Georgetown, Idaho, in about 1900. He spent most of his time with her but visited his second wife, Ann Elizabeth Waldron, and their eight children in Morgan several times a year, almost always at General Conference time in April and October.[32]

When the husband was in Canada and allowed to have only one wife living there with him, he quite frequently saw his Utah wives just at conference time. Heber Simeon Allen married his second wife, Elizabeth Hardy, who lived in Salt Lake City, in 1903. Heber served as president of the Taylor Stake in Raymond for 34 years, living with his first wife, Amy Louise Leonard, and their children while Elizabeth stayed in Salt Lake City. Elizabeth's youngest daughter, Amy Pulsipher, remembered that her father would come for conference twice a year and stay for a month. "Then he would go back to Canada because he had a large business there and he also had a large farm. He had other people run it, but he oversaw the operation of it. My memory of our father living with us is rather limited. He just wasn't around very much."[33]

As the husband and wives grew older, the husband would often stay with one wife most of the time. Brigham Stowell lived primarily with first wife Mary Olive Bybee after the family left Mexico. Wallace, a son of third wife Ella Mae Skousen, explained, "He did come to our home once a week to see that everything was in order and to see if he could help in any way. . . . It was understood after the father left Mexico that his first wife was the legal wife in the United States and he should live with her." As Karma Parkinson Parkinson put it, "The Church asked him to only live with one wife and it was the law of the land."[34]

Other husbands lived with one wife to help care for growing children. Asenath Skousen Walser said that her father, Daniel, lived with his second wife, Sarah Ann Spilsbury, because her mother, his first wife, "felt like Father's place was more with the younger children and my aunt had the younger family. Mother's children were all older." Nathaniel Hodges lived with his third wife, Charlotte, when he was older because according to William, a son of the first wife, Louisa Weston, his father might have over-extended himself and Charlotte's home was a peaceful place to escape from his business at the ranch where the first two wives lived.[35]

Compatibility and personalities played a role when strict rotations were not observed. Maude Nuttal Haws noted, "If father was working really hard on the ranch, he would stay with the other wife. Most of the time he would stay with Mother. When he went away to work, he took Mother with him. He lived with Mother most of the time until she died and then he lived with the second wife." Part of the reason was that "my mother had a home. It was always comfortable, and food and everything was always ready. I don't know about the other home."[36] Wasel Black Washburn said that she didn't think her father had a favorite wife, but "I think there were times that he would be more at ease and more congenial with my aunt because she was easy going. She liked fun; she liked to go and do things. My mother thought she had better stay home and keep things in order and look after the children. I think right down in his heart that he really didn't have a favorite. I think he loved them both." When asked if her father spent much time at the second wife Agnes's home, Roxey Rogers, a daughter of the first wife, replied, "Not that I remember. I don't think he felt welcome there. He used to go there, but he would never stay long. They were different people."[37]

Verda Spencer Adams and Teresa Richardson Blau identified simple living habits as affecting their fathers' schedules. Verda said that her father ate his meals at Aunt Louisa's because "it was heavenly over there. He could rest when he wanted to. It was quiet." Teresa said her mother liked to sleep with the windows open and since her father had weak lungs she encouraged him to stay at Aunt Rene's.[38]

Memories of Father/Husband Visits

When regular daily or weekly schedules existed, the wives and children looked forward to their visits. Viva Bluth Brown, a daughter of Daniel

Skousen and second wife Sarah Ann, explained, "We were always especially proud when Papa's time was with us. He would come with us for a week and then he would go with Aunt Mally for a week. I think a man is doubly blessed when he has this kind of treatment. . . . I know he got the best food in the world because we would save the best for when Papa would be with us and I think Aunt Mally would do the same thing." According to Annie Richardson Johnson, "We were all really happy when it was his time to eat at our place. The wives kind of humored him. . . . When Father was going to be there, they would cook the things he liked and we would have the best while he was there."[39]

There were times, however, when some wives and children had an advantage when the husband was gone. Hannah Skousen Call, Viva's half sister, remembered that her father didn't like onions, "so whenever we wanted onions we would wait until he was in the other part of the house." Elizabeth Acord Beck, the second wife of Erastus, said, "You will laugh, but when he was home regularly I used to sometimes be relieved when it was his turn at auntie's. It gave me time to get caught up on my work and do some things I wanted."[40] Maud Hodges, the youngest daughter of James and his second wife Fanny Martin Kearl, felt the same way. "Sometimes I'm sure we were glad Father had the other family to go to. It was a great relief not to have a man around the place to cook for and to look after. We girls and mother were such good companions that we got along just as well with Father there as when he wasn't there."[41]

Church Attendance and Social Occasions

Plural husbands also had to determine which wife to take to church and to social events. Sometimes the community's attitude towards polygamy and the laws against it influenced whether a husband could be seen with more than one wife at a time at a public gathering. Still, of the 51 families giving details on church attendance, nearly half said that the father attended with all of his wives and children. In about 14 percent, the father attended with the wife he was staying with on that Sunday. About the same number said that the families never attended church together. In nearly all cases the children simply accepted whatever arrangements existed and said it did not make a difference in relationships.

Marva Whipple Cram Little remembered "my brothers and sisters telling about when they were in Mexico. Dad would sit back behind the kids with Mom and Aunt Mary."[42] Lorna Call Alder remembered that when church met in "the Relief Society House" it was too far to walk. When she was older, she would drive her father's white top buggy to take the men to priesthood meeting and then drive home so the "mothers and children could ride. Then we would all go together. One of the women would drive the children up to Sunday School. . . . Then we would all come home again. The three seated buggy was just packed full when we all came home. . . . When cars came in, we had a car. It was the same way."[43]

Charles Durfee said that the children in his family usually sat with friends at church, and he was not sure what pattern his father followed. "I think he went to church the day that he stayed with Aunt Fanny and if my mother went in, [she] would probably sit on the same bench [with them]. If they didn't [sit together], Mother would sit with her [the other wife], but on her day he would go with Mother. They had no order about it."[44]

Children did not always agree on how the family got to church or who their father sat with there. Anthony Ivins Bentley remembered that all the family could ride in the buggy if they wanted to wait, but quite often the children walked while their fathers and the wives came together. His full brother Richard remembered that his father arrived with the wife he was staying with but did not sit with either because he was the bishop and sat on the stand.[45] Joseph Eyring remembered that in Arizona his father went to church with the wife he was staying with that week. But his half brother LeRoy recalled, "He would sit with Aunt Caroline [the first wife] in the audience in sacrament meeting whenever she was there. My mother was very careful to have other things to do so that it wasn't obvious she didn't have anyplace to go. For example, she was always in the choir. She had to be up in the choir during sacrament meeting. So it didn't present an awkward situation."[46]

Whether a husband with several wives took all or some of them to social activities depended on the circumstances. Obviously, during the underground period, he and several wives would not attend a social together. Otherwise, most husbands seemed to be willing to take more than one wife to church dances and to other community activities. Albert L. Payne remembered that his father took both of his wives to the Salt Lake Theatre two or three times a year after the families had moved to Provo during the 1910s. "There was no reason to hide. They didn't talk about it, but they did things together."[47]

Elizabeth Telford Hyer of Lewiston, Utah, second wife of Andrew Larse, said that he took both wives to socials, but took each in turn to General Conferences, leaving the other wife to manage the home and farm.[48] Anthony Ivins Bentley said that after his father married Maud Taylor, his third wife, the other wives realized "that every wife ought to have good times after she is married and so they rather encouraged, or at least tolerated Father showing Maud a special good time by taking her to dances and other ward functions. Then after that, he gradually settled down to all of them going together." In those early years, Maud also went to socials with her cousins because she was young and enjoyed more activities than her older husband. Lavinia Jackson, Maud's daughter, remembered that as her father got older he went to fewer socials but Maud continued to go with her children. "She was twenty-six years younger than Father, so there were some events he didn't go to like dances. He had only learned how to dance the round dances."[49]

Special circumstances sometimes determined who the husband took with him. Elizabeth Ann Schurtz McDonald said that her sister, the first wife, was shy. "She couldn't talk to people, especially strangers, so I went out with Pa [their husband] a lot when she wouldn't go." Their husband had the best team and rig in Heber City and was often asked to drive to Park City to get the visiting Church officials, and Elizabeth frequently accompanied him.[50] Florence Jackson, a daughter of Joseph and Mary Ann Stowell Payne, explained, "I think one of the big troubles in polygamy was the difference in ages. A man would take a young wife. Daddy was sixteen years older than Mother. When she wanted to go out, he wanted to sit home."[51]

It is impossible to tell what pattern the couples would have chosen if they had been free of external constraints. Wasel Black Washburn said that when her father and his wives "were younger, they would go to dances and parties together. After we left Mexico and were out here [in Utah, especially Salt Lake City], it was frowned on. Some people felt like they were too smart if they went places together. They got so they didn't go together . . . to anything." Katherine Cannon Thomas, whose father kept his three wives in separate communities, said that the families got together only for funerals or important weddings.[52] Frederick, the son of John Taylor and his fifth wife, Sophia Whitaker, said that his father "avoided being in company with two or more wives at the same time. This was consciously done to forestall any conflict that might arise out of the situation." When he traveled as President of the Church, he took a different wife each time, but in Salt Lake City, "he danced with all his wives and all the other men's wives too."[53]

Thus, a number of factors influenced living arrangements and visiting schedules. These varied over time as family needs and political considerations changed. Although the underground period during the 1880s affected the families, other considerations had more impact. Usually economic conditions and the ages of children played a larger role in determining lifestyle than the laws against polygamy. Living arrangements and visiting schedules were also significantly impacted upon by how the husband, wives, co-wives, and children related to each other. While it is impossible to define a typical schedule, for the most part the wives lived in separate homes usually next to each other in the same community and the husband lived in each home for a week or a night at a time. Attendance at church and social occasions also varied based on the age of the wives, family relationships, and individual personalities. What cannot be determined with any certainty is the degree to which decisions about these matters were made solely by the husband or by the husband in consultation with one wife or with all of his wives.

7

Daily Life and Family Roles

Although polygamous husbands shifted between households, daily life was about the same as it was in monogamous homes. Agriculture was the major source of income for Mormons throughout the West; families raised nearly all of their food and produced nearly everything they used. Men and women had specific work assignments. The men usually worked in the fields or in businesses outside of the home while women worked inside the home, in the garden, and with domestic animals. Men were to labor "by the sweat of thy face."[1] According to Brigham Young, "It is the calling of the wife and mother to know what to do with everything that is brought into the house, laboring to make her home desirable to her husband and children, making herself an Eve in the midst of a little paradise of her own."[2]

The Victorian ideal was that "women's God-given role was that of dutiful daughter, wife, mother, and homemaker" and that men's role was to be "a busy builder of bridges and railroads, at work long hours in a materialistic society."[3] In fact, these roles were far more important in determining life cycles for men and women and boys and girls than how many wives were married to the same husband. In his study of polygyny in Africa, Remi Clignet examined two tribes with very different life-styles to determine how polygamous families differed from monogamous families. He concluded, "Variations in type of marriage do not directly modify the existing principles of familial division of labor. Rather these principles are primarily cultural in nature."[4] In Utah, too, the predominant culture influenced the division of responsibilities more than the marriage pattern. This chapter will show that the roles of polygamous and monogamous husbands and wives and their children were basically the same in nineteenth- and early twentieth-century Mormon society. Men provided for their families by working on a farm or in a business. Women kept house, which often included caring for gardens and domestic animals, and children learned their future roles from their parents. Women and children stepped into men's responsibilities only when the husband/father was called on a mission or died. Then their work might involve engaging in paying ventures such as weaving, teaching school, or caring for the sick. Plural wives might share some responsibilities, but mostly they worked separately in their own homes.

Male Roles and Occupations

The husband's primary role was that of provider. Kimball Young examined male occupations in five categories: professional, proprietary (farm or ranch owner/operator, manufacturing, merchandising, and freighting), clerical and white-collar workers, skilled craftsmen, and semiskilled and unskilled laborers, and concluded that 80 percent of the men fit in the proprietary area. This figure included "slightly more than two-thirds" where "farming or ranching are the major source of income." Using the same categories, Vicky Burgess-Olson found that 53 percent of the 32 monogamous husbands that she studied and 70 percent of the 104 polygamous men were proprietors.[5] Of 185 polygamous and 118 monogamous husbands considered in this study, 58 percent of the polygamists and 62 percent of the monogamists were proprietors, using Kimball Young's definition. Of that number, 57 percent of the plural husbands and 59 percent of the monogamous husbands were farmers or ranchers. (See Table 13.)

Work for monogamous or polygamous farmers was the same. "Men and boys usually performed the most arduous or heaviest work, such as clearing the land, preparing the ground for crops, planting and cultivating, and building houses and repairing equipment." First, the land had to be plowed by hand. George Heiner of Morgan, Utah, described a plow a blacksmith made for his father. "The mold board of this plough was made of three strips of wagon tire."[6] After plowing, the land had to be harrowed, and the crops needed to be planted. Irrigating and weeding occupied much of the families' time until harvest, an all-out family effort. Annie Marie

Table 13

Economic Role of Polygamous and Monogamous Husbands

Survey includes 185 polygamous and 118 monogamous husbands.

Polygamous	Number	Percentage
Professional	38	20.6%
Proprietary	107	57.8
White Collar	12	6.5
Skilled craftsmen	25	13.5
Semiskilled and unskilled	3	1.6
Total	185	100.0
Monogamous		
Professional	14	11.9%
Proprietary	73	61.9
White collar	30	25.4
Skilled craftsmen	1	.8
Semiskilled and unskilled	0	0.0
Total	118	100.0

Darius of Ephraim, Utah, remembered that "my father used to cut the grain with a cradle and we children would rake it with hand rakes and my mother would bind the grain and then we would shake it up." Peter B. Johnson remembered, "We used to flail our grain. Wheat was placed on a bare ground and beat with a flail. Then we gathered up the straw and separated the wheat from the chaff by throwing it like we were sowing grain."[7] The farmers' families also had to care for work animals as well as food animals.

Since there was little cash available, most farms were basically self-sufficient; families raised nearly everything they ate and wore. Visits to stores were rare. Even if the main source of income was not farming, quite often the men were still responsible for caring for some animals and some crops. Still, the ever-present need for money made it common for men to have more than one occupation. Of those involved in farming and ranching, 24 percent of the polygamous and 20 percent of the monogamous husbands had additional occupations such as mining and freighting. Zaides Walker Miles and Nan Walker Atkins, daughters of Charles L. Walker's first wife, explained, "Father was a blacksmith, stonecutter, farmer in a small way and night watchman." Elwood Earl Larsen's father, a monogamist, had much the same problem. "We just had a small farm up there, twenty acres. Trying to make a living for the family is pretty tough on a small farm." Elwood's uncle, a salesman, convinced Elwood's father to distribute door to door Watkins and Raleigh products, which included spices and general household goods.[8] Of those not involved in farming, 32 percent of polygamous and 24 percent of monogamous men had two occupations at the same time. Lorenzo Watson, a polygamist, ran a tannery, made saddles and harnesses in Parowan, Utah, and had a soldier's pension from fighting in the Civil War. He also studied law on his own and passed the bar. George Black's monogamous father was a professional cook and a barber, but he also ran sheep and freighted.[9]

The typical nineteenth-century frontiersman, whether Mormon or non-Mormon, whether monogamous or polygamous, had a variety of occupations. Sometimes after graduating from the eighth grade or high school, he would travel, working on ranches, in mines, or freighting goods. After marriage, he might purchase a farm so he would not have to travel as much. When a farm did not produce a large enough income, he would supplement it with freighting, mining, or railroad work. Louis Mousley Cannon worked for Zion's Bank and then owned sheep. He felt the sheep took him away from his family too much, so he went into real estate and ranching. Edward Hunter Jefferies, the son of a monogamist, said that his father was a concert violinist before he married. Then because he was losing his hearing, he studied architecture. Later he farmed in Idaho and near Delta, Utah, worked as a carpenter, and when he was older, learned to repair watches and opened a shop.[10]

Making ends meet was a constant challenge. Franklin Lyman Stout explained, "My dad was a peddler. That is about the most he did. He had some land and tried to raise crops." He added, "I used to be awful critical of how he was doing, but now I wonder how he existed. I thought he had done an awful bum job. [But] he managed to keep himself and feed himself." Vera Anderson Christensen's father ran cattle and sheep in southern Utah. Because it was not sufficiently lucrative, he worked as a foreman for his brother Hakan on a large "cotton plantation" near Pima, Arizona. When the living arrangements did not work out and the climate proved too hot for him, he moved his family to Idaho and leased farmland.[11]

Andrew Jonus Hansen struggled to provide for his four wives and their children. He tried several occupations because "My family was steadily, and I might say rapidly increasing and their support depended entirely upon my daily labors." Yet despite problems with his business, Andrew told of several times where it seemed he was miraculously able to provide for his families. "I bear testimony in all solemnity that the Lord . . . [kept] His promise . . . and thus placed His stripe of approval upon our course and conduct, for we were never without bread, nor without actual necessities of life. Nay, we were better provided with food and with clothing. . . . Often our substance was multiplied in a manner marvelous and mysterious to us."[12]

Charles Edmund Richardson's experiences provide an example of how a man's economic situation changed. When Edmund first moved from Arizona to Colonia Diaz in 1889, he taught school, then started a blacksmith shop and a gristmill. When the stake president, Anthony W. Ivins, asked him to go to Mexico City to study law, he took his first wife and her four children and attended law school at the University of Mexico for four years, graduating with honors. His other business activities in Colonia Diaz provided for his three wives and their children while he was in school.

When Edmund returned from Mexico City, he purchased a large ranch, the Dusty Dale, in Colonia Diaz. He managed the ranch, and his wives and children did the daily chores. He traveled extensively while practicing law and moved his first wife to Colonia Juarez so he could be near Nuevo Casa Grande, the seat of the local government, and so his children could attend the Church-owned high school. There he married his fourth wife, Daisie Stout. Hazel Taylor, a daughter of the first wife, said her father "was as well-to-do as the average man was, but when he divided it up into four families, he had to watch his pennies. . . . We dressed well; we ate well; we had comfortable homes. But I wouldn't say that we were well-to-do. We never could afford to live lavishly."[13]

Edmund's life changed dramatically when he left Mexico in 1912, having to find a new career at 55 years of age. Some of his problems were directly related to the fact that he was a polygamist and had four large families to support. He was not licensed to practice law in the United States, although he returned to Mexico to help Mormons settle claims against the Mexican government. He drove his cattle from Mexico and sold them to buy a farm in New Mexico. Later he sold it and bought two others near Duncan, Arizona, property that was flooded when railroad drains overflowed. He then purchased some land called the Haven that he eventually lost in a lawsuit. He also tried to secure homesteads for his wives to prove up on. Daisie homesteaded some land outside Safford and then sold it to her brother. Becky, the third wife, took out a desert-entry claim near the Cascade Mountains in Arizona but lost it to ranchers who resented farmers.

Edmund tried a variety of other occupations without much success. He received a teaching certificate and taught Spanish-speaking students for three years in San Jose, Arizona, coming home to Thatcher on weekends. An elementary schoolteacher's salary was insufficient for his families, and he attempted unsuccessfully to mine. When he made plans to start a gristmill, the other millers in the area took him to court over the additional competition. By necessity, Edmund's wives began seeking paid employment.

Female Roles and Occupations

Though Harriet Beecher Stowe claimed polygamy was "a slavery which debases and degrades womanhood, motherhood, [and] family," some modern scholars have applauded polygamous wives for breaking out of the traditional female spheres and achieving greater independence.[14] Few Mormon women, either monogamous or polygamous, however, voluntarily worked outside of the home. Rather than being "decades ahead of their sisters in the American East in economic and professional opportunities," as Maureen Ursenbach Beecher at first concluded, their work "varied little from women's work anywhere else in the western civilization."[15]

In an article about Mormon women and the cult of domesticity, Kathleen Marquis emphasized that a plural wife's experiences were similar to those of a monogamous wife. Mormon "religious cohesion and spatial closeness nourished a strong group spirit that helped them survive and enabled them to prosper. In this setting a man's many wives (and children) enabled him to better operate his farm, though to the Gentile observer it constituted a harem."[16] Since the women made all foods from scratch and clothing by hand, extra hands made the load for each individual lighter and there was usually plenty for everyone to do. Even in urban areas such as Salt Lake City, families still were basically self sufficient. With these arrangements, it was possible for a husband to feed two wives and ten to twenty children.

Polygamy did not destroy the Victorian role for women and they were not forced to be economically independent. Of 225 wives, almost 9 percent of the wives received no support from their husbands and 3 percent received only minimal support and basically cared for themselves and their families. The remaining 88 percent divided the support of their families with their husbands. Of 46 monogamous families, 89 percent shared the task of supporting their families with their husbands. The other 11 percent (five wives) were widows and raised their families mainly by themselves. (See Table 14.)

The Pomeroy family was an example of a plural family where the second wife received almost no help from her husband. After Reuel Nephi, the youngest child of second wife Sarah Lucretia, was born, his father, Elijah, lived with first wife Mary Annette Coleman. Sarah bought and operated several farms with the assistance of her four young sons. When Reuel was nine, Sarah moved to Mesa, Arizona, where she was a store clerk. The next year, a son, Marion, died. His life insurance was used to pay off the mortgage on the city property and to fence the fruit trees. Reuel explained, "My mother told me many times that Marion wanted to see that place fenced, and he wanted to see it paid off. . . . He did pay it off; he did what he intended to do."[17]

The Brandley family received minimal financial support from the husband. When Louis's father, Theodore, went to Canada, he married a third wife, Eliza, while Louis's mother stayed in Richfield. Her husband sent very little money, forcing her to be more frugal. Louis reported that she wrote to his father, "We have thirty chickens; we are getting so many eggs a day. I want to get more chickens. I think we could have maybe a hundred chickens. If we could get a hundred chickens, we could do a lot more to support ourselves."[18]

In all families, though, the wives were expected to work and help support the family. Jonathan S. Cannon explained, "Daddy seemed to love all of us. . . . He provided the financial background for our home. . . . But he expected all of us, including my mother and all of us, to put ourselves to the wheel and work in the project of family living." Walter Haws said that he had never received a dime from his father. He felt "polygamous families always had to maintain themselves; they always had to take care of themselves. My father was a good man. He always kept the family in flour and sugar and stuff like that but as far as articles of clothing and food in the house, we always had to take care of our own."[19]

Both monogamous and polygamous wives assisted their husbands in traditional ways. Of 291 polygamous wives in this study, 20 percent worked outside of the home at some point during their married lives, but none did

Table 14

Level of Economic Support Provided
to Polygamous and Monogamous Wives

Survey includes 291 polygamous and 48 monogamous wives.

Polygamous	Number	Percentage
No support from husband	20	8.9%
Little support from husband	7	3.1
Male/female sphere division of support	198	88.8
Total support from husband	0	0.0
Total	291	100.0

Monogamous		
No support from husband	5*	10.7
Little support from husbands	0	0.0
Male/female sphere division of support	41	89.1
Total support from husband	0	0.0
Total	48	100.0

*All widows

---

so continually. They worked when necessary at very conventional jobs—
teaching, housekeeping, midwifery, and clerking—and returned to their
traditional roles as soon as possible. Another 46 percent, using their home
skills, sold farm goods, took in boarders or washed clothes to earn extra
money. Thirty-two percent did not work outside of the home for wages, but
helped support their families by frugally budgeting the goods their husbands provided. This study also examined 48 monogamous wives, and of
these, 13 percent worked outside of the home for wages at some time during their lives, but like the polygamous wives did not do so continually.
Thirty-six percent sold farm goods or used home skills, and 49 percent did
not earn additional money but made frugal use of the supplies that they
were given. (See Table 15.) In short, these statistics fail to support the
popular suggestion that "polygamy developed independent women who
bore much of the financial responsibility for their families."[20]

The duties and responsibilities were the same for both polygamous
and monogamous wives. Kimball Young explained that Mormon women
were to be childbearers, housewives, and companions. "The role of the
housewife followed the puritanical pioneer view. Wives were supposed to

Table 15

Economic Roles of Polygamous and Monogamous Wives

Survey includes 291 polygamous and 48 monogamous wives.

Polygamous	Number	Percentage
Outside salaried jobs	59	20.3%
Sale of excess farm goods	65	22.4
Use of home/home skills	68	23.4
Frugal budgeting of resources	93	32.0
Support from other family members	6	2.1
Total	291	100.0

Monogamous	Number	Percentage
Outside salaried job	6	12.8%
Sale of excess farm goods	11	23.4
Use of home/home skills	7	12.8
Frugal budgeting of resources	23	48.9
Support from other family members	1	2.1
Total	48	100.0

be thrifty, hard-working, 'to keep their houses, furniture and beds pure and clean,' to be good cooks and above all to be orderly, neat and systematic." Terrance Heaton said that his mother, a plural wife, "never did any work outside the home. She was a real homemaker." Bernitta Bartley described her mother, a monogamous wife, as "just a farmer's wife."[21]

The phrase "just a farmer's wife," however, depreciates the enormous amount of labor required. Any wife, monogamous or polygamous, spent a whole day each week doing laundry, a tedious and time-consuming process. Pressing clothes with sadirons, cast-iron implements heated on the stove, took another full day. Women made soap, vinegar, and cheese, and they baked bread, hauled water, scrubbed pine floors, and made rag rugs. In addition, they made straw ticks for mattresses, carded wool, spun thread, wove fabric, and sewed clothing. There was always plenty of work within the home.

And four walls did not limit women's work. They were often responsible for the garden, the milk cows, and the poultry. Plural wives had more responsibility for outside work because their husbands divided their time between several households. For example, more polygamous children than monogamous children described the garden as "my mother's" rather than "my father's." The plural wife was also more likely to milk cows and feed chickens than her monogamous counterpart. Reuben L. Hill, a son of George and his first wife, Elizabeth, said that each wife had her own chickens, turkeys, geese, cows, and gardens. Elizabeth, with the help of her sons, also did the garden work. Charity, the second wife, was not as energetic, so her cows and chickens did not do as well.[22]

Division of Labor

Of 59 families from this study that include information on how the plural wives divided their work assignments, 68 percent of the wives ran their homes separately or worked together only on special projects. Harriett Hutchings described an absolute division of labor in her father's homes. "Aunt Phoebus [McCarroll Snarr, the second wife] ran her place and my mother [Alice Thompson] ran her place. In our home, Mother had supreme authority. . . . No one ever tried to interfere with Aunt Phoebus's living; she did not try to bother in our living. It was just like two different families. We did not try to live together as a family. But we got along. . . . As far as managing the house . . . they both did their own." Ether Haynie explained that his father's two wives, Henrietta Parrallee Cecelia Gage and Mary Elma Wilson, "lived independently. They didn't have to depend on the other one too much."[23]

Thirty percent of the co-wives did some work together. Zina Dunford remembered that her mother, Sarah Thompson Patterson, and the first wife, Mary Thompson, her sister, would launder together. "We used to have two wooden tubs on a bench. Mother would be at one tub and Auntie would be at the other. One would scrub on the board, get the worst of the dirt off, and put them into the other tub. And then she would scrub." Louis Cardon said that although his father's second and third wives did most of their chores separately, "the one thing that the wives [had] in common were the beehives."[24]

In the Nathaniel Morris Hodges family, the first two wives, sisters Louisa and Anna Weston, lived together most of the time. Louisa enjoyed being outdoors and took charge of the cows, while Anna did most of the housework. They lived on the main ranch and supervised the workers, including some of third wife Charlotte Hancock's children who lived and helped at their home.[25] In the David Stout family the first wife was frail and did not do very much work, but the other four wives who shared the household divided the chores. Franklin Lyman, a son of fourth wife Sarah Lucretia Cox, recalled, "I remember one mother was always sewing and mending. My mother was the cook; she was cooking for everything. One of my aunts had a hoe. She was out in the garden hoeing weeds all the time."[26]

Elizabeth Acord Beck, second wife of Erastus Beck, recorded that she sewed for the first wife because the first wife could do only very plain sewing. When she made dresses for the first wife's daughter, she emphasized that she put the same care into them as she did for her own daughter. In return, the first wife would render lard for Elizabeth. They quilted, put up fruit, and cooked together. Elizabeth explained, "We found . . . we were far happier when we worked together and saw each other every day."[27]

Children's Roles

Children were assigned specific tasks in both monogamous and polygamous homes. Daughters usually worked with their mothers and sons worked with their father, learning the roles that they would have as adults. Brigham Young said that "both males and females" should have "mechanical ingenuity, and seek constantly to understand the world they are in, and what use to make of their existence." He sounded a familiar theme from the pulpit, encouraging mothers to teach their "daughters to be housekeepers, to be particular, clean, and neat; to sew, spin, and weave; to make butter and cheese." He added that there were some other things that girls could learn. "I have no objection to their learning to cultivate flowers, herbs, and useful shrubs in the gardens. It is good for their health to rise early in the morning and work in the soil an hour or two before breakfast. . . . [But] while you delight in raising flowers, &c, do not neglect to learn how to take care of cream, and how to make wholesome butter, and of the milk good healthy nutritious cheese; neither forget your sewing, spinning, and weaving." He also said to "teach little children the principles of order; the little girl to put the broom in its right place, to arrange the stove furniture in the neatest possible way, and everything in its own place. Teach them to lay away their clothing neatly, and where it can be found; and when they tear their frocks and aprons how to mend the rent so neatly that the place cannot be seen at a short distance; and instead of asking your husbands to buy them ribbons and frills, learn them to make them of the material we can produce."[28]

Eva C. Webb noted, "In Aunt Margaret's home eventually there were seven living daughters, trained to do their part so well that even the four year old could use dust pan and brush up crumbs that might fall from the table and those just older would wash and dry and put away the dishes."[29] Daughters helped their mothers with washing, ironing, and other chores, training as future wives and mothers.

When the fathers farmed, sons worked alongside them cultivating, irrigating, and caring for crops. When the fathers were not farmers, the sons were still responsible for chores such as milking cows and caring for animals. Just as the girls needed to learn order, Brigham Young said, "Teach the little boys to lay away the garden hoe, the spade, &c., where they will not be destroyed by rust; and let them have access to tools that they learn their use, and develop their mechanical skill while young; and see that they gather up the tools when they are done with them, and deposit them in the proper place."[30]

According to Jonathan S. Cannon, "When I was nine years of age, because my older brothers and the younger brothers were all getting larger and needed more room, my father moved us to Centerville, Utah, where we had quite a holding of land. We had a six acre multiple orchard with every kind of fruit you could imagine and several varieties of nuts. We had a five acre pasture, forty acres of hay, and six hundred acres of mountain land. . . . All the boys, seven of us all together, were able to find plenty to do in the way of work and activity." Sons also helped their mothers by turning the new hand-operated washing machines. They also weeded the gardens, and in nearly half of the families in this study milked the cows. They took care of the horses needed to draw the farm machinery and fed and cared for other animals. Jonathan, for example, helped his mother milk cows, sell fruit, and run a poultry business.[31]

Cecelia Peterson Bott Morris, the daughter of John H. Bott and third wife Cecelia Peterson, explained that the children were always working; her parents believed, "The devil finds work for idle hands to do." Sometimes they had make-work projects such as sorting old nails. At other times they helped with their father's tombstone business. Joseph Eyring's mother, Caroline Romney, was "the one if we wanted to take it easy would say, 'No son of mine is going to sit around the house. If you haven't got anything to do, go dig a hole and fill it up again.' "[32]

Families adapted a work pattern based on need. If a family had no sons or at least none old enough to work, the daughters often had more outside chores. Jeneveve Layton, a daughter of Emma Romney Eyring, recalled, "Mother had two sons. The first one died, and then there was Tony. Then she had five girls. Then she had a boy . . . which left a gap there without boys to work on the farm or to help with the milking. So Ethel got drafted for tramping hay. [Father] tried me a few times, but I was put aside as not being heavy enough." Jeneveve was also asked to help milk cows once, but her technique was so poor her father told her, "Daughter, you would dry the cows up before you even milked them." Her brother LeRoy, just two years younger, worked outside. She recalled, "I helped inside, and Ethel worked outside. That was kind of a division of labor that came about because of the arrangement of the family."[33]

Daughters also were called out at harvesttime when there was more outdoor work on the farm. Zina Dunford, a polygamous daughter, remembered, "We would have two crops of hay during the year. . . . The men folks would do the mowing and raking. The girls would help. . . . We [girls] would have to drive the horses to unload the hay. . . . We girls would . . . help tromp hay down on the load so that we could get more in." Caroline Olsen, a child of a monogamous family, "being her father's only large help . . . had to take the place of a boy and helped haul the hay and grain."[34]

Wives and Children Outside Traditional Roles

Sometimes both monogamous and polygamous wives and their daughters and sons had to step out of traditional roles. Although married men with children at home are no longer called to serve proselyting missions, they were routinely given such assignments in the late nineteenth and early twentieth centuries. Not only did they require some support — even in those days of traveling with little money, without "purse or scrip" as Jesus commanded his disciples — but the wives had full financial responsibility for themselves and their children. Lula A. Larsen's father went on a year mission in 1883 during which time a son died and a daughter was born. Although Lula was born after her father's return, she learned of the effects it had on her mother. "Those were hard times for my mother. I have heard her say she milked a cow and had some chickens. She made butter and sold a little butter. She sold eggs to support herself. Mother would try to send a few dollars now and again to Father, but they mainly went without purse and scrip."[35]

Laura Watkins's father, James Michael Andersen, was called on a mission in 1885 just as the grain was ripening. There were so many sun-flowers in the grain that a neighbor suggested that Laura's mother, Margaret Maria White, James's only wife at the time, just cut it for hay. Margaret was determined to get a higher price for the crop and so she took her two oldest sons, both under thirteen, to the field every morning to pull the sunflowers. She was home from the fields in time to milk the cows, sepa-rate the cream, fix breakfast, and assist the children. When the grain was harvested, it was an excellent quality, and her mother received more than the current market value.[36]

Henry M. Stark was 15 when his monogamous father left on a mis-sion. "My mother had to help quite a bit, particularly with the manage-ment. She didn't actually get out in the field and work doing hand labor that men would be doing, but all of her five children were deeply involved in that during those two years. It was a learning experience for us."[37]

Edward McGregor Patterson was called on a mission during the raids on polygamists. While he was gone, his two wives, Mary and Sarah, used to weave together on a loom. "That brought in some income besides the farm. . . . Of course, the wives took care of everything while he was gone. I guess there were many such women that had to provide for their families when the men were jailed or gone."[38]

Economic woes also increased women's involvement in family finances. After leaving Mexico in 1912, Sadie Richardson, Edmund's first wife, sold pans, his third wife, Becky, washed clothes, and Sarah and Daisie, the second and fourth wives, turned to their father's families for support. When Orin Elbridge Barney and his two wives, sisters Annie Matilda and Sarah Eliza Fenn, and their families left Mexico, Orin decided to live with Annie. He settled in Solomonville, Arizona, with her and their children while Sarah lived in Glenbar, Arizona, 12 miles away. Her son Jesse said that Sarah lived like a widow, taking in washing to support her sons.[39]

Death of a polygamous or monogamous husband also sometimes forced the wife into the job market. Heber Manasseh Cluff died in 1913 in Bluewater, New Mexico, just after he left Mexico. Sarah Ann Weech, his first wife, had thirteen children and Susan Carolyn Sims, his second wife, had seven and was pregnant with her eighth. Susan's son, Vearl, was not quite three when his father died. He remembered, "My mother had to work for every sort of a job that she could to support the children that were at home. She did tending of children for families on their vacations. She did laundry for the public. . . . She used to cook for a threshing crew that traveled around from place to place threshing grain in the summer."[40]

James Galloway Lowe died in 1905 and left Ann Eliza Doney with thirteen children and Elizabeth Ann Kingsford expecting her eleventh. Glen, a son of Ann's, was a year old when his father died, and he recalled how the wives supported themselves. "When the chore time came, you would see Aunt Lizzie starting down toward the barn. There would be about four or five larger children going down behind her. . . . It was the same way over to our mother's place. . . . There were around twenty-five and thirty head of cows for each family to milk." At "haying time" the two families labored together. "The work was divided half and half, but each helped each other." Glen's sister Jennie Huff said that after the death of her father, "Life went on just the same. The boys, the wives, and my brothers took over just like men."[41]

A. John Clarke's father moved his family to Magrath, Alberta, where he purchased a farm. He died in 1905 and left Margaret Green, his only wife, with seven small children. Although Margaret had been a schoolteacher before she married, her brothers and sisters decided that it was better for her to stay on the farm where she would have work for her six sons. Although the farm was large by Utah standards, it was very small compared to other farms in southern Alberta. John said, "I can remember her worrying particularly in the spring when she needed money for seed and in the fall when she had to pay her taxes." Reporting that "I'd rather be beaten than go see the banker to borrow money to take care of the farm," John said, "With that kind of background and the fact that she didn't have enough money to support us, she began to do other things like taking in washings."[42]

Daily life was very much the same in all Mormon families, whether monogamous or polygamous. Men worked in the fields with their sons or at a job away from the home and their sons helped with caring for animals and crops; women and girls worked at home or around the house. There were times when polygamous and monogamous women were compelled to take greater responsibility for supporting their children, but basically the division of labor was the same with both men and women playing an important role in the economic well-being of the family. Just as historian Julie Roy Jeffrey found that on the overland trail "women challenged domestic stereotypes by assuming male responsibilities and undertaking men's work," plural and monogamous wives both had different work when their husbands were away on missions.[43] But when the husbands returned, both again depended on their husbands for most of their support. Polygamy rarely made women more economically independent.

Victorian idealism was not viewed then as an attempt to suppress women. As Alexis de Tocqueville wrote, "Americans did not believe men and women should have "the same offices, but they show an equal regard for people because of their respective parts, and their lot is different, though they consider both of them to be equal." According to one historian, American society as a whole, like Latter-day Saint society in particular, "was characterized in large part by rigid gender role differentiation within the family and within society."[44] Mothers, daughters, fathers, and sons whether in an LDS monogamous or polygamous household followed these roles. Men were responsible for earning money, women took care of the home, and sons and daughters learned the roles that they would play in their future families. Departure from them occurred only in extreme situations, the pattern returning to the norm as soon as possible. Only death or divorce completely changed the family's division of labor.

8

Church Positions and Religious Activity

Just as the common stereotype has been that plural wives were economically independent, another stereotype has been that those who chose to marry in polygamy were more devout members of the Church than those who married monogamously. However, just as daily economic life was basically the same in polygamous and monogamous families, so was commitment to the LDS Church. Of course, it is much easier to determine that daily activities were the same by looking at work patterns. Deciding how committed people were to the Church requires examining feelings that may have never been recorded. One way to determine how devout members of the Church were, however, is to look at their Church attendance, their involvement in the Church, and their adaptation of worship in their individual homes. Church attendance is the most difficult to determine since going to meetings did not have the same emphasis then as it has now. As the LDS Church has a lay ministry, another way to determine religious commitment is to look at the positions held. While some scholars have argued that polygamous men were more likely to hold leadership positions than monogamous men, they have neither determined whether position or polygamy came first nor have they done a comparison of the positions held by the two groups. Statistical analysis reveals no significant difference between the positions held by monogamous and polygamous men except in stake leadership. A similar examination of positions held by wives also shows no significant difference. Religious activities in the home, especially family prayer and family gatherings, were also important in both types of homes. This chapter explores these areas of religious activity.

Church Attendance

Determining whether polygamous families were more likely to attend church services and participate in church activities than monogamous families is difficult because church attendance played a different role in the nineteenth century than it does in the twentieth. While today in the LDS Church exact attendance records are kept for all church meetings, during the late nineteenth and early twentieth centuries, no one counted those in attendance and turned in quarterly reports to Church headquarters. Attendance at church meetings was not considered as important as it is today. During much of the nineteenth century, rather than each ward having its separate sacrament meeting, there was only one service at a central location in the larger communities on Sunday afternoon. Even though the Church leaders directed each ward to hold its own worship service after 1894, attendance was still very low. As late as the 1920s, less than 20 percent of the members attended sacrament meeting. Jan Shipps suggested that "in the twentieth century sacrament meeting is a visible worship sign, whereas in the pioneer era more expressive worship signs were irrigation canals or neatly built and nicely decorated homes or good crops of sugar beets." Although some scholars have argued that church attendance was more important than Shipps implies, still attendance was very low at the meetings, and determining who attended is almost impossible.[1]

One way to determine church activity, however, is to examine positions monogamous and polygamous men and women held. The LDS Church is run entirely by a lay ministry who are not career trained administrators, and other than the General Authorities, those who direct the Church are not paid. Bishops who preside over a ward congregation, stake presidents who are in charge of several wards, Relief Society presidents who direct the women's organizations on the stake, ward, and general Church levels, and other leaders in Sunday School and youth, teenage and other auxiliary organizations on the ward, stake, and general levels are called to those positions by those in authority and receive little or no compensation for their work. Theoretically any priesthood holder could be selected to be a bishop or stake president or a counselor.

Comparison of Positions Held by Polygamous and Monogamous Men

Several studies have examined the relationship between Church positions and polygamy. Kimball Young concluded, "Most of our families reflect middle or high status among the Latter-day Saints. For our purpose we may say that median status is reflected in one's being a Bishop or counselor to a Bishop, and/or a member of the High Council of a Stake. High status . . . are stake Presidents, Patriarchs, and especially . . . the general authorities of the Church." He went on to argue, "In pioneer Utah it was often more a matter of ambition and enterprise, both in gaining wealth and in getting ahead in the Church, than the precise fulfillment of the spiritual norm that determined a man's going into plural marriage." He pointed out that while few Mormons had a great deal of wealth, "against the level of living of the time, plural families were generally recruited from among men of substance and of better-than-average church standing."[2]

Kimball Young presented no evidence to support this conclusion, and there are some major flaws in his reasoning. His classifications of middle and high status, for example, are misleading. A man would hold a variety of Church positions over his lifetime. He might be called to be a Sunday School teacher, a Sunday School superintendent, president of the Young Men's Mutual Improvement Association, a teacher in the religion classes, a bishop, and a high priest group leader, callings that would not come in any particular or escalating order. A man would not have to be a bishop before he could be a stake president or serve on the high council before he could be a member of the stake presidency. A bishop in Mendon, Utah, for example, was called to be on a high council after he was released and then later became a stake patriarch. Based on an examination of Church positions, there is no justification for placing the office of bishop and high councilor on the median level and patriarch on the high level. Rather than status, these Church callings reflect different responsibilities. Church members do not usually seek high positions in the Church but serve where they are called. So whether men were called to be Sunday School teachers, home teachers, seventy group leaders, bishops, or stake presidents, most accepted their callings as equally serving the Lord. Contrary to Young's view, most men would not have married plural wives to obtain leadership positions.

Young also does not consider when men accepted and decided to practice polygamy, assuming rather that husbands married plural wives to "get ahead" in the Church. The fact that General Authorities encouraged men in leadership positions to marry in polygamy, however, may indicate that leadership came first and polygamy came second. Elijah Pomeroy, the first bishop in Mesa, Arizona, "was ordained . . . in 1882 by Erastus Snow [an apostle]. It was decided by the high council and the stake down there that he should enter polygamy. He didn't want to, but he was persuaded to."[3]

Young pointed out that "facts regarding official church positions held by polygamist husbands are difficult to come by. . . . However, an estimate of polygamous Mormon men listed in the *Latter-Day Saint Biographical Encyclopedia* showed that a high proportion of those reporting plural families held offices of bishopric or higher order."[4] In their history of the Church, Leonard J. Arrington and Davis Bitton also saw a relationship between Church position and polygamy. "From the president down through the apostles and the Presiding Bishopric during the period, no general authority was a monogamist; the same was true of most bishops and stake presidents, as well as, for all practical purposes, their counselors. The privilege of polygamy was granted to the pure of heart and hence was a clear sign of worthiness for promotion in the Mormon hierarchy. Although no one ever explicitly said so in the nineteenth century, it appears to have been an effective device for gauging and assuring loyalty."[5] Neither study, however, meticulously examines those who held Church positions nor defines what a "high proportion" or "most" bishoprics and stake presidencies is.

At least three approaches can be taken to the relationship between Church positions and polygamy. One would be to start with the office-holders and then determine whether they were polygamists. Another would be to start with polygamous and monogamous men and determine what Church positions they held. And one could also examine what those living at the time said about the relationship between Church callings and polygamy and use anecdotal evidence to compare monogamous and polygamous men.

Kimball Young attempted to use the first approach, but his only source was the *Biographical Encyclopedia*, essentially a listing of prominent Latter-day Saints. In his study of bishops during the nineteenth century, D. Gene Pace made a more careful study of what bishops were polygamists. He found that of 835 wives of bishops, 58 percent were married to a man who had at least one other living wife, 30 percent had monogamous marriages, and 12 percent could not be determined if they were polygamous or monogamous. He concluded that a high percentage of bishops practiced polygamy because men who took plural wives had to be worthy spiritually and bishops more frequently met religious standards. Bishops were encouraged to marry in polygamy, and it was limited to wealthy families. On the whole bishops had more economic resources than the general population.[6] While a majority of the bishops' wives were married to a man who had more than one wife, 58 percent is not "most" of the bishops and definitely not the "high proportion" that the other studies suggested.

Another factor affecting Church leadership that Pace's study points out is that men — both monogamists and polygamists — who served as bishops and stake presidents during the late nineteenth and early twentieth centuries tended to hold office longer than in the LDS Church of today. According to his study of 1,205 nineteenth-century bishops, 29 percent served five years or less, 21 percent served six to ten years, 18 percent eleven to fifteen, 11 percent fifteen to twenty, 12 percent twenty-one to thirty, and 3 percent over thirty years. The median length of service was nine years, though Pace gave examples of wards that had only one to four bishops over a fifty-year period. As Earl Chadwick explained, "Only two or three people were bishop during your whole lifetime. I think all the time I was growing up in our ward we had two bishops." May Smith Morgan remembered that her father was always an elder (those serving in leadership positions such as in the bishopric must be ordained high priests), but he was very active in attending church and fulfilling church responsibilities.[7] In other words, it would be impossible for all men practicing polygamy — even if the percentage was very small — to hold leadership positions because the same people served for such a long time.

Pace's study has strengths as well as weaknesses. His conclusions are based on generally held views about men who practiced polygamy since there are no records available to determine a relationship between polygamy, Church leadership, and wealth. In addition, while bishops might have been expected to meet certain spiritual and economic conditions, these rules are not clearly spelled out, and examples in this study show that not only bishops but leaders of priesthood quorums in the local wards were encouraged to marry plural wives. Also, certain stake presidents and General Authorities seem to have been more active in promoting polygamy, and there was a higher incidence of polygamy in the communities where they lived.

The second approach is determining what Church positions polygamous and monogamous men held, information that can be obtained from this study. This approach, however, also has built-in biases. Since most of the interviews were with children, they did not always remember all the Church positions their fathers held. They probably recall the ones they felt were the most prominent. Holding multiple positions also creates problems in determining which positions should be counted. Rather than determining which was "the most important" or "most prestigious" calling each held, all of the callings that the sources listed were included. This study looked at the Church positions held by 166 polygamous men and 99 monogamous men. The total number of positions listed on the tables is more than the number of men since each man held several positions. When the sources specifically said that they did not know of any church callings or only told what priesthood the men held, they were listed on the table as "no known position." (See Table 16.)

Using the Chi square test to determine statistical significance, there was no significant difference between the positions held by polygamous and monogamous men except in stake leadership positions such as a member of the stake presidency, high council, patriarch, and stake clerk. In the other areas, including bishops and bishoprics, no significant difference was discovered. While this study examines monogamous and polygamous men who married during the last years the Church practiced polygamy and may not represent the same men used in the Young, Arrington and Bitton, and even the Pace study and do not represent a random sample of all monogamous and polygamous men, it does show that more careful study is needed before concluding that polygamous men were more loyal to the Church than monogamous men because they accepted the celestial law of marriage. Also, even though there was a statistical significance between the number of monogamous and polygamous men who held stake leadership positions, a number of factors determined if a man was called to serve in these positions, and polygamy was certainly not the only consideration. The figures also do not show when the man married in polygamy — before he was called to the position, immediately after receiving the calling, or many years later.

The final method of considering whether there was a connection between Church positions and polygamy is to examine anecdotal evidence. Although some ecclesiastical leaders were counseled to marry plural wives, threatened with loss of Church positions if they did not do so, or not given a position until after they had married in a plural wife, a man did not have to be a Church leader to practice polygamy. Mrs. Will Corbett, a daugh-

Table 16

Church Positions Held by
Polygamous and Monogamous Husbands

Survey includes 166 polygamous and 99 monogamous men.

	Polygamous	Monogamous
General Church		
Sunday School board	1	0
Stake Positions		
president	9	1
presidency	13	3
high council	32	9
patriarch	15	4
clerk	3	0
YMMIA superintendent	2	1
YMMIA	2	1
Sunday School superintendent	1	0
Sunday School	2	0
Ward Positions		
presiding bishop	2	0
bishop	50	21
bishopric	31	17
ward clerk	5	7
high priest leader	4	1
high priest quorum positions	4	0
seventy quorum presidency	5	9
elder quorum president	2	2
YMMIA superintendent	5	3
YMMIA superintendency	3	2
YMMIA	4	4
Sunday School superintendent	12	12
Sunday School superintendency	3	2
Sunday School teacher	9	13
other ward positions	19	13
Special Assignments		
temple president	2	0
temple presidency	2	0
temple worker	8	2
mission president	4	2
mission	40	31
No Known Position	10	16

ter of Hans J. Peterson, said, "Father had no church positions but he was valuable in the community as a shoemaker." John C. Larsen, who eventually had three wives, married for the second time one year before he was called to be a bishop, but explained, "A man did not have to have a church position before he could marry in polygamy." William, a son of Nathaniel Hodges, expressed the same opinion.[8]

If polygamous men did not have to hold Church positions, neither then were monogamists hindered from holding office. Bruce Gilchrist, whose father had only one wife, explained, "Dad was a very spiritual man. Although he didn't seek church positions, he was on the high council of the Rigby Stake." Roberta Allred said that her father, a monogamist, was president of the Los Angeles, California, Mission, in the Maricopa Stake presidency when he was in law school, the Young Men's Mutual Improvement Association stake superintendent, and on the high council when he died. "Father's whole life was the Church."[9]

Personal habits and situations also determined availability for Church positions for both monogamists and polygamists. The reasons why monogamous husbands did not hold Church positions varied, as Don Kofford Hansen explained. "My dad somewhere in his life took the habit of chewing tobacco. It seemed like he never could get over it. He had it under control enough that he would go to church. . . . He was nearly always a teacher in either Sunday School or priesthood meeting. . . . He was not in high positions because of his tobacco habit and he was never in a Sunday School superintendency." Vivian Elizabeth Haines said that her father was a ward clerk for a while but could not hold many Church positions because he worked away from home during the winters. Elvera Colledge Miles noted that her parents "just didn't have the opportunity. They were doing well to live and run the place." Ruth Jorgensen Cox pointed out, "My father was always real supportive of the Church, but he wasn't a real active person in the Church because he was quiet and retiring." Rather than holding Church positions, he worked with his team of horses on Church building projects. George H. Mortimer explained simply that his father didn't hold Church positions because "he was not thoroughly converted."[10]

Polygamous husbands might not hold Church positions either. Evan B. Murray pointed out that his father, who had two wives, "didn't attend church regularly and if there was work to do on Sunday he would do it." Orin Eldridge Barney, also a polygamist, went to church every week and considered himself a member in good standing but had no leadership role. Elizabeth Acord Beck said that her husband, Erastus, was a high priest, but did not hold positions and did not like to speak in public. Gladys Call Mallory added that her father stopped going to church when he could no longer hear, but he continued to raise money for Church projects and serve as a home teacher.[11]

In later years after the Manifesto, some polygamists such as Amos Russell Wright did not hold positions to avoid "advertising" polygamy. Karl Skousen also explained, "My father was never given a position in the Church other than high priest group leader in the time that he lived in Arizona as far as I know, even though he had been a member of the bishopric in Mexico. I suppose the Church wanted to keep him in the background. I think this was wise." In fact, the Church suggested that polygamists who had married plural wives between 1890 and 1904 be released from local Church callings where members would be asked to sustain them in the position.[12]

Comparison of Positions Held by Polygamous and Monogamous Women

Church positions held by plural and monogamous women are harder to determine. No other study deals with their Church callings as they do with the men. Two of the methods used to examine the husbands will be employed to look at the wives' callings: examining Church positions held by monogamous and polygamous wives and anecdotal evidence.

This study compared 115 polygamous and 90 monogamous wives. Since wives, like husbands, held a variety of positions over their lifetimes, all positions held by each woman were included in the total count. (See Table 17.) This method of comparison has the same weaknesses as the men's study. Since most of the reports came from children, they did not always recall all of the positions their mothers held. Wives' positions were in most cases cited less often than the husbands, and since the wives held positions that were less visible than the men and often in Relief Society, a meeting for women only, the children might not have known exactly what their mothers did. Women held positions on the stake and ward levels in the Relief Society, Primary, and Young Ladies Mutual Improvement Association as teachers, presidents, presidencies, and secretaries. They also taught religion classes and Sunday School and worked with genealogy,

Table 17

Church Positions Held by
Polygamous and Monogamous Wives

Survey includes 115 polygamous and 90 monogamous women.

	Polygamous	Monogamous
General Church		
general board YLMIA	2	0
Stake Positions		
Relief Society president	1	3
Relief Society presidency	4	0
Relief Society secretary	2	2
Relief Society worker	4	2
Primary president	0	4
Primary secretary	1	0
Primary worker	3	1
YLMIA president	1	1
YLMIA presidency	1	0
YLMIA	0	2
religion class	0	1
Sunday School	2	0
Ward Positions		
Relief Society president	17	20
Relief Society presidency	16	10
Relief Society secretary	7	5
Relief Society worker	47	20
visiting teacher	8	17
Primary president	13	12
Primary presidency	5	2
Primary secretary	1	1
Primary worker	13	10
YLMIA president	10	8
YLMIA presidency	5	4
YLMIA	10	0
religion class	3	3
Sunday School teacher	12	6
music	10	6
Special Assignments	5	2
No Known Positions	8	11

music, and drama, and in the temple. Running a Chi square test showed that there was no statistical significance between the positions held by the polygamous or the monogamous wives.

Anecdotal evidence provides more information on the positions wives held. Lorna Call Alder's mother, a fourth wife, was president of the Mutual Improvement Association and a counselor in the MIA. She also taught the Social Service lessons in the ward Relief Society and was a member of the Relief Society and MIA stake presidencies. Joseph C. Bentley's first wife, Maggie, was president of the Primary, his second wife, Gladys, worked in the Relief Society, and his third wife, Maud, served in the MIA. Emma and Caroline Romney, the plural wives of Edward Christian Eyring, both served as Relief Society and Primary presidents in Arizona during the 1920s and 1930s. Monogamous wives were also active in the same positions in the wards and stakes. John Murray Nicol's mother was Relief Society and Primary president in her ward, and Xarrissa Merkley Clarke's mother taught the Relief Society literature lessons and served in the ward Relief Society presidency.[13]

Women in monogamous and polygamous marriages gave similar reasons for not holding Church positions. According to Rhoda Ann Knell, the third wife of David Henry Cannon, "None of us worked much in the Church, though we all attended and we did some in the Relief Society. But we were all too busy with our families and taking care of him [their husband] and people who came to stay with us."[14] George S. Pond reported that his mother, a second wife, expressed regret that she did not hold more positions in the Church. Bearing a child every two years "kept her tied quite a bit. She asked the Lord to forgive her for not being active in the Church because it was almost impossible with her family responsibilities, and she promised him that she would dedicate her family to the work in the Church. That is exactly what she did. Everyone of her family was very active in the Church." In a biography of Edward James Wood, Melvin J. Taag called the first wife, Mary Ann, "naturally retiring in disposition, but [in] her quiet unassuming way [she] was always willing to make it possible for her husband to serve the Church long and generously."[15]

Earl Chadwick, a son of a monogamous family, reported, "My father was always very active in the Church. Of course, Mother had ten children and she didn't have too much time. She worked in the Church, but she didn't have any real high positions." Howard J. Engh's mother "wasn't very active," he guessed because she was shy and as an immigrant did not speak English very well. According to Vivian Elizabeth Haines, "They didn't give the ladies jobs in the Church at that time like they do now. She had enough to do to take care of her children." With unconscious irony, though, she then added that her mother was a Relief Society president.[16]

Family Religiosity

Family devotional services, important in both monogamous and polygamous families, could be another way to determine whether polygamists were more devout than monogamists. Rather than being simply a Sabbath-day observance, religion was to be an important part of everyday Latter-day Saint life. Prayer together with all members of the family was especially a common practice. This study examined family prayer in 79 polygamous families (a husband and his wives counted as one family) and 76 monogamous families. Ninety percent of the polygamous families and 85 percent of the monogamous families held daily family prayers. Prayer was, therefore, nearly as common with monogamous as polygamous families.

Children of both monogamous and polygamous families discussed the value of family prayer. Reed W. Warnick, a child of a monogamous family, said, "Nobody ever ate a breakfast in my father's home until after we had family prayer, no matter what they were doing or where they were going. I believe that has contributed more to the success of our family life than anything else." The Alexander F. MacDonald family also felt that prayer helped their family. The first wife, Elizabeth Graham MacDonald, wrote, "The rule of our family has always been to attend to family prayer. . . . By attending to [them], we received strength from the proper source to remember our covenants and obligations to each other and to help us to avoid trespassing upon each other's rights."[17]

For most families, prayer was a ritual that took place at the same time and place every day. For those who prayed at mealtime, the chairs were turned with the backs towards the table and each family member would kneel for prayer before the meal was served. Evening prayers were held in the dining room or living room and the family would kneel together.

Individual families reported considerable variations in who prayed, although quite often the father took that responsibility. Wallace Wood, whose father had two wives, remembered, "I never ate a meal in my mother's home but what my father would kneel. Everyone would kneel around the table. He would offer the prayer. He would get up and set the table. He would ask one of us to say the blessing." Everett Mark Hamilton, a son in a monogamous family, recalled, "Dad and Uncle Rueb did all the family praying at night." Grace Viola Jorgensen Hadfield, also from a monogamous family, noted, "Mother and Dad did the praying. Most generally nowadays the little children will take part, but then the parents did it." That was not always the case though. Mary Westover Carroll said, "We took turns as soon as we were able to give a prayer."[18]

In both monogamous and polygamous homes, family prayers continued in the husband's absence. Olive LeBaron Greenhalgh's monogamous father was a freighter. "When he was away, our mother would take care of [prayer]." In polygamous families, the father was gone regularly, and the mother had to take charge. Lavinia Jackson, the daughter of Maud Taylor Bentley, her father's third wife, remembered, "Everything that my father started to do, she would follow through. So we had family prayer when he wasn't at home." In such cases, either the mother or one of the children would pray. Elizabeth Graham MacDonald wrote, "If our husband was not at home it devolved upon me to pray or call upon another wife or upon one of my sons to do so."[19] Harriett Snarr Hutchings, whose father had two wives, recalled, "It was almost always my father who said the prayer. The little ones did not ever say the morning prayer. If my father was not there, the older boys would say it." In very few cases did the wife turn the responsibility for prayer over to a son who held the priesthood. As Anthony, the son of Margaret Ivins Bentley, a first wife, explained, "My mother was not a stickler for the deacon of the home to preside. Some mothers want to emphasize the priesthood in that way. She thought that was unnatural and so she presided and conducted when [my father] was not there."[20]

A few polygamous families had family prayer only if the father was there. Ruth Cannon Thatcher, whose father came once a week on Wednesdays to visit, said, "When father was there, we all got down and we knelt. He prayed and prayed. When he wasn't there, we just usually said the blessing. We didn't get down and pray for everything." Only 1 of 79 polygamous families and 5 of 76 monogamous families never had family prayer. Ollie Marie Allsop Schoepf, who grew up in a monogamous family, said, "We never had family prayer because Dad didn't believe in it I guess."[21]

Though scripture reading and family home evening are current practices in the Church, very few children remembered reading the scriptures together and very few read them at all except in connection with Church meetings. In 1915, the First Presidency issued a statement asking "that the presidents of stakes and bishops throughout the Church set aside one evening each month" for a "Home Evening" where "fathers and mothers may gather their boys and girls about them in the home and teach them the word of the Lord" and "upon such evenings no other Church duties should be required of the people." The First Presidency then added, "If the Saints obey this counsel, we promise that great blessings will result. Love at home and obedience to parents will increase. Faith will be developed in the hearts of the youth of Israel, and they will gain power to combat the evil influence and temptations which beset them."[22]

A few families, both monogamous and polygamous, started holding regular family nights during the next few decades after the First Presidency's announcement. Anson B. Call Jr. recalled, "Shortly after we returned to Mexico . . . President Joseph F. Smith told the people if they had family night . . . we would be blessed. Father felt that he should obey this because he was the bishop at the time." He remembered that they met on Wednesdays and the two wives would take turns having it at their homes. "Father would read the scriptures to us, and we would then sing songs generally to start with. Probably some of the children would have a recitation or song. . . . Then there was always some treat for us."[23] Edward Christian Eyring especially encouraged his plural families to have a weekly family home evening. According to his son Joseph, "My father was determined to keep the two families as close as he could. I think it was more his promotion than anybody else's that we got together as much as we did. I don't think our mothers were that much concerned about it."[24]

Alberta Lyman O'Brien, whose monogamous family lived in Blanding, Utah, said, "Long before family home evening was really pushed, my father [who was in the stake presidency for 23 years] had been holding family home evenings . . . because Joseph F. Smith had suggested it. . . . We called them home meeting or little meeting. . . . It took top priority on everything. . . . I learned more about the gospel, about family and about life's values in these little meetings than in any and all church meetings put together." The majority of families, however, did not follow the suggestion. According to G. Alvin Carpenter, "We didn't have a regular organized family home evening. I don't think it came out like we have it now."[25]

Although family home evenings were not organized in all families, according to Glen Lowe, "Every evening and every night was a home evening. It seemed like it was just like you are supposed to have home evening now. . . . We would all get together around the big table and discuss things. . . . Our older brothers would tell us stories. It was enjoyable because we looked forward to every evening when we were at home."[26]

Family Celebrations

Although all families did not have family home evenings, being together as a unit was an important religious activity. Holidays were also significant shared events in both monogamous and polygamous families. Of 63 polygamous families who talked about how they celebrated holidays, 40 percent said that all the families were together for holidays such as Thanksgiving or Christmas, and 35 percent said that they celebrated them separately. Eleven percent said that they celebrated only Thanksgiving together, and 6 percent said that the father visited both homes on a holiday.

Lorna Call Alder remembered that her family had a big Thanksgiving dinner at the first wife's home because she had the most room. The wives divided the food preparation and made their specialties. Theresa made pies, and Julia, Lorna's mother, made gravy. Karl Skousen said that his father's two families celebrated Thanksgiving together and sometimes they had dinner with Uncle Willard, his father's brother, and his two families. Karl's father's families, however, would not get together on Christmas. Marvin Ezra Clark said that his father's two families often celebrated Christmas separately but then would visit. When they arrived at the door, the first one to say "Christmas gift" received a small present. Asenath Smith Conklin said that Joseph F. Smith's families met for Thanksgivings and Christmases.[27]

If the polygamous families did not celebrate together, the father had to decide which house to visit. Karl Skousen's father stayed at the home he was scheduled to live at that day. Loretta Merrill Rigby's father, Apostle Marriner W. Merrill, took turns coming to each home. With eight wives, Loretta's father did not see her very often on Christmas. David Cannon's father spent time with each family on Christmas day.[28]

In monogamous and polygamous families, extended families often celebrated together. Married children would return to be with their parents on Christmas and Thanksgiving. Alba Jones Anderson remembered spending Thanksgiving with her Grandma Jones. For Christmas, several families would stay with Naomi Selman Thatcher's parents while on Thanksgiving, the relatives would gather at either set of grandparents.[29]

Like aunts, uncles, cousins, and other relatives getting together for outings, polygamous families also joined together on other occasions. Maybelle Farr Dickerson remembered both of her father's families going in the wagon for swimming parties and picnics. "When we would get together for things like that it was always one big family. It wasn't one family this time and one family next time. It was all together." Goldburn L. Knudson remembered that the children from both of his father's families went on summer trips up Provo Canyon but the first wife who lived in Payson, Utah, would not come, partly because she was ill and partly because the second wife's family had very little contact with her.[30]

In some plural families, gatherings took place regularly. Miles Park Romney liked to have all four of his families together for big meals on Sunday. Both of William A. Murray's families had Sunday dinner at the first wife Sarah's home because the second wife, Amanda, and her children came in from the farm to go to church. When Sarah and her children went on outings, they went to the farm. Esther Phelps Whatcott described less frequent and more impromptu gatherings. "Once in a great while maybe we would get together Sunday afternoon and have a big freezer of ice cream."[31]

Both polygamous and monogamous families had basically similar religious activities as members of the Church of Jesus Christ of Latter-day Saints. Although polygamous husbands were more likely to hold stake leadership positions, monogamous men also had some of these positions and were active in Church callings. Monogamous and plural wives held basically the same callings. Family prayers were important in both monogamous and polygamous families, and scripture reading and family home evenings were also stressed in a few of both types of family units. Marital status did not seem to make a difference in religious activities at home. Family gatherings were also significant as faith-building events. In a Church where all aspects of life were important to the religious atmosphere, home life was an essential part of worship in monogamous and polygamous families. Although polygamous husbands and wives chose to obey the principle of plural marriage as a commandment of God it does not logically follow that the monogamous men and women were less devout. To both groups the Church was the establishment of the kingdom of God on the earth.

9

Relationships of Wives and Husbands

As the chapter on daily life and family roles pointed out, husbands and wives worked in two separate spheres. Carroll Smith-Rosenberg explained that the "rigid gender-role differentiations within the family and within society as a whole" led "to the emotional segregation of women and men." Each sex had its own realm of influence and their expectations were "complimented by that for the other: the husband was supposed to be dominant, the wife submissive; the husband was asked to provide for his family, his wife was called upon to care for the home and children."[1] Women, therefore, quite often worked with other women, relatives, and friends, while men worked in the job market with other men.

In Mormon society this division of labor was sometimes enhanced even more because the priesthood holder—the man—was supposed to be the head of the home. His wife was to be his companion and follow his lead in righteousness. Jesse Smith Decker's monogamous father "was a man of very definite opinions. He felt that as a priesthood holder he was the one that would govern all the activities of the home." Sarah Perkins described a deferential relationship with her husband, Benjamin Perkins, "I never had a fight with my husband. I respected him as the head."[2] Joel Hills Johnson explained that God had commanded Eve to obey Adam and Paul had admonished wives to submit to their husbands. In reviewing domestic problems, he felt that his wives were not obedient. He wrote a "poem" entitled "The Cause":

> Good Adam's greatest wishes
> To do his Father's will
> By Eve was disregarded
> While gloom upon them fell.
> The great imposition
> On man as times records
> Is wives while disregarding
> The wishes of their Lords.[3]

During a domestic argument with his wife Janet, he wrote another "poem" telling of his sorrow about her disagreement. He concluded:

> Then cleave to me with all thy heart
> And let no evil spirit dare
> To cause our friendship to depart
> And crowns of glory thou shalt wear
> With me when mortal life is past
> And while Eternity shall last.[4]

Of course, when men and women interacted, both the husband and wife had to make adjustments and concessions. To what extent was adaptation complicated by the addition of a second or third wife? George Q. Payne, who grew up in a polygamous family, described plural marriages. "A man and his wife are like . . . objects tied at each end of the string. No matter how you move it, they move together, but add a third element and they have to all step together or they get tangled."[5] Providing equally for all family members, expression of affection, and settling disputes were problems common to families in general, but what unique aspects "tangled the strings" in polygamous families?

Dividing limited resources between several families was a major concern. Sometimes less jealousies and disagreements developed if the husband determined what each wife received and attempted to divide supplies equally. Husbands also had to be careful when giving emotional support to wives and children. Other than the few guidelines just mentioned, there was no set pattern on how to achieve equality. As in all aspects of polygamy, each family determined the best way to deal with its members. Plural husbands also had unique problems helping their wives get along, and plural wives had unique periods of loneliness. In all marriages, occasional conflicts arose that needed to be resolved between husband and wife, but in polygamy, there were also conflicts between the husbands and wives and just between the wives themselves. One of the primary factors that made plural marriage work was the religious commitment that convinced them to marry in the principle in the first place. Since they felt it was an essential religious practice, husbands and wives overlooked possible jealousies and problems. Polygamous and monogamous husbands and wives were also committed to their marriages and did not consider separation, resolving to keep their families together.

Allocation of Economic Resources

Mary E. Croshaw, the fourth wife of George H. Farrell, said that financial matters caused most domestic disagreements in polygamous families.[6] Thomas E. Taylor's letters to his third wife, Brighamina (Minnie) Christensen, indicate some of the financial problems and the disputes they could cause. During most of their married life, Thomas lived in Salt Lake City and Minnie in Sanpete County, Utah, usually in Gunnison. While Thomas was on a mission in England, he wrote several times expressing regret that he had no money to give his wives but his debtors had not paid him. In several letters following the mission, Thomas again explained his financial problems and asked for Minnie's help. At one time his first wife, Emma, also wrote to Minnie. She explained that she was sorry that there was no money to send her, but added if she came to Salt Lake City, they would find a way to help her. Minnie complained in a letter that she had no money to buy stamps and she would have to stop sending letters if she did not receive more funds. She also expressed concerns that she had not received the things that she had requested.[7]

These types of pecuniary problems were typical in a polygamous family. Questions that had to be resolved included: Who should divide the goods? Should they be divided equally among the families or should amounts be determined by the number of children each wife had? Should wives receive an allowance, have free access to a common storehouse, or ask for what they needed? In most cases (65 percent of 49 families), the husband divided the goods. Few had rules in writing, but David Candland's regulations are an example of how such plans could be made: "All articles of clothing that I bring into the house I will dispose of to my judgment. Same to apply to groceries. My wife [Mary Ann Burton, his first wife] to have some for under her charge for general company and under my direction she will deal out weekly supplies to each woman as her week to do work comes round."[8]

Anthony Ivins Bentley recalled that his father, Joseph, divided the food, clothing, and other supplies that he brought from El Paso to Colonia Juarez. When he brought clothes, the children would choose their favorite item, but Joseph always made the final decision. When Joseph was gone, the division of goods was "oft times dramatic. Sometimes my father would not make a decision about how the fruit should be divided and so forth. There was a little bit of trouble reaching decisions like that if he was not available."[9]

Robert Daines had one orchard, and Lydia, a daughter, remembered that he would decide how the fruit would be divided when it was still immature. Each family received a percentage based on the number of children in the family, and Robert "was very particular." Clarence Allen's father, James Carson, would go from Cove to Brigham City, Utah, to buy peaches, dividing them up equally between his two families.[10]

In about 20 percent of the cases, the first wife apportioned the goods, and in most situations, the other wives cooperated and accepted the first wife's decision. Lydia Romney, the daughter of John Conrad Naegle's sixth wife, reported that when her father had the family wool made into cloth the wives could choose the material that they wanted, but Louisa, the first wife, always had first choice.[11] Ether said that his mother, Mary Elma Wilson Haynie, "always told the first wife to go through the dry goods and whatever Father brought back for her to select what she wanted. My mother would be satisfied with taking the other." He recalled that his older half brother Lynn wore bib overalls and he wore dresses until Lynn's overalls "got old. . . . I was happy for them because they had good pockets in them." The second and third wives of Samuel Rose Parkinson "always deferred to the first wife when there wasn't enough to go around. They thought that she ought to have the first choice."[12]

In a very few cases, having the first wife divide the goods exacerbated already existing problems. William Hendricks Roskelley's first wife, Margaret Ann Wildman, divided the supplies with his other wife, her sister Agnes. Rebecca Lewis remembered her mother Margaret split the raspberries, eggs, and milk based on the number of children. She placed the second family's share on the pantry window of her home, and Agnes's children came to pick them up. Since Margaret had twelve and Agnes had four surviving children, Margaret kept more. Rebecca added, "They tried to be fair, really!"[13] Lula Mortensen, Agnes's daughter, resented the food division. She felt that the first wife divided the goods so that she could keep track of the other family. "The pantry window had so many memories attached, . . . the peg for the mail pail, the bucket for the eggs and mail and other things that were meant for us. This was sort of a watchtower to observe the happenings at our home and keep close tabs on everything."[14]

Keith Romney said that his father, Miles Archibald, "used to lean over backwards to be just and divide up things according to the size of the family. My mother [the first wife] had eight children and Aunt Lizzie had eleven I believe. Aunt Lilly had one. Aunt Emily had five or six. . . . He would try to be very fair about the way he divided up the sugar, the meat, the potatoes."[15]

Joseph C. Bentley divided goods based on the number in the family, but Maud Taylor, his third wife, "would proceed to try to have things divided up in thirds even though the other families were a little larger."[16] After his second wife, Gladys, died, and the first wife assumed care of her children, Viv, a son, recalled, "There were twenty-two in the three families and fifteen in ours then, so Father divided everything in one-third and two-thirds, the two thirds to Aunt Maggie's house. . . . I think that one of the main troubles was a man would take a younger wife and she would make her mind up that she was going to have everything. She would demand and insist and get more than the other wives."[17]

If the husband or the first wife did not partition the supplies, they were divided by all the wives or simply divided based on need. Warriner Abez Porter would go from Colonia Pacheco, one of the mountain colonies in Mexico, to Colonia Juarez to sell lumber and buy dress material. Mabel Amelia Carroll, a daughter of the first wife, Mary Melinda Norwood, remembered, "When he came home, one time he would take the stuff to Aunt Rachel and another time he would take it in to Mother." Rachel made unilateral divisions, but Mary "always took it in to her to help divide."[18]

In nearly 60 percent of 32 cases, supplies were split evenly. Dividing goods could vary from sharing food to buying large appliances or cars. Merle Gilbert Hyer and Estell Hyer Ririe tell the story of their father buying a car. "I remember Ed Parson and Will Homer came to sell Father a car. They saw him two or three times. They couldn't hardly talk him into buying a car. Finally he decided he would. . . . Ed turned around and went out of the shop and went towards the bank. He got up there just a little ways and Father came out of the door and whistled. He said, 'Come here, young man.' Ed thought, 'Oh, my gosh, he has changed his mind.' He came back and [Father] said, 'Bring me two of them.' "[19]

Wallace Wood said that if his father, Jonathan David, bought a phonograph for his mother, second wife Kathleen Blanche Bird, "the other woman," first wife Eliza Hess, would see it and "right now she had to have one too. He got one right now." If the wives went shopping with him at ZCMI and one saw gloves that she wanted, he would tell them they could both have a pair of gloves. "If Dad papered one room in Mother's house, he had to paper one in the other house because she would tear the paper and get it so it had to be. That is what I used to say, but I would get my ears boxed if I said it. . . . It worked the other way too. If the other wife got new linoleum in her kitchen, Mother also got it. I never heard Dad complain."[20]

Eliza Boyle, a daughter of John and second wife Eliza Bowen, recalled her father would buy two sacks of flour and two bolts of cloth of different colors and then bring candy for all the children. Other purchases were based on need. When her mother got a new stove, the first wife, Hannah, didn't need one so she got a new picket fence. John tried to give equal gifts. For example, he gave both wives knitting machines, but Hannah didn't use hers.[21]

Because of the problems division of goods could create, some husbands required their wives to consult with them before buying things or else made the decisions themselves. William Daines's wives had to ask him for even a loaf of bread. His son Rudgar encouraged William to give the wives allowances, but William always controlled the finances. Samuel Rose Parkinson bought supplies when they were needed, but they were not necessarily the same for each home. Rosalia Payne, third wife of Edward William, said Lucy, his second wife, wanted to have an allowance after the families left Mexico because she liked to keep records, but since the families never had much, everything was divided equally. "Theoretically I think a definite allowance is the best way but we got along better without it. If either of us were selfish that way, each wanting more than the other, we couldn't manage as we do, but we each try to work for the best of the family."[22]

In other homes, allowances were seen as a way to avoid problems. As one wife explained, "We never knew what debt was. We were provided with the necessaries of life, purchased in wholesale quantities and each home received a certain allowance weekly." Leah Reeder and Margaret White, daughters of John D. Rees's second wife, said each spouse had an allowance and could buy what she wanted. The wives took care of the purchases because "Father was a very busy man, and he didn't have any time to attend to any of the buying. Of course he always had such staples as flour and potatoes sent out as they were needed." In large polygamous homes like President John Taylor's, the wives could go to a common store-house to draw supplies as needed. The families also operated a school, a blacksmith shop, and a nail factory — "a community in and of itself."[23]

Whatever way the financial resources were divided, the husband "would have to be really considerate of both wives," as one son put it. "I'm sure under the circumstances eyes would be open if one wife had more than the other. Jealousy crept in. I think that applied to polygamy in general with the exception of a few of the families. A husband living in polygamy should have the same for one wife that he does for another." Thomas E. Taylor expressed similar feelings in a letter to his wife Minnie. "I have no purpose in view than to make you as comfortable and happy as I can, but when a man has a number of families he has to be very circumspect and careful in both actions and words."[24] George S. Tanner felt that his father, Henry Martin, tried to be fair, but each wife was sure that the other one got more. He said that the second wife's feeling that the first wife got more was probably accurate, but "it was a practice of the Church, at least at that time, that the first wife had a little priority over the other" even though that was never official Church doctrine. George went on to say that if his father went to Holbrook, Arizona, 10 miles away, he brought home gro-ceries and left a sack with each wife. "He probably left a little more at our place because there were more children. But I don't remember particularly that my mother had things that Aunt Emma didn't have. She may have had."[25]

Demonstration of Affection

Just as most husbands tried to divide their economic resources fairly among wives, they also tried to demonstrate equal love and emotional support. Luke William Gallup wrote in December 1866, "A woman needs but one man at a time. . . . She has no right to be any other man's wife while he lives for she has given herself to him. The husband belongs to no woman, and can lawfully receive other women, if they come to honorably. Then it is his right and duty to love them all that belong to him. Such a course is no more wrong than it is for a woman to love several children of her own at the same time." Esther Huntsman said that her father, Christian Anderson, was affectionate with his wives and joked he needed three to take care of him. Silas Derryfield Smith described the love that he felt for his wives. "The same love burned in my heart for Maria as ever came in the love affairs with Ellen; that does not mean that I loved Ellen less nor Maria less. The heart of a man grows and expands with knowledge and understanding of the correctness of the plural wife system. I do know and assert that we did start our family right and that pure sincere love has always burned in my soul, and I thank Heavenly Father for it."[26]

Living in polygamy and overcoming natural jealousies and selfishness took considerable effort. Alice Louise Reynolds said that her father, George, "always manifested an extreme solicitude for women and especially his wives. He moved heaven and earth in order to keep them together."[27] Elizabeth Graham MacDonald, first wife of Alexander, explained that her polygamous marriage was successful because "I have had a husband amongst a thousand. Although he was always firm and decisive he was always kind and had a great deal of forbearance. . . . A good deal of good can be done in a family of many wives when the man takes a wise course. It is in a man's hands to make his family happy or unhappy to a very good extent; when they are striving to do right, if he is unwise in his course he will make them unhappy; and he can be to his family sunshine or shade. A man should be possessed of great wisdom in presiding as the head of a polygamous family."[28]

Ida Walser Skousen, the first wife of James, described her husband as "one of the best men in the world and one of the kindest and fairest." Beulah Stout Limb said that her father did not have a favorite wife. "There was just too much love there. He would never play favorites at all. He was the kindest and gentlest of men." When asked which of his three wives — Susannah Titensor, Mary Ellen Titensor, or Emma J. Howland — he liked best, John C. Larsen replied that "he'd be willing to be hung or shot for any one of them."[29]

Husbands varied in the ways they demonstrated affection and gave attention to their wives. Ida Walser Skousen said her husband explained several times, "Don't you get on my ear. I've got all I can stand with Emma, and I can't have you cross and complaining." She said that she was pleased he felt she was easier to get along with than Emma, and therefore she was more willing to do things to please him. Ida added, "This, however, is as far as his telling goes. Each wife knows that he respects her confidence." Other husbands also knew that it was impolitic to compare one wife with another. Edith Smith Bushman said, "Father was very wise. He never carried the stories from one family to another and he never made a comparison."[30]

Not all were so careful or so wise. Laura Moffet, the second wife of W. F. Jones, said, "I came, as he grew to love the children, to have a place in his heart." For a while after she married him, the first wife, Ella, had to tell him when he was slighting Laura. Though the hurts gradually lessened, Laura noted, "He never came to love me — to love me as he did her. I don't think it is possible for a man to love two women at once, not in ways that are the same."[31]

The struggle to maintain peace in several households was not always successful. Sometimes the husband took the path of least resistance and supported the first wife or the wife who was the "squeaky wheel." William Roskelley usually sided with his first wife to prevent difficulties, Roxey Rogers remembering, "Dad told me later in life, 'I have made many, many mistakes, and if I had it to do over again, I could see now where I could have done better. But at the time I thought I was doing the right to keep peace.' "[32]

Occasionally the efforts at equality backfired. Edward Christian Eyring recorded in his autobiography, "My idea of plural marriage is a strict equality which I have striven to practice all these years."[33] His son Joseph, however, explained the situation from a different viewpoint. "My father expressed to both families very often that when he was a boy and where there was polygamy, there was always a favorite wife. That was the older wife. She had a lot of advantages. He determined in his marriages that he would have strict equality. I suspect that caused more friction than the old system that my mother had thought would exist when she agreed to polygamy. She thought she would be the queen bee as it were instead of strict equality."[34]

Clearly, favoritism is a highly subjective perception. David Guymon, who came from a polygamous family, said, "Uncle Jim Carroll . . . came the nearest I believe of treating them pretty much alike, like they should be treated." Yet Wayne, one of James's children by first wife Mary Bell Black, felt that the second wife, Annie Eliza Burrell, received preferential treatment. "When I was growing up . . . ..sometimes I would speak of my father as Thell's dad. . . . When Thell was born Aunt Annie nearly died. I felt that in some ways Dad favored Aunt Annie. Aunt Annie said it this way, 'I left all my folks; we came here with your mother's folks.' I think that was part of what Dad was trying to compensate for."[35] Jesse, the son of second wife Sarah Eliza Fenn Barney, said that he felt that his father favored first wife Annie Matilda Fenn "because she was the first wife, the first love." His full brother Orin, however, felt, "We couldn't see that Dad treated anyone any different than anyone else."[36]

The stereotype of a favored younger wife and a resentful older one also had some basis in fact. Walter, the son of first wife Rebecca Josephine Cluff Haws, said, "If I said something, it might be recorded and maybe hurt someone's feelings. [But] after my dad married the third wife [Martha H. Wall], then we kind of felt and also my mother felt that he spent more time with the new wife and the younger kids which I guess is only natural. . . . There was never any friction in the family until the third marriage. . . . Sometimes we would feel that the other family had a little advantage which is understandable because this wife had these little kids where we were a little more grown up. There were never any hard feelings." Rhoda Ann Knell Cannon, the third wife of David Henry, described a similar situation, but did not see it the same way. She said that some viewed her as the preferred wife because she was the youngest, but she felt that her husband did not favor any of his wives.[37]

Sensitive to potential family difficulties, many of the children hedged when answering. Lawrence Leavitt stated, "I think he [my father] cared a lot for my mother" but then implied that she was not the favorite wife. Catherine Scott Brown began, "My father was rather partial," then paused before concluding, "I will just say this; my mother wasn't the favored wife. I won't say anything more about it."[38]

Separation and Loneliness

Even if the wives felt equally loved, they encountered feelings of loneliness — especially when the husband was at another home. Martha Spence Heywood, who lived in Nephi, Utah, while her husband and his other two wives lived in Salt Lake City, recorded in her journal, "My feelings have been rather calm during the last week though I meet with little rubs that I anticipated. It is rather trying to a woman's feelings not to be acknowledged by the man she has given herself to and desires to love with all her heart.[39] Oara Pace reported, "My mother was a very lonely woman. When my father died, my mother was only thirty-eight, and she lived to be ninety-one. She lived most of her life without him. Even then [when he was alive] she was sharing him with another woman." Sarah Dearmon Pea Rich asked her husband, Charles, when he was on a mission, "How do you suppose I feel with seven children and not a man about the house?"[40]

Loneliness was not unique to the wives though; husbands also expressed such feelings. When away from all of their wives on missions, some wrote about desires to be with their wives. William Broomhead wrote to his wife Sylvia, "I want to see you as bad as you want to see me I think. I shall come as soon as I can."[41] Thomas E. Taylor wrote to Minnie on 14 April 1894, "I am commencing this love letter in the morning," and went on to describe how he would like to "raise the curtain that separates us and look upon you at the present." The next year on 24 December 1895 he wrote, "I can imagine you are with me tonight. The day has been full of anxiety and care. You are weary in body, distressed in mind and your spirit restless and uneasy. Having bowed ourselves before the Lord, after committing ourselves to his care, and craving his protection for the night, we go to bed. You turn from me, and presently I can feel that you are crying, but not liking to disturb you, I only draw closer to you, passing my hand over your body." Even when he returned from his mission and was living with his first two wives in Salt Lake City, he wrote of missing Minnie who was still in Gunnison. "The Lord bless my beloved wife, may she view with the spirit of inspiration her husband, and be able to bear with complacence real or imaginary faults which may appear to her. I would have her consider him the man above all others she would have for her husband, even with her past experiences of his imperfections."[42]

Husbands' Views of Wives' Relationships

Wives that got along well together were a high priority with polygamous husbands. Ida Stewart Pacey noted that her husband's father said that his happiest time was when all three of his wives said good morning to each other. "In this period of my life, though one of toil and poverty, surrounded by jealousy and hatred and ingratitude, I look back as the happiest of my life," wrote Benjamin Johnson of 1858, "for then all the mothers of my children loved me and honored me and I was assured of their confidence and sympathy." In a letter to his wives while he was on a mission in England, Charles C. Rich wrote, "I am glad and thankful so far as I know that there is a kind and friendly feeling among you. I hope and pray that this spirit and feeling may increase among you till you will be one as the church of God is one." Robert Gardner wrote in his autobiography that his life at the mill in Cottonwood was "the happiest time of my life, for all was peace and good feelings, and no one need tell me that there cannot be peace and enjoyment in a family where there is a plurality of wives in one home, for I have tried with three wives and all their children."[43]

But anxiety abounded when wives did not get along. David Candland wrote in his journal in March 1859 shortly after he married his second wife, "I find much annoyance and vexation of spirit as well as much schooling of the feelings in polygamy. My wives Anne and Hannah are much dissatisfied one with another and hence jealousy, bickering and strife is the result. I hope years, experience, and the absurd folly will be made apparent." However, when the wives did not get along better, he recorded, "I have removed Hannah to another home. Her conduct became more and more unbearable and puts me to much trouble. . . . I absent myself sometimes for weeks then she craves forgiveness." Phineas Cook described marrying in polygamy as "the beginning of all my sorrows . . . notwithstanding I was converted to the doctrine of plurality." John Jacob Walser said that his second wife, Mary Louise Frischknecht, was "selfish and jealous and wanted too much. I would take her aside and talk to her and tell her how things must be, but she kept being jealous and I was sometimes disgusted with her."[44]

Resolution of Marital Conflicts

Disputes over the divisions of time and resources were handled in various fashion. George W. Terry recorded in his journal, "October 12, 1889 Saturday Fannie very rebellious, stubborn and hateful this morn. with me. Afterwards begged for pardon but kept up meanness with Eliza." He took both of his wives aside to discuss the problems, and as a result, Fannie agreed to fast for three days. Arabelle Daines, the daughter of Samuel Rose and his third wife, Maria Smart Parkinson, said that when quarrels broke out between the wives, her father would have one of them prepare dinner for him and the other wife. During the dinner, they would discuss their problems, and he would not let them go to bed until they were settled. Most of the quarrels she recalled were incidents of wives defending their children. According to Benjamin Julius Johnson, "I didn't notice trouble among the families when I was a boy. When I grew up, I realized that there were some. You can't put seven families together and not have some trouble. There were always some jealousy among the wives, I expect. When they had difficulties among them, they had to settle it. Father wouldn't let them bother him."[45]

It is clear, however, that the children were not privy to many marital discussions. Elizabeth Acord Beck said that her children noted she was "so meek and submissive." She explained, though, "I never quarrelled with their father or opposed him before them. But when I wanted a thing settled, I went to him in private. Of course, we were somewhat inhibited, but we lived pleasant lives and our children did not know quarreling and bickering." G. Milton Jameson said, "I am sure there were difficulties, but they were kept from the children. I don't know what the problems were. The relationship between my father and mother always seemed happy. . . . Knowing the problems that a man and wife have, I'm sure that they would have had at least as many problems and maybe more." Likely most problems were resolved the way Maud Farnsworth remembered: "I know that they had differences like most double families do. . . . They didn't see eye to eye on everything, but I could see that would be the way with most any family. . . . I think my mother was hurt lots of times. We could tell that things didn't go just right but she was not one to say anything. She never said a word and never did tell us anything."[46]

Factors That Made Plural Marriage Work

While the negative aspects for women such as having to share a husband and not having his full attention and possible positive ones for men such as having more sexual opportunities are usually pointed to, both oversimplify a complex situation. While plural wives experienced loneliness when their husbands were gone and the husbands sometimes received special treatment from several wives, quite often the wives worked closely together in common interests. Yet special treatment and common interests were the main reasons that plural husbands and wives accepted polygamy and learned to live with it. Just as they married in polygamy for religious reasons, they saw their efforts to live it as part of that same commitment.

Thomas Lowe explained to his wife while he was on a mission, "We must be tried in all things to see if we will endure but the time will come when we will get a reward if we will only stand true to our commands and the kingdom of God. Will, dear wife, cheer up. All will be well yet and we will live together in peace." Christopher Layton said after his third wife, Sarah, died, "She was true and faithful to the principles of the everlasting gospel to the end of her mortal life, and is gone to await the resurrection of the just." Andrew Jonus Hansen, describing his wives, said, "I feel that it would be selfish indeed if I recorded only the trial that this circumstance [polygamy] was to me, without recognizing the wonderful fidelity and devotion to men and to the laws of the Lord made manifest by my wives, Aunt Bengta and Aunt Caroline. Cheerfully did they make the sacrifice for what they believed to be right."[47]

There were rare cases though where the religious motivations backfired. Josephine Vance said of her mother, Janey Smith, second wife of Alma Spillsbury, "Mother felt very bad about everything and I've heard her say that unless she got better treatment from Father she didn't want to see him in the next world. Father said many times that he didn't want to meet his first wife on the other side unless she was more just to Mother."[48]

Comparison of Monogamous and Polygamous Relationships

Although polygamy may have created or exacerbated marital conflict, children of monogamous marriages cited economic concerns and lack of affection as causes of jealousy. However, cultural norms downplaying confrontation meant that open disagreements were rare. It was probably true as Alice Smith Kartchner described the polygamous home she grew up in. "We had little ups and downs, but I don't believe we had any more trouble between us than just regular families with one wife." Irene Larsen Whitehead said that usually their monogamous home was very calm, but in times of stress, her parents would revert to Danish so that the children could not understand them. Mabel Moody Whitmer, a monogamous child, said of her parents, "We never heard them quarrel; we never heard them say a cross word to each other. If they disagreed, we never knew it. In fact, he would wake her up about five o'clock every morning when she was sleepy and want to talk things over. They settled a lot of their problems without us children knowing about it." Not having to care for another family did not eliminate feelings of loneliness, though. About the relationship between his monogamous father and mother, Elbert Hans Anderson said, "I think at times that Mother felt that Father didn't take enough time to spend with her."[49]

The commitment to marriage per se imposed a calming context on disagreements in polygamous and monogamous families. Henry Earl Day said that his parents' monogamous marriage was "very good. They would have some arguments, but it never was anything that turned out serious. There wasn't any chance of their separating. We thought it was terrible to hear about people getting a divorce." Monogamous child Fenton L. Williams said that his mother was unhappy a lot of the time because his father was not all she wanted him to be. But, he added, "they were married; they knew they were married, and that was it. Nobody broke up in those days because of those things. Their life together could have been better."[40]

In both monogamous and polygamous families, husbands and wives needed to work together to overcome problems. Where extreme difficulties existed, they originated in personality differences — intensified by plural marriage but not caused by it. As Ida Walser Jackson explained, "Not all the families got along. It was the people though and not the institution. It was the way the man handled it a lot and the way the women themselves accepted it. When selfishness crept in, they couldn't live it properly. There was jealousy among some, but many of them just got along beautifully." Anthony Ivins Bentley's statement matched that of many other children of polygamous families: "My father was the personification of peace and fairness. Whatever he felt for a particular woman was not obvious. . . . I prefer to believe that he had the ability to treat each as an individual and in terms of her unique characteristics. I didn't see any partiality. I was never critical of him on that basis."[41]

Husbands and wives of both marital persuasions had their disagreements. Although problems sometimes resulted in divorce, in most cases they were able to resolve, overlook, or live with them, often without their children even being aware that there were difficulties. Unique to polygamy were providing equal treatment in financial affairs and in expressing affection. Ways of solving these problems included having the husband divide goods equally between the wives and spending equal time at each home and not comparing wives. Sometimes rules — whether spoken or unspoken — helped overcome problems. But each family established its own guidelines. On the whole, plural families were able to work through or suppress their difficulties because of their religious commitment to the principle.

This commitment, coupled with the cultural norms of the time, kept many couples together. For these nineteenth-century couples, divorce was not an option. This applied to monogamous and polygamous Mormon families, and while there were problems unique to polygamy, plural husbands and wives had much in common with nineteenth-century monogamous lifestyle.

10

Relationships between Wives

In a twentieth-century context where romantic and sexual relationships are assumed to be the basis of marriage, the most immediate question polygamy elicits is how a woman regarded another woman who shared her husband's affections and bed. Since most Mormon plural wives lived in separate homes, they did not have to deal with each other constantly, but most tried to establish and maintain cordial and courteous relationships. Orson Smith's second wife even felt "to make polygamy successful you've got to love the man and the woman both."[1] Religious commitments that led the wives into polygamy also motivated them to overcome jealousies. For the most part, they adapted their monogamous traditions to get along with their husband's other wives. With no pattern of how they should treat a co-wife, the wives used relationships from their Euro-American background to define their activities, including mother-daughter (if there was an age difference), friends, and, most commonly, sisters. Although there were differences and even jealousies between wives, most were minor and easily resolved or suppressed. Polygamy emphasized some of the differences since the wives shared a husband, but differing personalities and unfulfilled expectations were usually the cause of problems. Relationships were not dynamic though. Over time, wives grew closer together or farther apart depending on their acceptance of each other and the amount of interaction. Whatever the problems, though, they usually pulled together, especially in times of illness, childbirth, and death.

Seven of Brigham Young's wives. In most cases plural wives had harmonious relationships and overlooked or suppressed minor jealousies. LDS Church Archives.

Harmonious Relations

Religious commitment was the major incentive for the wives to work together closely. An interviewer remembered observing Charles White's wives as a child. "The wives were friendly and kind to each other. They were always helping each other, sending food, helping with the sewing and they took a deep and real interest in each other's children, but there was an undercurrent of feeling between them that I as a child of twelve could detect." He hypothesized, "They couldn't rest; they had to be doing something to prove to themselves and to the world that polygamy was right." Alice Smith Kartchner said of her mother, "I know it was hard for Mother at first, but through her obedience, they got along and were congenial in a good way."[2]

Rosalia Tenney, the plural wife of E. W. Payne, said, "I married with an intense desire to make a go of it." When asked if she got along with the second wife, she answered, "I'd get along if it cost me my skin. . . . I felt that I was living a holy principle and that I must conform my life to it. Polygamy makes people more tolerant, more understanding, and more unselfish. It gives them more contact with reality and a wider circle to love. . . . It's not an easy way to live. We never fully conquer ourselves. And always it is the little things that make it hard, the little foxes always upset the vine you know. It's not jealousy so much for I had my mind made up to that, but the constant pressure of adjusting yourself to another woman."[3]

Some wives had little or no contact with each other. Ida Pacey, a daughter of Andrew and his first wife, Melissa Riggs Stewart, said the wives had "mutual admiration and respect," but because of their age differences, only visited occasionally. According to Iona Jackson, her mother, Janette Hamilton Tanner, the second wife, and the others had a "good relationship. [But] they didn't have to live together at all. . . . She lived out of town a little ways. . . . They had different dispositions."[4]

Many wives, however, did associate regularly and quite often modeled their relationships on monogamous patterns. For example, when the first wife was considerably older than the second wife, they sometimes developed a mother- daughter relationship. Jane Flake, second wife of Peter Woods, said, "I loved Sister Woods. She was like a mother to me and she died in my arms." Claude Hawkes described the relationship between Mary and Sarah, the wives of his father, Joshua, as like mother and daughter because Mary served as a midwife for Sarah. Mary Elma Wilson Haynie spoke highly of her husband's first wife, Henrietta Parallee Cecelia Gage Gagwell. According to Mary's son, Robert, his mother told him that Henrietta "just took me in. I was more like one of her own daughters instead of sharing her husband because I was so young." He added that his mother "never felt to question [the] authority . . . of the first wife. She was glad to have an elder person to teach her. This first wife was able to teach her in homemaking. . . . She didn't have a mother of her own for half the time after she got big enough to where she could have learned from her."[5]

Sometimes the wives were companionable friends. Edgar L. Cazier said of his father's wives, "They got along as well as any two women could get along. Just neighbors didn't get along any better than they did." Isaac B. Ball analogized that his father's wives were like David and Jonathan in the Old Testament "and were never happy when separated." Florence Anderson said that her father's second and third wives, Melissa Stevens and Anna Lowrie Ivins Wilson, "were always best friends. They had been best friends for a greater part of their school years." Louis Brandley described the friendship between his mother, the second wife, and the fourth wife — neither the preferred one: "My Aunt Emma Biefer and my mother were the closest of friends. They shared the same faith, the same trust, the same hopes and the same husband. Significantly, they [also] shared the same frustrations, the same poverty, the same loneliness, the same widowhood."[6]

Sometimes the term used to describe the wives' relationships was sister. Ida Jackson told how her father's wives, Ida Rosette Whipple and Mae Adelia Robinson Walser, lived together after he married Mae. "They were like sisters. They would tease Father. Once when he went to play at a dance late they put a broomstick in the bed. When he got in bed, he pulled what he thought was a wife over towards him and it was the broom. . . . They were always playing tricks on him. Mother was full of humor." Mary Diantha Cox Sherratt said that Aunt Lettie "was my father's first wife. My mother and she were like sisters. I never heard them quarrel about anything. She had her own home, and Mother had her home. Aunt Lettie was to our place as much as she was to her own home." Martha Cragun Cox described the closeness that she felt for her husband's other wives. "To me it is a joy to know that we laid the foundation of a life to come while we lived in that plural marriage, that we three who loved each other more than sisters, children of one mother love, will go hand in hand together down all eternity. That knowledge is worth more to me than gold and more than compensates for the sorrow I have ever known."[7]

Sororal Polygamy

In 25 percent of the families sampled in this study, the wives literally were sisters. Kimball Young also reported that 20 percent of the men in his study married sisters. Some Latter-day Saints believed if the wives came from the same family that they would not have as many disagreements and that they would already love each other. This was not always the case, though. Just as in African varieties, in Mormon polygamy "sharing the same background, and hence the same past may induce co-wives to cooperate with one another or compete against one another. Similarity of past experiences may minimize the frequency and the intensity of the conflicts most likely to develop among co-wives. . . . But it may also breed jealousy."[8]

In Mormon families, many sisters who were co-wives had congenial relationships. Mike Butler married two half sisters. Mary Ann Stowell Jackson, a sister and half sister to the other remembered that they "were so unselfish with each other. When it came to a question of one of them going with Mike when the other must stay home, they would always try to get the other to go. One would nurse the other's baby if the other was busy." Later he married Mary Ann's full sister Matilda. Although the other two wives didn't like the idea of the third marriage, "I guess they were glad the way things turned out." Matilda helped the other two wives when they were sick. When they died at nearly the same time, Matilda raised their children.[9]

Edward McGregor Patterson's wives, Sarah and Mary Thompson, were sisters, and, according to Sarah's daughter, Zina Dunford, that was probably one of the reasons they got along so well. "I never did see any friction. . . . They used to share the work load. Usually sewing for the boys was done by Auntie, and the girls' sewing was done by Mother. . . . They both did the gardening and the cooking. . . . Father built a loom where they used to weave carpet. They did the carpet weaving for everybody in the valley." Mary explained that "we took up the trade of weaving. When I say we, I mean my sister Sarah and family. We are all one family."[10]

Sisters did not always relate well, but as Kimball Young pointed out,

"When the wives fell into serious conflicts, the matter of being sisters or not may have had far less to do with it than personality divergence, economic problems and sense of differential treatment by the husband." William Roskelley's family is an extreme case of sisters at odds. William married his childhood sweetheart Margaret Wildman and then later married her younger sister Agnes. The wives did not openly express their differences and had no major confrontations; they just did not associate except for occasional conversations when they worked in the raspberry patch. They did not visit each other's homes even when their other sisters came from out of town. Roxey Rogers, a daughter of Margaret, remembered, "In my day Mother and Auntie were not close at all. . . . I just always felt like they didn't want to be close and forgive, no matter what. . . . I have sat at church more than once with Mother on one side and with Auntie on the other side of me. They didn't speak."[11]

All three reasons Kimball Young mentioned—personality differences, economic concerns, and the relationship with the husband—cooled the affection between Margaret and Agnes. Lula, Agnes's daughter, remembered asking her mother, "But, Ma, how could you consent to marry Pa with Aunt Maggie being the first wife? You must have known what a troublemaker she was as your older sister." Agnes replied, "Well, I guess we expected everyone to be about perfect, living in the principle." The first and second wives' children described Margaret as a domineering woman who usually got what she wanted. Even her own children sometimes found it hard to get along with her. Agnes, as Margaret's daughter Rebecca Roskelley Lewis put it, had no "spunk" and was very submissive. William was easygoing and he usually gave in to Margaret because he wanted to maintain peace in the home.[12]

Jealousies and Conflicts

Although the Roskelleys are atypical, their situation highlights some of the jealousies that plural wives felt. In a study of women's views of polygamy in Nigeria, Helen Ware asked women to list the negative side of sharing a husband, and 85 percent included feelings of "envy, jealousy, hate, chaos, devilishness or murder" towards the other wives. The women use a Yoruba word for co-wife that means rival or competitor.[13] Given this backdrop of expected disagreement, Mormon plural wives seem surprisingly congenial. Of 197 families for which information was available, almost half the wives had minor disputes. Only about 13 percent reported jealousy that induced a wife to leave her husband or avoid the other wives completely. About 30 percent gave no indication of jealousy. Certainly, since much of this information came from children, they might not have known of the minor disputes or their mother's hidden feelings. Some even admitted that they had no way of knowing. Nearly 10 percent of the wives had little or no contact because they lived in different towns.

All families could expect moments of jealousy and disagreement. Joseph F. Smith, namesake and grandson of the Church President, was told that his grandfather's first wife, Julina Lambson, and third wife Edna Lambson disagreed on which grandson should bear their husband's name. Julina felt that the name should be given to her oldest grandson, but Edna's grandson was given the name since he was born first. Joseph added, "I understand this was a sore point for years. However, when my first sister was born, both these wives waited upon my mother and Aunt Julina was the midwife in charge. Aunt Julina treated me personally quite as cordially and affectionately as she did her own grandchildren." Sarah, the second wife, liked to give things to the other wives, but when Edna tried to give her some eggs, she returned them with the comment that she was not starving, an exchange that occasioned hard feelings.[14]

Some people are inclined by temperament to be more jealous than others, reading malice into innocent events and brooding over fancied slights. They view many acts as attempts to hurt them. The oldest daughter of Charles White's second wife said that "if a woman was phlegmatic, she might get along, but Mother was too high strung, too emotional, and she could not help being constantly upset." Laura Moffet Jones, a daughter of a plural family, said, "Mother was overly sensitive. I think she spent half of her life crying. She could never stand up for her rights and Aunt Olive took advantage of her. I can remember her crying and crying. . . . I think polygamy helped to make Mother sensitive but she was sensitive anyway. She used to imagine slights and be so hurt over everything." Caroline Pederson Hansen explained some hidden jealousies that her husband's first wife had. "Aunt Bengta was a good woman, in that she was willing to share her husband with me. But she proved to be of a very jealous disposition and had a very violent temper."[15]

Other wives were easy going and not inclined to jealousy. Harriet Snarr Hutchings remembered, "My mother always said that Aunt Phoebus had a lovely disposition. They never quarrelled or had words. Some of the women in the colony did fight over little things like a piece of calico, but our families never did fight." Robert Haynie noted, "My mother said she never did have a fight with the first wife. . . . Mother wasn't that nature." Bessie Jameson Judy said that her father's families got along well because "everyone's needs came before Mother's. . . . I think that was the thing that saved them because Mother was perfectly willing to let others be helped."[16]

Role and Personality Variations

At times the first wife in plural families played the same role as in some African societies where she had the unique responsibility of giving consent to other marriages and serving as a special counselor with her husband. Benjamin LaSalle Farnsworth stressed that his mother "wasn't a plural wife. She was a first wife." Juanita Brooks, granddaughter of Mary Ann Stucki Hafen, explained that the first wife felt that she was superior, and she always took the best and gave the rest to the other wives. Although the husband tried to be impartial, the first wife always dominated him. Lestra Marison, a daughter of Andrew J. Stewart, said that her mother, the first wife, was a good adviser and the other wives sought her wisdom.[17]

The first wife did not always play the dominant role, though. William, a son of John Horsecroft and his third wife Betsey Leavitt Wyatt, said, "There is usually a little bit of jealousy. . . . There is always one [wife] that is a stronger character and they kind of domineer over the other one." Nilus Stowell Memmott told of the conciliatory behavior of her mother, Mary Olive Bybee. After the exodus from Mexico, her father, Brigham, was living with Olive, his first wife, in Thatcher, Arizona. "My Aunt Rhoda [Olive's sister] was more domineering than my mother." When Rhoda decided to come to Thatcher to live, Olive agreed and moved to Miami, Arizona, with her children. A year later when Rhoda decided that she did not want to stay in Thatcher, Olive moved back to live with Brigham.[18]

Were information available, documenting changes in the wives' relationships over time would prove enlightening. A few insights do appear in the interviews. Miles Archibald Romney married his first wife, Frances Turley, in 1889 in Colonia Juarez. Then he married three Burrell sisters: Lilly in 1898, Elizabeth in 1902, and Emily in 1909. Keith Romney, a son of Frances, said that his mother's resentment to these plural marriages "affected the relationship with the other wives in an adverse way. But as the years went by, I noticed a softening and an acceptance of the situation. They really lived together in harmony, but it was pretty tough at first." Dennison Romney, a son of third wife Elizabeth, added, "Aunt Frances didn't want to go into polygamy. She was not in favor of it, but he did. . . . I guess this could have been an irritant for the first wife as she wasn't in favor of it. But I grew up and didn't know that. Maybe the other kids did."[19]

Dennison said that his mother, Elizabeth, "was more high strung or outgoing. So naturally she didn't get along as well with Aunt Frances maybe as Aunt Lilly, the peacemaker." Rulon, Dennison's full brother, likewise remembered Aunt Lilly in the same way. "One evening [Lilly] came over to our house and said, 'Lizzie, the sun is about to set and you haven't said you are sorry for the bad things you said to me this morning.' My mother went soon after this visit over to her house, and they settled their differences." Rulon recounted the differences between the wives by describing their laughs. "My father had a real funny sense of humor, and he kept the four women laughing most of the time. It seemed to me that Frances laughed the loudest. Then Aunt Lilly chimed in on a high pitched cackle. My mother and Aunt Emily would giggle without much noise." He added, "It seemed to me at times that the women competed for his attention."[20]

Dennison reported a telling example of how the wives related to each other. As Lilly had no children, Lizzie told her that if she had her baby on Lilly's birthday, she could care for it. Dennison was born on the specified day, and Lilly raised him for about twelve years until she died. He explained, "Actually all four wives as far as I was concerned were mother to me since I was [then] an only child really in a polygamous family that eventually had twenty-six. I remember all the attention I was given. I guess I was probably spoiled as if I was the only one on earth with Aunt Lilly. She gave me 100 percent of her time and her attention." When Lilly died, he lived with Emily, then with his own mother. Frances's children were all raised, and she insisted that she should have had Dennison. His father settled the disagreement by returning him to Lizzie, his mother. However, Dennison commented, "If they had given me a choice or if they had said, 'You're going to live with Aunt Frances,' I would have gone. Why? Because it would have been the same situation: I would have been pampered."[21]

Despite personality differences, these four wives worked together on large projects and took care of each other in need. Frances and Lilly studied art together. When Lilly was sick, Frances and Lizzie took her to El Paso, Texas. During her absence, Emily's house burned down, and she moved into Lilly's home. During Lilly's final illness, Emily took care of her. While there were some jealousies, the wives "all visited each other. They were congenial with each other."[22]

The six wives of Samuel Roskelley also illustrate a spectrum of relationships. Mary Jane Rigby, his fourth wife, lived with Mary Roberts, his second, in a one-room log house. "We had our first babies there and did all our work together." The two wives worked "shoulder to shoulder," according to Mary Jane, and "got along famously." Mary Jane confessed jealousy sometimes when Samuel went places with the other wives and felt tied down by her little children, yet "I believe he loved me as much as any woman he ever had. I've got letters to prove that." After they were established in separate homes, the wives visited on holidays but generally did not see much of each other because they were busy with their own housework. Emma Hansen, a daughter of the fifth wife, Margaret Rigby, said that although her mother and Mary Jane were sisters, her mother was closer to Mary, the third wife. "Aunt [Mary] Jane was high strung. . . . She just seemed a little harder to get along with than the rest."[23]

When Samuel Roskelley married a sixth wife, Sarah Maud Burton, Mary Jane said that none of the wives got along with her. Maud was much younger, and Mary Jane expressed suspicions of her motives in marrying the bishop. She stated, "If he had only left Maud alone, we were all one big family. But he was older and she was younger and you know what kind of situation that makes. I used to hear that when you can't get along with anybody, you should just let them alone. That is what we did with Maud. We didn't treat Maud ugly, but we just let her alone." She noted with resentment, "Brother Roskelley spent more time with her than with us. . . . She could have things that we couldn't have." She could make him "believe the moon was made of green cheese. She's caused me more trouble than a little bit. I don't mind saying it, because she knows." Maud apparently made overtures by visiting the other wives, but she was not made welcome.[24]

Reactions to Illness and Death

Moments of need — particularly those related to health — usually saw extra helpfulness and even reconciliation. This matches John Faragher's conclusions about women in American society as a whole. "Perhaps women's most important relations with each other were expressed in the sisterhood of the sick bed. Women took it upon themselves to act in nurturant and nursing roles for the sick . . . and most especially for stricken women." Lucile Barlow Clark said, "Aunt Fanny [Call, her father's first wife and her mother's sister] and Grandmother Call always helped Mother [Sarah] until she was able to take care of the new baby and family." Karl Skousen said, "Whenever Mother was confined with a new baby, the first one there to take care of her and look after her was Dad's other wife, Aunt Ida, and vice versa." Eunice Stewart Harris remembered though, "It was not an easy thing to do, making all the baby clothes for the second wife, but that was the only thing [I] could do." L. Oliver, a son of Anthon and his second wife, Caroline Flygar Skanchy, said that his father's wives were usually cold towards each other and often gossiped about the other, but in times of sickness and childbirth they would work together.[25]

James Douglas Harvey's wives, Nancy and Sarah, were friendly when they lived in Mexico, but according to a son, Bernal, disagreements arose because Sarah "always got more than Mother did." James was killed during the Mexican revolution, and the wives moved to different places in Utah after they left Mexico in 1912. Years later, when Sarah learned that Nancy was dying of stomach cancer, she moved with her young children to Blanding, Utah, to care for Nancy because her daughters were too young to help much. After Nancy's death, she took one of her young sons home to raise.[26]

A daughter of Flora Bingham Taylor wrote, "For years Josephine [the first wife] was somewhat frail in health and it was necessary that Flora should assume the responsibility of performing some of the heavier tasks about the place, especially in Levi's absence. But she accepted conditions in a practical cheerful spirit and did whatever was necessary in a prompt, thorough manner."[27]

The death of a husband and resulting economic and emotional problems could bring either closeness or separation. An example of a bond that endured was the lifelong affection between the wives of Henry Smith Tanner. Helen Watkins remembered taking her widowed mother to see another wife dying of cancer. " 'Oh Belle,' she [the other wife] said, 'I have always loved you so.' Mother said, 'And I love you.' " Her mother went on to explain, "We still love each other; we've always loved each other. You would think Dad [their husband] would be the one that held us together but he has been gone since 1935." Helen added, "When the next to the last wife was in a rest home, she was real old and sick and wanted to go. She thought that the first wife should come and get her. She would keep saying, 'Why doesn't Reta come and get me?' "[28]

When James Michael Andersen died, his two wives, Margaret Maria White and Susan Eliza Stevenson, "lived together until Aunt Sue's daughter got married. They [the wives] would come down to the temple [in Logan] once or twice and go back to Lewiston [about fifteen miles]. . . . Finally they decided it was a long drive, so they rented their home in Lewiston, . . . rented a little home [in Logan] and worked in the temple. . . . Then Mother finally got to the point where she felt she couldn't keep up with her end of the bargain. My mother couldn't see very well and Aunt Sue couldn't hear. They got along with each other as long as they could." When they could no longer live together, each went to stay with her own daughter.[29]

When Eldon Payne's father died, "each family tried to take care of their own mother. But we still worked together; we still played together." After Frank Romney's father, Miles Park, died, the farm was sold to a brother who built new homes for the wives that were no longer next door. "That was the saddest day of my life when my [half] brother Vernon and I were separated," he recalled. "After that our lives were pretty much apart most of the time." After Oara Cluff Pace's father died, his wives who lived in Thatcher and Pima, Arizona, turned to their own families for help and rarely saw each other. Frances Grant Bennett summarized this type of experience. "After the Grant wives separated and they didn't have any man to hold them together, they really drifted apart."[30]

And a wife's death sometimes called forth revealing tributes. Eunice Stewart Harris wrote in her autobiography, "December 1922 I was called to Boise by the sudden death of Annie Wride Harris, my husband's wife. . . . With her passing the world lost one of its noblest women. A truer or more devoted friend no one ever had than she was always to me. In the family she was always charitable, unselfish, and kind. . . . During the 36 years of our association together in our large family there was ever harmony and love."[31]

Although any given set of human relationships is complex, the relationship of plural wives, though sometimes strained, was surprisingly rewarding in many cases. Motivated to accept polygamy as a religious practice, plural wives tried hard to treat each other with respect and love. With no model to follow, they established their relationships based on monogamous traditions. In many cases the wives were like mother and daughter, friends, or sisters. There were jealousies, but the women learned to overcome, deal with, or suppress them, and still love each other. Relationships changed, especially with childbirth and sickness, and brought the women closer together. A husband's death, depending on the family situation, could draw a family closer together or pull it apart.

11

The Children of Plural Families

By the nineteenth century, children were no longer just small adults who were an essential part of the family economy. Childhood had evolved into a distinct, sheltered period in which to grow up. Simultaneously the Victorian ideal of separate spheres for men and women expanded, and caring for the home and children became more a female role. According to one historian, "From every available source, it is clearly evident that girls and boys were raised by mothers who were faithful to the standards of motherhood." "Women became primarily responsible for child care and for maintaining the emotional and psychological well-being of the enclosed family unit; men concerned themselves with the work outside the home and viewed the family as a refuge from the competitive world of industrial society." Given these assignments of responsibility, "many boys were estranged from their fathers, not only because sons did not see their fathers often enough to get to know them, but also because there seemed a latent tension between a mother and father."[1]

Since in the typical American family of this time children were the responsibility of the mother, were relationships between mothers, fathers, and children changed with additional wives? This chapter examines kinship between mothers and children, fathers and children, and between siblings themselves. Since children of polygamous families only personally knew what life was like in a polygamous home, they could only imagine how it would have been different growing up in a monogamous family. Most children simply accepted polygamy as part of their lives. While some scholars have suggested polygamous wives were closer to their children, very few children saw a special relationship develop because of polygamy. The Victorian ideal was that the mother took care of the children while the father worked out of the home, so a closeness, an identification, with the mother was expected.

Some children commented that they were not as close to their fathers as they would have liked to have been. There were cases where a closeness did not develop because the father was gone, dividing his time between his work and another family. Even though fathers were gone from their plural families, their children were still important to them. In relating to their father's other wives, the children, like their mothers, adapted their monogamous traditions, often referring to and treating the other wife as an aunt or another mother. The relationship between a plural wife and children can be compared to that of a stepmother and children. Personalities, however, not polygamy — especially in cases when one plural wife died — were the deciding factors. Another way to examine relationships between parents and children is to look at discipline. In both monogamous and polygamous families, mothers did most of the disciplining. In polygamous families, fathers were not as active since they were away from the home more. Most mothers corrected their own children and not those of their co-wives. Half brothers' and sisters' relationships were determined more by personality, age differences, and location. The relationship between the father and his wives and between the wives themselves determined how much and how well the children interacted.

Mother-Child Relationships

Since polygamous wives did not have the complete affection of their husbands and since children saw their fathers only a few times a week at best, some scholars have asked, "To whom did female Saints turn for emotional outlet? Women turned to their children and often to other women, in compensation." This is similar to what some African scholars have discovered — "a co-wife in a polygamous family tends to have less affective attachment to her husband than to her children. . . . Marriage is diluted, and the relationship with the children tends to become more important than the other relationships in the woman's life." Examples of this sentiment are found in Mormon polygamy. Annie Clark Tanner, second wife of Joseph Marion Tanner, described the emotional needs her children fulfilled. "I had the attitude of many Mormon women in polygamy. I felt the responsibility of my family. . . . A woman in polygamy is compelled by her lone position to make a confidant of her children." Caroline Eyring Miner explained, "Mother's children were her own. I think in a polygamous family that is sometimes quite characteristic. The mother gets a tremendous satisfaction out of her children. That was one thing she didn't especially want to share that much." Archie L. Jenkins reported, "My mother was the stalwart of our family and the backbone. . . . It was through her we learned love and affection for each other and kept us united." Loretta Merrill Rigby said, "These polygamous wives were the ones who raised the children. Father would drop by occasionally but to stay overnight."[2]

Although some mothers and children expressed a special relationship because their husband and father had responsibilities elsewhere, this was not the typical response. It is true that the man could not be home as much, and as Wasel Black Washburn explained, "A woman wouldn't like to be left with her family on her own. She wants a husband there to teach and help and to be a patriarch of the family. If he has to be gone most of the time, that leaves all of that responsibility to her." But the same situation could happen in some monogamous families. Ada Howlett said that in many cases the mothers were "the mainstay" since the fathers were "quite busy."[3] Polygamy was not the sole factor that determined the relationship between a mother and her child. Personalities and individual circumstances proved equally significant.

Usually a close bond developed between a mother and her child, which one would expect to find. Mothers looked forward to the birth of their children and valued them as special gifts. Martha Spence Heywood, who lived in Nephi, Utah, away from her husband and his other wives, remembered when her first child was born. "I enjoy day by day my sweet babe and find that in possessing him my cup is full, such as it has not been before and I am willing to bear some little difficulties in the possession of him." On her first anniversary she said, "My child is the consummation of all my earthly wishes." Lorna Call Alder said of her mother, "Her home and her family meant everything in the world to her."[4]

Children also experienced a special closeness to their mothers. Jeneveve Eyring Layton declared in her interview, "Oh, my mother! She was wonderful. You know how you feel about your mother." Her half sister, Rose Eyring Calder, said, "We idolized our mother. She was a marvelous woman, just a marvelous woman." Then referring to Jeneveve's mother, she said,

During the nineteenth century, children were no longer considered little adults, and childhood became a distinct sheltered period in which to grow up. The John Parry children here represent the new forms of play. Utah State Historical Society.

"Aunt Emma was a fine woman, too, but Mother was a most outstanding, supportive woman." Sometimes that relationship with a mother had nothing to do with the relationship with the father. Both were close, but the child felt a special attachment to the mother. Ara O. Call said, "I guess everyone thinks their mother is the greatest and I certainly think mine was." Describing her, he added, "She did have a great influence on my life. I was probably closer to my mother than I was my father although I wouldn't want it understood that I didn't love my father. I was close to him. But Mother was a close confidant of mine all her life."[5]

Just like other Victorian families, the mother spent more time with the children and was responsible for teaching them. George S. Pond said, "One of the first recollections I have after I came into this world was the fact that I had a wonderful mother. My father stood behind her in all that she did in disciplining and in helping us to become good citizens and good members of the Church." LDS children often remembered some of the specific things that their mothers taught them, religious values being some of the most significant. Albert L. Payne said, "Mother was a very religious person and had a very sensitive keen conscience." She taught her children how to pray and what was wrong and right to such an extent that "we didn't let Mother down by doing wrong." Anson B. Call Jr. said that his mother "was just as strict as far as the Gospel was concerned as Father and maybe a little more so. If any of us children went astray, it wasn't because we didn't have good teaching." Mothers also preached the value of education. Abraham Stout said that all his father's wives "believed in education and the development of talents and did all in their power to supply these things for their children."[6]

Sometimes the individual personalities of parents determined the relationship. Rita Skousen Johnson said, "My relationship with my mother has always been most precious. It was the same with my father. My father was more strict and more stern. My mother was more loving." William Walser remembered that his father paid him a penny a piece for killing gophers. He carefully saved his money, only spending every tenth penny on tithing. When his mother wanted to buy a new couch and could not quite afford it, he gave her money so she could get it. His brother Alma did not assist his mother in the same way but spent his own money. Because of the special help that he had given, William's mother praised him as "more of a father than a son." Jonathan S. Cannon explained that he was very close to his mother and "I always felt that Mom trusted me more than she did the other boys."[7]

In cases where there were closer relationships between mother and children there were often special circumstances. Mary Ann Stowell, the second wife of Joseph Jackson, explained why she moved from the family mill outside of town to Colonia Juarez. "A man doesn't come first when there are children, I tell you." Other wives also moved with their children to towns so they could have a better education. Sometimes when the father had to be gone a great deal, having children helped combat the loneliness. Ellen Clawson said of her six-month-old baby, "She is so much company for me while her father is gone I don't know how I should live without her."[8]

Annie Clark Tanner, who felt that "a woman in polygamy is compelled by her lone position to make a confidant of her children," also had a special situation. For the first years of her marriage, her husband was on a mission and she was on the underground. "My husband's interests were many. His other homes, as I have said, were sixteen miles from mine. His law office was also in Salt Lake and he traveled for the Church throughout Utah and the adjoining states, and even into Canada and Mexico." Later, he moved to the Mormon settlements in Canada. "He wanted me to go to Canada and was greatly disappointed when I hesitated about selling the home." He sent Zina Card, a friend and a plural wife, to discuss the situation with her. Annie asked her, "What would you do . . . if your husband had increased his family from three wives to six, some of whom you had never even seen? Were there just the three of us, I'd make any sacrifice, but am I justified in robbing my children of an ideal home, situated among all my people, and where they have the opportunities for an education?" Zina answered, "If that is the condition, keep your home." Unsure of her decision, Annie even went to Joseph F. Smith, the President of the Church, who advised her, "Don't give up your home unless Brother Tanner invites you to a better one." Although her children spent time on the farm in Canada, Annie remained separated from her husband. She said of the wife that did move to Canada, "One of Mr. Tanner's younger wives, a cultured and educated young woman, had been induced to leave the educational field where she was an eminent success and move to the Canadian ranch. . . . She was young and in love with him, and nothing had happened to mar her confidence in her husband's judgment." Annie encouraged her children to visit Canada but return home so they could get an education.[9]

As the discussion on living arrangements and visiting schedules pointed out, Annie's circumstances were atypical of polygamous families where the father and his wives lived in the same town and he visited daily or weekly. When most of those interviewed described their mothers, they did not detail their relationships; for them, that closeness was probably a given. Rather, they described physical appearance, family backgrounds, activities in the home, teachings, discipline, and cooking. Since their only experience was as a part of a polygamous family, they did not compare their mothers to those in monogamous ones. Their mothers were simply their mothers — someone who was expected to take responsibility for their rearing.

Father-Child Relationships

Children's separation from their fathers, like closeness to their mothers, was also a given. At first it might appear that monogamous children were closer to their fathers than polygamous children. Of plural families whose children talked about their relationships with their fathers, 13 percent had no attention, 52 percent had little interaction, and 35 percent had close relationships with their fathers. In contrast, 84 percent of the children from monogamous families reported that they were close to their fathers. At first, these figures suggest overwhelming support to the theory that not only were polygamous children closer to their mothers but they also lacked a special relationship with their fathers. However, that conclusion might have been arrived at too quickly. This study looked at over 200 polygamous and 150 monogamous families, and only 63 and 49 respectively specifically mentioned relationships with fathers. (See Table 18.) Just as with their mothers, rather than discussing specific relationships, children usually talked about their fathers' occupations and Church positions. Given the Victorian ideal, they expected to be closer to their mothers than their fathers since the fathers were out earning a living and did not spend as much time at home.

Special circumstances arose from polygamy in which children did not feel a special closeness to their fathers. According to Annie Clark Tanner, "As I have observed monogamy, the husband and wife rearing a family

Relationships between fathers and sons were not always close — especially when the father was much older. Here George Reynolds poses with his sons. Utah State Historical Society.

Table 18

Father's Relationship with Children

Survey includes 63 polygamous and 39 monogamous families.

Polygamous families	Number	Percentage
No attention from father	8	12.7%
Little attention from father	33	52.3
Close to father	22	35.0
Total	63	100.0
Monogamous families		
No attention from father	0	0.0%
Little attention from father	8	16.3
Close to father	41	83.7
Total	49	100.0

have a common interest. They are a team working together for the advantages of the children. In polygamy the man's interests are scattered." Archie L. Jenkins after describing a closeness to his mother went on to say, "My father never showed any sentimental feelings toward our family to speak of, which we felt like we were missing as we grew up. . . . We respected Father but he never gave us a chance to really love him as non-polygamous families seemed to enjoy with a father patriarch dedicated to one family."[10]

One of the reasons these families did not feel close to their fathers was because their interests were spread between several families. Fern Cluff Ingram said that her father "was gone so much that he was almost a stranger." Marjorie Cannon Pingree recalled, "I was not neglected, but it seemed to me that I grew up with very little regulating because my father had another family that he lived with a part of the time. He supervised us as best as he could, but I can't remember that I was ever forced to study or guided in my assignments."[11]

When the father had married a plural wife later in life, it could impose added burdens on his relationship with his children. Robert Haynie said, "There are not too many memories that I have as far as my father goes because he has always been an old man in my eyes. I didn't get a chance to play with him . . . like the older brothers did because he was an old man by the time I came along. I always figured he was quite stern. In other words, I got robbed out of a childhood father and son relationship."

Alvin Heaton also had sons of various ages from his two wives. This photograph was taken in Moccasin Springs, Arizona, in 1907. LDS Church Archives.

Joseph T. Bentley remembered that his father was "quite a bit older. He seemed to be more like the bishop than the father as I remember him. . . . He was busy; quite often he was away."[12]

In extreme cases, the father spent almost no time with one wife. Reuel N. Pomeroy's father did not live with his mother. "I don't remember my father at all until I was seven years of age. . . . I can remember it as though it was yesterday. We were eating supper. My dad, Elijah Pomeroy, was at the head of the table, and my mother was on the side. I went up to her, whispered in her ear and asked her who that man was. . . . Of course, she told me." The next day Elijah asked Reuel to get something for him and was upset when Reuel stopped to play. "He asked me why I didn't bring it in and mind him. I said, 'You're not my boss.' " When he threatened to hit Reuel, his mother intervened, "Don't hit that boy. . . . He doesn't know who you are." Then she explained what had happened the night before. Later Reuel got to know his father better working with him on some mining claims. "My personal relation with my dad was pretty close and satisfactory. I never got any fatherly advice from him that I can remember. My impression is that in those days the relationship of father and son was not spelled out and dwelt upon . . . in the Church as it is today."[13]

Even though polygamous fathers were often away from their families, their children were an important part of their lives. Men who rarely mentioned very much about home life in their autobiographies and journals at least noted when their wives gave birth to children. For example, John Brown recorded, "February 3, 1857 — My wife Elizabeth gave birth to a son, William Crosby," "July 7, 1858 — My wife Amy gave birth to a daughter Mary Ann," and "June 11, 1859 — My wife Margaret gave birth to a daughter Julia Ann." Thomas E. Taylor wrote to his wife Minnie in Gunnison, "Time does pass quickly. I remember so well the evening 4 years ago when you were in confinement and you remarked to me, 'I think this little affair would have been over before you got here' and how soon after I arrived you were delivered. We have so much to be thankful for and that Alfred is strong."[14]

Fathers also took special concern in their children by giving childrearing advice. Thomas told Minnie, "On account of [Alfred] being your only child, you must not neglect that he is taught correct principles. He seems to be getting along well with his teeth." Lyman Andros Shurtliff wrote to his daughters, "Girls, learn all you can and obey Melissa [Lyman's first wife] and hearken to her counsel. Help Altamira [his second wife] all you can with her work so that she can make up the clothes for herself and children." They were also proud of their offspring. Christopher Layton wrote of his children, "My sons were now a great help to me for they were trusty boys and very obedient. I always tried to be a kind and affectionate father and maintain my place at the head of the family and they loved to obey me and seemed to regard my word as law to them."[15]

Relationships with Other Wives

In polygamous families, children had "other mothers" — the father's other wives. Again, just as the children did not detail their relationships with mothers and fathers, they did not discuss their relationships with the other wives. Only 57 families gave much explanation about how they interacted with them. When asked to describe them, most, just as they did with their mothers, talked about physical appearances and positive and in some cases negative qualities. Of those who described their relationships, over half mentioned some closeness with the other wives, one quarter felt that they were especially close, 11 percent had no relationship, and 12 percent had little contact. Since polygamy was the only way of family life that they knew, they just accepted their father's other wives. Joseph W. Pratt's mother taught school, and Aunt Dora, his father's other wife, "was just like a mother to me, especially being Mother's own sister. She was always the cook and housekeeper. Aunt Dora kept the house and took care of us all. . . . I thought at the time that was just the way things ought to be . . . but after I got older I decided Aunt Dora was something special."[16]

Just as the wives adapted monogamous patterns to determine relationships with each other, the children used monogamous terms to describe interaction with other wives. Yet only a small percentage of the children interviewed in this study called the other wife mother. Elma Jane Jones Anderson saw that special relationship: "Some of the younger children didn't know which was their mother." She recalled a time when one child told another, " 'Mother wants you.' She said, 'Which mother?' They said, 'Well, the mother we have had the longest.' "[17]

Age differences affected how the children viewed the other wives and what they called them. When the first wife was considerably older than the second wife, the title the children used reflected the difference in years. For example, Esther Webb Pope said that she and her brothers and sisters called the first wife Sister Webb. When the second or third wife was closer in age to the children of the first family, she might be more of a friend. Catherine Scott Brown said, "We always called her Zilly; she was just like one of the girls."[18]

Just as many wives considered their husbands' other wives as sisters, most children referred to the other wives as aunts. As pointed out earlier, 25 percent of the polygamous wives in this study actually were sisters. Yet in an even greater percentage of cases, children referred to the other wives as aunt, probably feeling the title of Sister or Mrs. was too formal, the first name was not respectful enough, and that it would be confusing and inaccurate to call a number of women "mother."

Although most of the children called the father's other wives aunt, their actual relationships took on a number of forms. In her master's thesis,

Dorothy Geneve Young Willey examined the interactions of children in polygamous families with their fathers, mothers, and the father's other wives. She found that of 37 cases, 27 percent saw the other wife as a second mother, 49 percent as an aunt, and 14 percent as just a neighbor. Thirty-two cases gave more specific feelings about their relationship, and of these 34 percent said that they loved the other wife while 31 percent said that they "liked" her.[19]

Alma Uriah Jones described his father's other wife as "a mother. I have given Mother's Day talks. I have said on every occasion that I have at least two mothers in heaven to go back to." Annie Richardson Johnson said, "It was real nice to have more than one mother because then we had the benefits of the talents of all of them. If one could sing and play the piano, they would teach the others."[20]

Ada S. Howlett relates a humorous story illustrating the same point. "When my uncle, Johannah's son, was a little boy, he said he had two mothers. The other kids said, 'You haven't got two mothers; no one has two mothers. . . . I bet you daren't ask your other mother to give you a piece of bread and butter.' . . . So he went to Grandmother and he said, 'Mother, can I have a piece of bread and butter?' She said, 'Of course, you can, my dear.' The kids said, 'Well, I guess you have got two mothers.' "[21]

Morris Hodges was also very close to his father's first wives. "I lived with Aunt Louie and Aunt Anna until I was married when I was twenty-two years old. They were my mothers most of the time. . . . They treated me just as if I were their own child. They took care of me if my socks needed to be mended. . . . If I needed a spanking, I got that too."[22] Albert L. Payne explained, "My Aunt Lucy was just like a second mother. When I needed something, I could go to her or go to Mother, either one. Normally you would go to your mother more because you are there more and naturally closer to her, but I always felt free to go to either one. All who came to Mother were mothered and Aunt Lucy mothered me and the rest of the family." Glen Doney Lowe recalled, "In the case of emergency, she was just like a second mother. She was right there to help in sickness or anything."[23]

Though certainly proximity to other wives helped shape feelings of closeness, personality was probably the decisive factor. Rinda Bentley Sudweeks, the daughter of third wife Maud, said that Aunt Maggie, the first wife, was so much older "I sort of felt just as I did towards my mother's sister. . . . I used to go up there sometimes and wish she would give me a piece of candy. But I didn't dare ask for it." LeRoy Eyring said that his father's first wife was "certainly not a grandmother. We called her Auntie. That was the proper address for her. I suppose we thought of her more like an aunt, but certainly a very stern aunt and one that I, at least, was afraid of." Caroline Eyring Miner, LeRoy's half sister, said that her relationship with his mother, her aunt, "was not comparable in any way to my relationship with my mother. I liked her and thought a lot of her, . . . and I thought often if she had been just an aunt removed, we would have been very close to her or maybe closer."[24]

Occasionally jealousies and problems developed between the other wives and the children. In Daniel Skousen's family, the older children were only a few years younger than the second wife. Viva Bluth Brown said, "When Papa married Mama [Sarah Ann Spilsbury when she was 18], Polly [an older daughter of the first wife who was 15] in a way had to take a second seat. . . . Mama tells that one of the first times she ever went to El Paso with Papa after she was his wife, Polly just couldn't accept it because she had been the one that had been used to going" since the first wife was ill. When Polly found that the second wife was sleeping with her father, Polly felt "it was more than I could take." Sarah also explained, "Polly and I sometimes had hard times because our ages were not too far apart, but we managed. I feel like I did much for her and in later life she repaid me well." The first wife's younger children who were born after their father had two wives accepted Sarah as another mother.[25]

When a mother died, the other wives often felt a special commitment to her children. According to Bessie Jameson Judy, "My sisters had decided . . . they would take Mother up to Salt Lake and get her a little apartment. . . . Then Aunt Amelia died, and we got word of it. Mother walked the floor for two nights. The next morning she came and said, 'Can you girls get along without me? I feel that I must go to that young family. They need me.' " Her mother moved and took care of the five children for the school year. At the end of the year the next oldest son Alex was graduating from high school. He told Bessie's mother, "When school is out, I will go over to Big Indian [Mine where his father was working] and see Dad because I don't feel like I can graduate in these clothes." She "was quite a seamstress for boy's slacks. . . . Unbeknown to him, she took his school sweater and had it cleaned. Then she made him some lovely slacks. When he came from school, she said, 'I wonder if you could graduate in this outfit.' He softened his heart and threw his arms around her."[26]

Children as well developed new relationships with the other wives when their own mother died. Zina Patterson Dunford's mother died of appendicitis when Zina was nine and her sister Venna only a month old. "Auntie just took over the care of the baby, and she was just a mother to her. Of course, she was the only mother that Venna knew, and she always called her Mama. To the rest of us she was Auntie. She was just marvelous. . . . We all loved Auntie. She just took over and was a mother to us. I'm sure it was easier for us to grow up normally because of her."[27]

Hannah Skousen Call's Aunt Sarah addressed her letters to "Dearest Daughter" after Hannah's mother and father died. "She claimed my children as her grandchildren as she did her own children's children. She would write often and always say, 'from your other mother.' When she died, I sang, 'That Wonderful Mother of Mine,' the same song I sang for my own mother." Elizabeth Adams, the third wife of John McFarland, said, "The children in the other families treat me as if they were my own. Now that their mothers are dead, they look to me whenever they can and are dear to me."[28]

Some children acknowledged, however, that the wives were not interchangeable. Abalone Porter Hurst was very close to her mother who died when she was only 12. Aunt Mary "was never exactly like Mother to me. I don't mean to say that she wasn't my mother and didn't treat me just as good as our mother would. . . . I just worshipped [Aunt Mary]. She was just everything that a person could ask for. I always got lonesome for Mother."[29]

Louis Brandley praised his Aunt Eliza for her willingness to care for their children after the first wife and his mother, the second wife, died. She gave them "a full measure of family care as though we had been her own flesh and blood. . . . As soon as we got there she took us into her home and into her heart and treated us well. If we got sick, she cared for us. There was no difference between my mother's children and Aunt Marie's children in her mind and in her ideas." But he added, "She was devoted to her own children and she guarded them like a mother hen. That was understandable."[30]

In rare cases, bitter feelings separated the children from the other wives. When Pearl Jarvis Augustus's mother died, "Dad sent for his first wife to help him with us six children. He took us back to old Mexico to live. The stepmother or first wife stayed with us. Her name was Fanny Godfrey Jarvis. We had to call her Aunt Fanny. When Father brought her to the house I heard Father tell her that she had to do it. . . . . She said, 'I'll take any of the other children, but I don't want anything to do with Pearl.' My name was the same as my mother's. . . . But Father told her that she had to stay there. But she didn't stay too long and there was a lot of unhappiness. Then Father died when I was twelve." After her father died, Pearl stayed with a number of families, helping however she could to earn her room and board.[31]

Relationships with Monogamous Stepmothers

In a monogamous family when the father remarried after his first wife died, the children reported the same variety of encounters with their stepmothers. Viva Skousen Bluth Brown recalled, "I'm a second marriage; I married into a family that was not polygamous but a family where their mother had died. Then they found somebody that was coming in to be with their father. They had lost a mother and now . . . they had lost their daddy in a way because he was a husband to me and he had to treat me like a wife. It is quite an experience." She added that Polly, her half sister, must have felt the same way when Viva's mother married Polly's father as a second wife.[32]

Abraham Marion Bergeson explained that his mother became very ill when he was 12, so his father sent to Sweden for a housekeeper. His mother "talked Aunt Milloy into marrying my dad after she died so she could stay and take care of the kids. She did, and it was such a blessing for us kids. A more wonderful woman you never could find. I always said that most women are good mothers, but it takes a special woman to be a good stepmother. She was really a good one." Harry Moroni Whitmer said, "It is hard to be a stepmother and it is hard to be a stepchild. But you have to have them at times. She [his stepmother] was good to us kids and took care of us."[33]

Just as a polygamous wife sometimes favored her own offspring, a stepmother would sometimes treat her own children better than the first wife's children. Everett Mark Hamilton said, "My stepmother . . . had a daughter who was a half sister to me. As soon as she would bring the meat on, she would see that her daughter got the first helping. . . . Then she would pass it around to the rest of us. I guess that is natural for people to do those things." Roberta Allred resented her stepsister who was just a year younger. "Still today there is not the closeness between me and my stepsister that there is between me and the other sisters. I think it is just because of differences in personality. . . . We had plenty of clashes. It was not easy at all; it wasn't smooth. I'm sorry it wasn't."[34]

Disciplining Children

Discipline dramatizes the role polygamists actually played in their children's lives. Many of those interviewed saw discipline as purely physical punishment for disobedience rather than part of the process of how parents convinced children to obey. A few children of both monogamous and polygamous families said that their parents never had to discipline them because they were never disobedient. Most mentioned mild corporal punishment such as slapping, spanking, or "switching" with a willow. Many also listed lecturing or scolding. This was typical of nineteenth-century America. According to one historian, "Another sign of the change in outlook was the decline in corporal punishment of children. . . . Children were still punished, to be sure, but more usually through withdrawal of affections by parents, . . . through denial of privileges, rather than by beatings, as had been commonplace in the colonial years."[35]

Both mothers and fathers in monogamous and polygamous families imposed discipline; in both types of families, mothers were always involved in correction, fathers sometimes playing a more passive role. Polygamous fathers had less responsibility for their children than their monogamous counterparts because they were gone more often. Mothers did most of the correcting in 40 percent of both monogamous and polygamous families. In 28 percent of the polygamous families, the mother and father split the responsibility, and in another 26 percent the mother was totally responsible when the father was gone. (See Table 19.)

Mothers spent more time with their children while the fathers supported the family and thus were more often on hand when discipline was required. Polygamous child Teresa Richardson Blau said, "Mother had so much [disciplining] to do alone that I think Daddy just kind of left it to her when he was there too." According to George E. Hancey, a polygamous child, "I don't recall my father ever laying a hand on one of the children regardless. . . . If there was any punishment to be meted out, he would leave it to Mother to do it." Hazel Richardson Taylor, the daughter of the first wife, said that her father "very seldom" disciplined. She recalled a time when he "attempted to correct one of the children. They turned to him and said, 'You're not the boss; my mama is.' " Edward Hunter Jeffries explained that his monogamous mother "was the most outspoken of the two. We were always around her more than we were around Father, so she had the bulk of the disciplining to do." Agnes Ford Johnson, a child of monogamous parents, said, "Father was gone to work, but Mother took the brunt of it [disciplining] when he was gone."[36]

Fathers were partially responsible for discipline in half of the families — both monogamous and polygamous. Anthony Ivins Bentley, a son of the first wife, said, "I knew that my father would learn about what had happened while he was gone. My mother was just as much in harmony with what he would want as he was in harmony with what she would want." Clark Hamblin, a son of a monogamous family, explained, "I guess my mother probably was the one that kind of corrected us, but when it got to be something she felt was a little bit serious, then Dad entered. When Dad entered the picture we knew we had to straighten up then."[37]

Twenty percent of both monogamous and polygamous fathers had very little to do with disciplining the children, and in only 11 percent of polygamous families were fathers totally responsible. Ione Naegle Moss, whose father had more than one wife, explained, "My father was the disciplinarian when he was home. He was still the disciplinarian when he was away. We would get a spanking when he came home." Seneth Hyer Thomson, who was also from a polygamous family, recalled, "The mothers never interfered with us. If anything was to be said, it was told to our father who straightened us out. That didn't happen often. Father was the disciplinarian."[38]

Another 13 percent of the polygamous fathers disciplined when they were at home. Laura Andersen Watkins said that both her parents disciplined. "I think if Father was there, he would be the one that would stick up, but if Mother was alone, she would be the one." Lavinia Bentley Jackson, the daughter of the third wife, said, "My mother did most of the disciplining. Father would talk to us, but he never did any spanking. . . . Once in a while he would get real firm if he thought you weren't minding what he was telling you to do." Richard Ivins Bentley, the first wife's son, said of punishment, "I guess the wives had to do most of it. Of course, my dad licked me a couple or three times."[39]

Fathers were responsible for all discipline in 27 percent of monogamous families. Kenneth E. Weight remembered that his father was in charge "because Mother, as long as I remember, had rheumatism. She couldn't

Table 19

Discipline in Polygamous and Monogamous Families

Survey includes 127 polygamous and 88 monogamous men and 106 polygamous and 81 monogamous women.

Discipline by father	Polygamous		Monogamous	
	Number	Percentage	Number	Percentage
All	15	11.8%	24	27.3%
Occasionally	62	48.7	45	51.0
None or almost never	27	21.3	17	19.3
When there	17	13.4	0	0.0
Outside	3	2.4	0	0.0
Boys	3	2.4	2	2.4
Total	127	100.0	88	100.0
Discipline by mother				
All	44	41.5	33	40.8
Occasionally	30	28.3	44	54.3
None or almost never	0	0.0	3	3.7
When father not there	28	26.4	0	0.0
Inside	1	1.0	0	0.0
Girls	3	2.8	1	1.2
Total	106	100.0	81	100.0

use her hands very well." Xarissa Merkley Clarke called her father "quite a strict disciplinarian. . . . Father was the head of the house and he was law." Earl Chadwick remembered his father as very strict. The children also obeyed his mother but "any request Mother made Dad would back her up in. We never could talk back to our mother. . . . If Dad ever heard us, we were in trouble."[40]

Since polygamous homes were usually separate, each wife was responsible for her own household and her own children. In most cases, the wives did not correct another wife's children. Edgar L. Cazier said, "I never remember my Aunt Susan ever saying a cross word to me about anything." Wasel Black Washburn said, "I don't think my aunt disciplined us in any way. . . . I don't remember there being an occasion for her needing to."[41]

There were exceptions. Just as some children in polygamous families considered the other wives as second mothers, so they were disciplined by them. Franklin Lyman Stout said, "Aunt Retty used to bat my ears down. She would beat us more than all of them put together. . . . It seemed to me she was whacking me on the head all the time." Elma Jane Jones Anderson said, "If we did something bad, either mother would discipline us, and we would accept whichever mother corrected us."[42]

But in the same way that some children had little contact with their father's other families, they were unaware of how disciplining was done in their father's other homes. For example, Hazel Richardson Taylor said that she felt her father's other wives "taught them correct principles, and then they lived the lives that they should." She added, "But as far as discipline was concerned on the outside, you didn't see it. But I suppose there were rules, regulations, and standards in the home that they had to live up to."[43]

Sibling Relationships

In polygamy, children also developed bonds with their "aunt's" children. Frank Romney gave a typical reply: "I had a friend call me one day, and she said, 'Are Gaskell and George Romney your half brothers?' I said, 'No, I don't have any half brothers. They all have two eyes and two ears and two arms and two legs.'" Frank added, "Although I was the youngest, I always felt right at home in any of my brothers' and sisters' homes just as much as I would have in my mother's sons and daughters." Rulon Romney, Frank's nephew, said, "My childhood life was especially happy because of the many brothers and sisters that I had. I had eight full brothers and sisters and sixteen half brothers and sisters. My half brothers and sisters sometimes treated me better than my immediate family members did."[44]

Close proximity of the homes helped in developing close friendships. Mercelle Farr Atkinson said that her father and mother taught them to love members of the other family just as they loved their own. "We were brought up that we were just one big happy family. I guess we spent as much time eating in one place as we did at our home." The children worked together on the farm, played together in the swimming hole, and celebrated holidays together. "We had a lot of good times. I really can't ever remember a serious fight or argument that one of us had. If I had them, I've forgotten them. . . . I can remember a little squabble over a skate, a tin can stilt or something like.that. I don't remember any bickering ever in our families."[45]

Mercelle's half sister Winnie was almost her age. "We did everything together. We worked together; we played together all the time. There was never any separation. If you had seen us going to or from school or Sunday School or Primary, we were always together. In fact we were best friends." Viva Skousen Bluth Brown remembered, "Aunt Mally had a little girl, Caroline. She was just the age of my sister Leah who was just younger than I. They were twins really. One was born in March, and one was born in May. Caroline was very blond and Leah was very dark, but they were just always together. They would dress alike in most ways and they were very close."[46]

Differences in age separated Esther Webb Pope's family. Her half brothers and sisters "were all older. They could tell us what to do. . . . My father's oldest son was the same age as my mother." Douglas Cannon's father married a second wife eight years after the first and a third ten years after the second. Because of the age range and the underground, Douglas knew only one of the first wife's children; and although he lived near the second wife he didn't associate with her children. Georgina Bollette Critchlow Bickmore explained that her half brothers and sisters "were all old enough to be my mother and father. My father was twenty years older than my mother."[47]

In a few cases, half brothers and sisters did not get along, but the variable seemed to be personalities of the children and relationships between the mothers. George S. Tanner's mother, Eliza Ellen Parkinson, and the second wife, Emma Ellen Stapley, were not close. Speaking of his half brother, Clifford, who was four months older, George mused, "We should have been the closest of friends. We should have enjoyed each other thoroughly. . . . To be perfectly honest and candid, the feeling between the members of one family and the other was never what it should have been. . . . This brother of mine, Clifford, and I battled." George pointed out that he was bigger than Clifford and he was ahead of him in school. "He started to school one year before I did and I caught him. . . . Before he graduated from the eighth grade, I was two years ahead." George then went on to explain, "There was jealousy between my mother and his mother and there was jealousy between me and him."[48]

Sibling relationships evolved over time. Rose Brown Hayes, the daughter of John Brown's third wife, explained, "I don't remember of there ever being any quarreling or strife. We children loved each other dearly." However, when the children got older and started going to school, they wanted more and sometimes felt that the first wife's children got more.[49] Rudgar H. Daines remembered his father saying, "We never had any problems as far as the two families are concerned until the kids got old enough to be teenagers." Then jealousies started developing.

As the years passed, the closeness returned to the Daines family. Rudgar was going to work for his half brother when he retired from teaching in 1969, but his brother died that year. "When he died, I was the first one that his wife turned to. . . . I took care of her as much as I could." Mary Lucile Clark Ellis explained, "As we grew older, we were closer and more understanding." A half sister offered to take care of their father when he was ill and staying with Mary. She declined the offer, but appreciated the half a beef sent by a half brother.[50]

Most children felt closer to their full brothers and sisters. Wasel Black Washburn explained, "There were times when they would fight against each other and say things that they shouldn't. I think that each family was closer to their brothers and sisters than the other family." Seneth Hyer Thomson played with her half brothers and sisters and felt comfortable in their home. But "there was a difference. I do feel just a little bit closer to my full sisters, of course, but a whole lot closer to a half sister than the cousins because we worked together; we played together; we lived together." Terrance Heaton said, "I had about the same relationship to my half brothers and sisters as I did to my cousins. My mother's family was a very close family. . . . I had six cousins that I grew up with in Orderville all my age or within a year."[51]

Mary Lucile Clark Ellis described her family's current situation. "We are all very warm and friendly. In fact, one of the brothers passed away just recently and we all went to the funeral. They had us stand right in the receiving line by the casket. We are just one happy family." Andrew Larse Hyer called a special meeting in 1909 of his plural families and encouraged them to meet often. In 1978 the family held its seventieth family reunion. According to his daughter, he desired that these meetings take place as long as two of his children were living.[52]

Pearl Jarvis Augustus, despite rejection from the first wife, learned to love and appreciate her half brothers and sisters. After her sister had a spiritual experience in the Provo Temple about the two families uniting, they started to work on a family organization. "I don't know how it is all going to turn out but there are a lot of resentments and feelings that have been in the family. Most of them are older than I am. But if we can establish peace, that would be a good thing to do."[53]

Some polygamous families run into the logistical overload — unmanageable reunions a generation sooner than monogamous families. Esther Webb Pope said that they continued to have reunions "up until the children had families of their own. Then it got too many because we didn't have [large enough] facilities." In others such as Edward Christian Eyring's family, everyone gathers for a reunion every other year and for funerals.[54]

The relationship of children to their parents, to the other wives, and to each other depended largely on the relationships of the husbands and wives and the children's personalities. As in American society as a whole, polygamous children were closer to their mothers than their fathers. However, since life in polygamy was all they knew, they simply spoke highly of their mothers. They also praised their fathers, although some commented that they were not as close to them as they would have liked. The other wives played varying roles in their young lives based on location and individual personality. For some children their father's other wives were like other mothers. More referred to them as aunts, and while close to them, they were not as close as they were to their own mothers. Death led to close bonds with other wives, although in a few cases it was a dividing point. A comparison can be made between plural families and step families. Just as the relationship between a stepmother and the children depended on the personalities and the willingness to make the relationship work, plural wives and their husband's other wives' children got along if they lived close to each other and were willing to work together. Personality and distance were also the factors in determining how well the siblings — full and half brothers and sisters — got along. Families related well if they lived close together and they were willing to work together. As in all other aspects of polygamy, each family was unique.

12

Divorce and Inheritance in Plural Families

As has already been pointed out, external legal pressures from society at large, changes in Church policy, economic stress, missions, and death, just to name a few, all affected relationships between plural family members and forced husbands and wives to re-examine their life-style. In most cases, when difficulties were resolved, the family remained intact. However, in others, problems created enough stress that the couple decided to divorce. Because records were not kept, it is impossible to determine if there was a greater percentage of polygamous than monogamous divorces during the nineteenth century. While some divorces were a direct result of polygamy, others were the results of simple incompatibility. Another pressure point that could alter family relationships was when the father died and his estate had to be divided among heirs. In many cases the father left a will or the family members decided how to divide the property. At times no arrangements had been made and the family could not come to an agreement. Although some laws passed against polygamy made provisions for inheritance for children born before a certain date, cases were more likely to be resolved in Church courts. This chapter examines these problems — divorce and inheritance — and their effects on Mormon polygamous families.

Divorce Among Mormon Polygamists

Finding out just how many divorces were granted to polygamous couples and determining an accurate divorce rate is made difficult in that plural marriages were not officially recorded. The territorial legislature, in an "intent to protect plural marriages," passed an ordinance in 1852 that allowed registry of marriages to be kept by the Church rather than by civil courts who did not recognize plural marriages as being legal. According to Carol Cornwall Madsen, especially in the early days, "The aggrieved spouse presented her complaint to a bishop who after granting a hearing for both spouses sent his recommendation to Brigham Young for final adjudication. In many instances women and men appealed to Brigham Young directly. Young, as President of the Church, retained authority for the final disposition of the cases." George Reynolds, testifying during the Reed Smoot hearings in 1903, explained divorces were granted "for plural wives . . . on application, without any action of the [civil] courts, because the courts will take no action, as they do not recognize the marriage.[1]

Given these limitations, several attempts have been made to determine the number of divorces granted to plural couples. Eugene E. and Bruce L. Campbell point out that divorce was probably more common than is usually assumed. Using records in the Historical Department of the LDS Church, they found Brigham Young granted 1,645 divorces during his presidency. The Campbells explain that although no records show that these were polygamous marriages, "there are reasons to believe that most if not all of these certificates were issued to polygamists" because many of the men were General Authorities and stake and ward leaders. In some cases a husband was divorced from two or more wives on the same day. They added, "More conclusive evidence is the fact that Brigham Young had no authority to grant civil divorces terminating monogamous marriages, but as president of the church he alone had the right to sever polygamous relationships."[2]

Since plural marriages were also performed during the administrations of Presidents John Taylor and Wilford Woodruff, the Campbells conclude, "It seems logical to believe that they also granted divorces. If they granted them in similar numbers, it is likely that there were well in excess of 2,000 divorces granted prior to the 1890 Manifesto. Since there were only an estimated 2,400 men practicing polygamy in 1885, 2,000 or more divorces would be considerably higher than the national divorce rate in 1890 which was about one divorce per 1,000 existing marriages per year."[3]

Several obvious problems are evident in this conclusion. The Campbells determined the number of men practicing polygamy based on B. H. Roberts's statement in *A Comprehensive History of the Church of Jesus Christ of Latter-day Saints* that "male members practicing polygamy represented only 2% of the church population."[4] They conclude that since there were 120,000 men in the Church in 1888, that would mean an estimated 2,400 men practiced polygamy in 1885. This study and others have shown that more than 2 percent of the Church practiced polygamy, and, since some men were divorced from more than one wife, divorce figures cannot be equated by simply looking at the number of divorces and the number of men practicing polygamy.

Carol Cornwall Madsen explains some additional problems with the Campbells's conclusion. "Although President Young authorized approximately 1,645 divorces, three-fourths of these were in the first two decades of his administration. During the last decade of leadership the number of divorces dropped approximately 30 percent while the general population increased by nearly 65 percent. In the decade following his death in 1877, the population increased by nearly 42 percent but the number of divorces granted by Brigham Young's successor, John Taylor, decreased again by nearly half to 266. After the Woodruff Manifesto of 1890, Church divorces continued to decrease." Lacking formal records, Madsen concluded that it was impossible to make "comparative statistics on the ratio of marriage and divorce in Utah until 1890."[5]

Rather than giving a ratio of marriages and divorces, Phillip Kunz used family group sheets to determine what polygamous and monogamous marriages resulted in divorce. Based on a random sampling of group sheets found in the Genealogical Department of the LDS Church, he found that 6 out of 683 or 0.9 percent of monogamists divorced while 28 out of 1,029 plural marriages (counting each wife as one marriage) or 2.7 percent were divorced. Eight of 315 first wives or 2.5 percent were divorced. Based on these figures, a higher instance of divorce is evidenced in polygamous than monogamous families.[6] Family group sheets as a source present problems, however, since family members submitted them and not all divorces are listed. Also, since Kunz's figures are not based on a number of divorces per thousand per year it is difficult to compare it to the national averages.

Reasons for Divorce

Given these problems, most divorce studies, including Kimball Young, the Campbells, Madsen, and R. Collin Mangrum's study of Mormon courts, are anecdotal. These examples, though, reveal some interesting trends in divorce cases. The Campbells suggested that the major reason for divorces was the lack of rules governing polygamy. "In anomie [normlessness] circumstances, if the only voice of possible regulation is muted or ambivalent, a fluid marriage system may be expected." Madsen explained that the Mormon view of "post-mortal marital and familial ties" resulted in a higher rather than a lower divorce rate as would be expected. According to John D. Lee, a polygamist, "It was a sin for people to live together and raise and beget children in alienation from each other." Madsen found that from the time of settlement in Utah to 1847 to the first territorial legislature in 1851, only the Mormon ecclesiastical courts granted divorces. Domestic cases, mostly divorces — which were between 10 and 20 percent of their caseload — were granted for "verbal and physical abuse, non-support, abuse toward other families by the husband, even marriage by deception, but the decree was handed down on the basis of incompatibility."[7]

Brigham Young encouraged couples to stay together, but he did grant divorces, and he was more likely to consider a woman's appeal than a man's. One of Young's clerks explained, "As a rule, the Prest. never refuses to grant a bill on the application of the wife, and NEVER when she INSISTS on it." On the other hand, Young told men, "If you have drawn a red iron between your legs and scorched yourself, bear it without grunting, and if it smarts, grease it. It is not right for the brethren to divorce their wives the way they do. . . . I do not want to grant divorces." Jane Synder Richards recorded, "If a marriage is unhappy, the parties can go to any of the council, present their difficulties, and are readily granted a divorce." David Candland wrote in January 1855, "My wives Lucy and Bertha [both plural wives] became so possessed with evil to demand a bill of divorce. After much . . . counsel and the sanction and approval of Pres. Young and all who knew the matter I gave them the bill."[8]

Examples of divorce cited in this study help reveal some of the reasons why divorces were sought. As Madsen pointed out, it was more likely the wife than the husband who sought a divorce or requested separation. In some of these cases since the government did not recognize the marriage and only a church divorce would have been granted, no official steps were made to terminate the marriage; husbands and wives simply no longer lived together. Children interviewed were not always aware whether a divorce had been requested.

Out of 29 cases examined, it is possible to determine cause for divorce in only 25 cases. The main reason (10 out of 25) was lack of compatibility expressed by the wife. Two husbands sought divorce for the same reason. Three wives left their husbands because they would not financially support them. Three more were jealous of other wives, and another four decided that they could not live in polygamy after they had initially agreed to it.

Determining what actually caused divorce or separation is difficult though, since usually only one side of the story is available. Warren Foote, who wrote very little about his family life in his autobiography, went to great lengths to explain his separation and divorce from his plural wife Maria, so that his family would understand how he saw the situation. He wrote that in 1856 "during the summer and fall there had been a jealousy between my wives who caused a great deal of trouble. My second wife did not use the wisdom that she should have done, and I sometimes begin to think that such a state of things would end in apostasy and the breaking up of my family."[9]

Problems resurfaced in 1875. Maria had a store in her home, but because Warren thought it was crowded, he moved some of the goods to his first wife's house where there was more room and "the public" could get to it better. Maria objected because he had done it without her permission, so Warren decided not to allow a store on his property at all. "Maria got very mad and made some threats but seemed to be about as usual after her passion was over. I always wanted to treat my wives impartially and it was not for benefitting my first wife" that the goods were moved. "In fact I never consulted my first wife about it and I supposed that I was the head, and was able to judge in those matters."[10]

Problems came to a head when Maria encouraged her daughter Olive's marriage to a man that Warren objected to and when Maria decided to marry a non-Mormon after separating from him. Just before they were divorced, Warren and Maria and their children exchanged letters hoping all could be reconciled. In the end, though, Maria wrote a letter addressed to "Mr. Warren Foote" and signed "your once loving wife Maria" in which she asked for a divorce.[11]

Edward William Payne married his first wife Emily Bean in 1889. After 10 childless years, Edward asked her if he could marry a plural wife, and she agreed. He married Lucy Alice Farr in 1899 and Rosalia Tenney in 1903. Eldon, a son of Lucy's, remembered the first wife "didn't stay [in Mexico] all the time but she was there quite a bit of the time." Her childlessness remained a constant source of unhappiness. Eventually she returned to the United States and Edward had very little contact with her although they were not officially divorced until 1917. After the Paynes left Mexico in 1912, Rosalia began envying Emily's comparative comfort and security. Eldon remembered later when he and his brothers and sisters were grown that Emily "was kind of wanting to get back in the good graces of the children to see if they would take care of her I think. But we were all struggling, just getting started and didn't have anything. We couldn't take care of her. If she would have stayed with the family, we would have taken care of her some way. . . . The younger ones just didn't know about it, but some of us older ones that knew about it didn't have quite as much sympathy as we would have had if she would have stayed with the family." Rosalia said that Emily became close to the younger children and sometimes brought them presents.[12]

Belle Harris Merrill Nelson Berry, second wife of Clarence Merrill, gave economics as the reason that she left her first husband. "I said that my failure in marriage to Clarence Merrill was not due to polygamy but he could not support me and I could not endure it because I was ambitious for myself and my children." In another case, Price Nelson said that his second wife left him because she felt that she could earn more money as a midwife if she was separated from him and she "couldn't accept a man to be the head of his household. . . . I told her that I felt to promise her that if she would come back . . . [and] go to the Temple and get a blessing I would take her back and that she would have well, strong children. I arranged the time when I could meet her, but she didn't come. She told me she didn't get the letter, but I know she did. She was too independent and wanted to make money of her own."[13]

Arthur Day was not sure why his father's second wife left but hypothesized, "After the Manifesto, they weren't allowed to live with more than one wife. I think she just more or less left on her own and went off to Manti and started teaching. I'm sure she and Father saw each other occasionally and visited. . . . As far as being around our family, she wasn't around at all." When asked how his father felt about his wife leaving, Arthur answered, "I'm sure it bothered Father a great deal to have to give up one of his wives. . . . I'm sure that he felt very bad about not being able to live with both his wives because I'm sure he loved both very dearly."[14]

Joseph Holbrook Call's second wife, Martha Esther Williams, moved to Blackfoot, Idaho, from Afton, Wyoming, when her mother became ill, and "it finally drifted that he [Joseph] stayed most of the time at [the first wife's] place." When asked why Esther did not return to Wyoming after her mother died, Truman, a son of first wife Sarah Isabel Barlow, replied, "I don't know. I guess her and Father didn't get along well. I never heard of any quarrels with them. . . . I went with him several times when he would make a call on her. He never would stay there. He would just go and talk to her a while and then we would go on."[15]

Edward Franklin Turley married Annie Martineau Walser, a widow with two children, in Mexico. After having five children, they left Mexico in 1912. Already in financial straits, they faced a bleak future. According to Clarence, a son of first wife Ida Elizabeth Eyring, "When they got to El Paso, the government gave the people . . . free scrip to anywhere they wanted to go in the United States. So Aunt Annie took her family and went to Logan." Clarence's mother stayed in El Paso with Edward and her children. When they returned to Mexico two years later, Annie "got a divorce from Father. . . . We never did know why. I told some of the other children that I never did know why my father and Aunt Annie separated. My sister . . . said, 'I figured I didn't have the right to ask my mother, and I never asked her.' " Clarence continued, "I've wondered if it wasn't because of my stepbrother and sister. Maybe she felt that Dad didn't treat them right. . . . If that isn't it, then I don't even have an idea what the trouble was because she and Mother got along just wonderfully well."[16]

While Charles Edmund Richardson's families struggled to make ends meet after leaving Mexico, Daisie Stout, the fourth wife, had an especially difficult time. Crippled with arthritis, she was unable to work like the other wives. Edmund tried to give her a little more, but there was little to give. At one time he suggested that she ask Becky, the third wife, for some money, but Daisie did not want to impose. Yet she could not pay her water bill and was barely able to feed her children. Finally she consulted with the stake president and was counseled to leave Edmund. She moved to Logan where her father helped raise her family. Her problems were only economic though, and she did not ask for a dissolution. Her son Justin explained, "When I was a grown man, I put the question squarely to my mother, . . . 'Do you love my father? Do you want to maintain the sealing that you have with my father?' She said, 'Yes, I do. I can live with him if there is justice available.' "[17]

From their interviews, the Campbells conclude, "Perhaps the number of marriage failures and divorces among Mormon polygamists should not be surprising, but the fact that so many succeeded in developing happy marriage relationships and producing fine families should command both wonder and respect." Despite pressures and problems, a strikingly high number of families held together. Keith Romney said that his mother, first wife Francis Turley Romney, "wasn't the type that fit into polygamy too well. But she stayed with it. As a result, we are together as a family."[18]

Inheritance

A predictable and nonetheless disruptive crisis was distribution of either parent's estate. Here polygamy seems to have had a clearly negative impact. Of 119 polygamous families with information on inheritance, 29 percent mentioned disagreement over its settlement. Out of 41 monogamous families, only 3 identified any disagreements and one involved a stepmother, making it similar to a polygamous situation.

Since plural wives were not wives by law, the husband had to make some type of provision for them and their children. After the LDS Church announced the practice of polygamy in 1852, the territorial legislature passed laws giving rights to polygamous families. In regard to inheritance, men who left a will could of course divide their estates any way they wished. However, for those men who died intestate, the statute stated that "illegitimate children and their mothers inherit in like manner from the father, whether acknowledged by him or not, provided it shall be made to appear to the satisfaction of the court that he was the father of such illegitimate child or children." This act, while accepting the rights of children to inherit, also acknowledged the non-Mormon belief that the offspring of plural marriages were illegitimate.[19]

Federal laws passed against polygamy complicated inheritance matters. The Morrill Act, passed in 1862, included a clause that voided the inheritance laws the territorial legislature passed. The Edmunds and Edmunds-Tucker Act included provisions on inheritance. Section 7 of the Edmunds Act, passed in 1882, legitimized all children born prior to 1 January 1883. All future children of polygamous families were therefore declared illegitimate. The Edmunds-Tucker Act of 1887 strengthened the previous law, Section 11 stating: "No illegitimate child shall here after be entitled to inherit from his or her father or to receive any distributive share in the estate of his or her father." The law was not retrospective. The Utah state constitution of 1896 accepted polygamous children as legitimate.[20]

These laws determined how the estates were divided if no provisions were made or if the families could not agree on how the property should be apportioned. Sometimes the husbands had already distributed the property, usually deeding the wives their homes with the farmland being divided upon his death. They left either a formal will or an informal listing of how the property was to be divided which the heirs accepted and followed. In most cases, the laws did not have to be applied since there was some type of arrangement made by the father before his death. In cases where there was a dispute, the family members occasionally went to Church courts, still avoiding the state's inheritance laws.[21]

Sometimes after property was divided among them, a son purchased it from the rest of the family. In other cases, the children turned it back to their mother for her support. Personal property as well was distributed. Either all the wives and children received a percentage of the estate or each wife received a half, third, or quarter of the estate, according to the number of wives, then distributed it to their children at time of death. Sometimes the first wife received most of the estate while the other wives received a child's portion or only the home deeded to them.

The Mads Christian Jensen family shows some of these common elements. Each of the four wives owned a home and some land. Mads's will directed that his property be divided so each child received a fair share. Emma Rasmussen, a daughter of the second wife, said that each daughter received $125 from the estate. With Jensen's oldest son, Denmark, in charge, the children divided all of the personal property after the funeral. One daughter who owed her father a hundred dollars asked that the debt be cancelled as her share of the personal property. Hyrum, a son of the fourth wife, explained, "There was no dissention. Some wanted the things others got but nothing was said." According to Mary E. Croshaw Farrell, the fourth wife of George H. Farrell, the wives received all the property except the personal things and some small pieces of real estate. The sons divided the personal property by drawing names from a hat.[22]

Zerah Pulsipher left a formal will giving "to my three wives one-third of my Estate to be divided equally among them. I appoint my son John, assisted by his brothers Charles and William to divide the property and take care of the remaining two-thirds for the benefit of the family that shall most need it." After Zerah's death, his son John explained, "I have reported progress in settling of the estate . . . a dozen times, so the court has been posted in regards to the business." After dividing the one-third between the wives, he gave money to the Church "to keep Father's honor good" and then "endeavored to take care of the helpless ones of the family, the old and the young the best I could."[23]

According to Lavinia Jackson, her father's estate "was put in the hands of my [half] brother, Harold," the son of the second wife, Gladys, who had died earlier. Maud, Lavinia's mother and the third wife, according to Lavinia, "loved Harold. . . . I don't think there was ever one word of jealousy or one word of where the money went or one word of what happened."[24] Harold, however, remembered differently. "Aunt Maud did get everything. There was a little rough stuff. There were the personal things of the first wives. The first wife was a great artist in a way down there. . . . Her house was full of oil paintings. Aunt Maud wanted some of them; Father wanted some of them. Father was hurt because all of Aunt Maggie's family sided against him." Harold went on to say that although his father had no will, he had some written instructions for him because Joseph said that Harold "will see that everything is treated fairly. . . . I was down there visiting. I did it and when Aunt Maud heard about it, she got those who would support her. They came and threatened to ride me out of town." Harold said that he went to his father and explained that because of family disagreements he did not want to administer the estate.[25]

Archie L. Jenkins said that he didn't know much about his father's estate. "I know that when my father sort of divided his land, his property, all stocks . . . we didn't get any of that. He did have land in my mother's name. It wasn't even deeded directly to her. We used to get a tax notice . . . that was in Mother's name. It seems as though as years went along though that some of the land wasn't there." Archie also said that his father promised to give him some land when Archie returned from World War I. Years later when he asked for a deed, his father said that he had given it to a half brother. "I felt just a little bit hurt about that. I don't know whether he was pressured through the family to turn that over . . . or whether he had forgotten that he had said he would give it to me. . . . I never held that against him because it didn't mean that much to me. I thought I would get along anyway, and I have." Francis Moulton said, "The first family seemed to get everything and we didn't get anything, never had a dime of dad's property and we were quite bitter for a long time."[26]

In these cases, only hurt feelings resulted. In others, the estates had to be taken to Church courts for settlement. In 1899 a "CL" died intestate, and Apostles John Henry Smith and Anthon H. Lund arbitrated the case. All four wives received $600 and the 55 children $375 each. One wife was allowed to keep property that had been deeded to her before "in consideration of the large number of minor children she had to rear and educate."[27]

Joseph, the oldest son of Nathaniel and Anna Weston Hodges, the second wife, said that the third family "stood against me when the time came to divide up father's property." His father left property but also debts and it took several years to settle them. According to Joseph, "Father's will provided that in event of any dissension, the stake presidency should act as arbiters. So when the third family preferred charges against me, the stake high council sent an investigating committee which cleared me entirely and which ordered the distribution of the property."[28]

William, a son of Louise Weston, the first wife, said that he and Joseph favored Charlotte, the third wife, who had a farm and a house in her own name. The other wives had nothing in their names. Still Charlotte felt she was treated unfairly and took the matter to a Church court. It decided Charlotte and some of the sons had received their shares of the estate and the rest should be divided among the other heirs.[29]

Morris, a son of the third wife, saw the situation differently. He said that his father was proven incompetent after he had a stroke, so "they divided the big ranch all up over there. The mills and all his property was divided between three wives. That is one thing that we never were satisfied with as the third family because the other ones got a little more than we thought they ought to. Father didn't have it fixed hardly tight enough. They were old enough to be members of this Hodges Land and Livestock and Milling Company. I wasn't nor my brother. They got the biggest part of the property. So that was about the only time that was a discord there."[30]

These problems were probably not more intense than in some monogamous families today, and through the religious atmosphere and love that developed among the wives and children, they often worked closely together to settle and share the estate. Rulon Romney said of his father's estate, "My mother Elizabeth was of the opinion that Frances [the first wife] should have preference if there was to be any. Frances was of the opinion that it should be equal with no preference."[31]

Zaides Miles and Nan Atkins, the daughters of Abigail Middlemass Walker, the first wife of Charles Lowell, reported that their mother divided her co-op stock with the second wife, Sarah Smith, after their father died. The daughters praised their mother as "absolutely just with her." Sarah remarried, the second husband passed away, and she lived with her children. When Abigail saw how poor they were, she asked Sarah to come and live with her. Nan and Zaides thought that their mother had gone beyond "justness," and asked their mother why. Abigail replied that she could never face their father if she had not "done right" by Sarah.[32]

Even though the second wife, Annie, divorced Edward Franklin Turley, Ida, the first wife, told her sons that "she wanted Aunt Annie to have half of the field." Clarence Turley, Ida's son, explained that he managed the estate property for years, sharing the profits with his half brothers and sisters. When he decided to sell the property, he paid both his full and half brothers and sisters. "They were tickled to death. They've shown it by the letters they've written."[33]

Divorce, separation, and death all had special ramifications for polygamous families. Since the law did not acknowledge plural marriages, the Church granted divorces. Sometimes rather than seeking official divorce husbands and wives simply separated. Economics was one of the prime reasons; others included incompatibility and inability to accept polygamy. With death came the division of the estate, and although laws passed against polygamy included inheritance provisions, most cases were not taken to state courts. Instead, husbands provided that property be distributed after death by transferring title or by stating their wishes in formal wills or informal listings. In many cases when the husbands left no records, the families could simply divide the estate among themselves. When problems arose, they could be referred to state or Church courts. Although there were some disagreements as to how estates should be settled, few were major problems and could usually be settled within the family.

13

Participant Evaluation of Polygamy

It would be unusual, given the complexity of polygamy, if husbands, wives, and children did not have mixed reactions to it. What is surprising is the degree of unanimity and the willingness of the participants to work out problems. They accepted and lived polygamy because of their religious beliefs. This chapter will examine what women, men, and children said about the practice of polygamy and then try to determine the success of these families.

The Female Point of View

Marrying in polygamy was the fulfillment of a "divine principle revealed to Joseph Smith," according to Alma Elizabeth Mineer, the second wife of Joseph Felt. Caroline Pederson Hansen wrote after her decision to marry in polygamy, "We were very happy in our innocence that day, little dreaming of the trials ahead of us which we would have to endure in trying to live together under those conditions."[1]

Mary Jane Done Jones, the first wife of Timothy, expressed similar feelings, stating she saw many women pray for polygamy who regretted it once their husbands married again. "Polygamy was a great trial to any woman. And it was just as hard on the man. He had to learn to adjust to his women and his troubles were made worse by the women having to learn to adjust too." She not only accepted polygamy though, but she saw virtue in it. "Polygamy was a great principle and we were taught to believe

187

in it. I know that it does bring added blessings if one lives it the best she knows how. It makes one more unselfish and more willing to see and understand other people. After you learn to give in and consider other people, it makes you less selfish in all your relations. I never wanted polygamy, but I don't regret that I lived it."[2]

Margaret McNeil Ballard recorded, "On October 4, 1867 my husband married my sister Emily for his second wife. Although I loved my sister dearly and we knew it was a commandment of God that we should live in the Celestial marriage, it was a great trial and sacrifice for me. The Lord blessed and comforted me and we lived happily in this principle of the Gospel and I have thanked the Lord every day of my life that I have had the privilege of living this law."[3]

Lucy Walker Kimball explained that polygamy was a "grand school. You learn self control, self denial, it brings out the nobler traits of our fallen natures, and teaches us to study and subdue self while we become acquainted with the peculiar characteristics of each other." Alma Elizabeth Mineer Felt concurred. "When people had what I call the spirit of polygamy they were happy and they raised good and happy families. They had bitter times of course. No woman can help being jealous of another and if all the wives did not have the spirit of polygamy then there was suffering. It was a hard principle to live, but when it was lived at its best, it was truly a divine principle. Women learned to control themselves and develop resources within themselves that they would not have done otherwise."[4]

Most polygamous wives did not blame their hardships on polygamy. Although Sarah Lucretia Phelps Pomeroy had to support herself and her children barely knew their father, she told her son Reuel before she died that "she, of course, wished that her life had been different, but she was glad it was polygamous. . . . She was always very, very sorry that this bitterness had crept in and had been in the family, but the principle of polygamy was just as valid as far as she was concerned as baptism was." Elizabeth Acord Beck said she had hard times, but she was happy as a polygamous wife. "Perhaps I should not say that because there were times when I felt that I had more than I could bear and I became disgruntled. But those things happen to any wife in monogamy and on the whole I was very happy."[5]

Mildred Bennion Eyring, a daughter-in-law of Caroline Romney, said, "I have never known anyone else who came so near to being the Pollyanna of fiction. When she [Caroline] was staying with us in Salt Lake a few weeks before her death she said one evening, 'I'm glad Papa and Emma will have some time by themselves — Anyway, I guess I'm glad.' She was still trying to see the bright side even at the time of her death." Looking back as an adult, Nilus Stowell Memmott realized, "I was brought up very sheltered from a lot of the problems. My mother never was one to cry to her children about things. . . . I'm sure it was a heartache to my mother. . . . But still she felt that it was her duty." Clarence Allen said, "Mother naturally was hurt to think that her love for Dad had to be divided with another woman. Even though it was her sister, she didn't approve of it. She had to go along with it because in those days that was the style, that was the trend of marrying in the Church in polygamy."[6]

The Male Point of View

Like the women, men believed that living plural marriage was obeying a higher law. Edward Christian Eyring wrote in his autobiography, "This record shows that at least part of the families making up this account have lived in Mormon polygamy. This will no doubt be obnoxious to some who may read it. Even some of our descendants may wish it had been otherwise. I wish to impress this fact upon the minds of my children that to discredit the principle of plural marriage is the same as discrediting any other principle of the Mormon Doctrine. . . . I testify to you that I know my father entered into the principle in full faith of receiving a generous reward from our Heavenly Father for this honest effort to live it properly. The same can be said of my father-in-law, Miles P. Romney and I testify to you myself after twenty-eight years experience in trying to live it that I know the principle is divine."[7]

Men gave many of the same reasons as the women did for accepting polygamy. Esaias Edwards recorded in his journal on 27 March 1874, "I have entered into the order of plural marriage and have been living in and practicing the same with good effect. . . . I have enjoyed more of the Spirit of the Lord living in that order than I ever had in any period of my life." George Q. Payne, a son of a polygamous family, said, "Polygamy is one of the truest and greatest principles of our church. . . . It took big men to live it. . . . It was an ennobling thing, if lived rightly. I know of no other way of living that made men more self reliant, more unselfish, and more self controlled."[8]

John J. Esplin gave a semihumorous view of his situation. "It wasn't meant for all men to have two wives and maybe I wasn't one of them. It's hard on a man that's kind of nervous. It is more than he can stand having to worry about them and seeing that everything is all right." Harriet Jane Hakes, the second wife of Benjamin Julius Johnson, was certain that "polygamy is harder on the man. He has to put up with two women and when he does anything, he has two pairs of eyes watching him and two people to account to."[9]

After asking his housekeeper to marry him, Martin B. Bushman wrote, "It was then I realized the responsibility that I was taking upon myself being a young man only twenty-six years old and in poor circumstances. So I went to the Lord in secret prayer and asked that if it was his will that I should marry her that it would be so. If not, may something turn up to stop the marriage. I had learned by reading the revelation on the subject that men may marry more than one wife and if it done for a righteous purpose it would be attended with blessings and after living in that order for forty years I have been blessed with means to provide homes for my families and school for my children and have had joy in doing so."[10]

Children's Views of Polygamy

Children who grew up in polygamous families accepted the system as God's commandment as well. Conrad Naegle, a trained historian, regrets that he did not ask his mother how she felt about polygamy. But "polygamy was not something that bothered me. I wasn't ashamed of the fact that I was a Mormon; I wasn't ashamed of the fact that I was a product of polygamous families because they lived the law of the Lord. . . . It was something that I accepted on faith. . . . Who am I to question it?" Harriet Snarr Hutchings, who grew up in the Mormon colonies in Mexico, explained, "We never thought of polygamy because everybody around us was living like we did, so it was just one of those things. That was the way to live."[11]

Ivan R. Richardson explained, "If I was to judge polygamy solely on the basis of what happened in our family, I would have to say I'm in favor of it. It made us better people. It taught me to be unselfish. It taught us to work for a common goal with others. It was a social trial. Abrasive though it might be, it made better people. I would have to say it was a good thing as far as our family was concerned." He added, "True we were called bastards by some Mormon people in the same community that we lived in.

We had to undergo quite a bit of persecution in that valley because we were polygamists. . . . But within the family itself we had peace and love."[12]

Many children felt that they could not condemn the practice of polygamy. Louis Brandley said, "From my childhood I have accepted polygamy as the Lord's way for my mother and her family. My first feeling is that it brought lots of misery to the people who tried to live it mainly because they weren't prepared. My next feeling is that I can't discount polygamy because it was responsible for my birth." When Winnifred Newton Thomas started her interview, she explained how polygamy was part of her testimony of Brigham Young and Joseph Smith. "As far as I am concerned, polygamy is a good thing when the Lord decides it is to be used. . . . If it weren't for polygamy, I wouldn't be here, so who am I to say that polygamy is right or wrong? I only say it is right."[13]

Although most polygamous children accepted the principle, some, especially those born after the Manifesto, had mixed feelings. Florence Jackson Payne explained, "I believe in polygamy, of course. It seemed natural to live in. In spite of what we went through Mother always taught us that it was a great and true principle. I told my husband when we married that if ever polygamy should be lived again, I'd not stand in his way of marrying, but I don't know whether I could promise that again. I hope it will never be necessary for me to live it." Mabel Amelia Porter Carroll noted, "I always said that I was glad it was done away with. I wouldn't have wanted to have to live it, but I would have tried if I would have had to." Esther Phelps Whatcott said, "I never felt but what I could live in polygamy and be happy. Some people say that they couldn't accept it. I didn't have a jealous hair or any jealousy about me."[14]

Some children reported having to deal with hurt feelings. "When I say I'm a polygamous child," commented Jennie Lowe Huff, "so many people look at me kind of funny. I can't understand because it just seemed like it was so natural. But it has kind of hurt me. They didn't even have to show it; I could feel the feeling they felt within them. They wouldn't hardly believe that we could live that way." Emma Scott, the oldest daughter of William and his second wife, Emma Hoth McNeil, said, "All my girl chums thought mother and we were getting a raw deal and that father was unjust. Oh, yes, I had spells of bad feelings about it." Keith Romney admitted, "I had three older sisters [who] were old enough to get in on the traumatic experience of my father taking these extra wives. They had a tendency to blame the Church for it. Consequently they weren't very close to the Church after that happened."[15]

Polygamy is sometimes even more difficult for the third and fourth generations to comprehend. With their monogamous traditions and the Church's stand against polygamy they have a hard time understanding how their grandparents and their great grandparents could have agreed to marry in polygamy. Steve Faux, whose grandparents were polygamous, prefaced a paper that he wrote at Brigham Young University with compelling curiosity. "The real reason for writing this paper comes from my obsessive desire to understand my polygynous ancestry. Thus this paper really represents my search for personal conclusions on the matter in the absence of convincing answers from familial traditions or standard histories."[16]

Measuring the Success of Mormon Polygamous Families

In some of the interviews in the LDS Family Life Oral History Project, the interviewers asked, "How would you measure the overall success of your family?" Quite often those questioned would respond, "What do you mean by success?" Does success mean economic advantages? Does it refer to continued Church activity? Does it refer to the emotional and social relationships within a family? Kimball Young and Vicky Burgess-Olson attempted to measure the success of polygamous families based on economic security, housing arrangements, the attitude of the first wife and family towards polygamy, and the relationships between the families. Although these elements were important for a successful polygamous family, this study found that even the presence of all or nearly all of these elements did not completely eliminate problems and conflicts. While it is easier to define economic success, it may be more important to examine how well the families got along, how much acceptance or conflict there was between families, and how well the wives, children, and husbands accepted the principle of plural marriage. These questions are more difficult to answer since feelings are difficult to quantify.

Anthropologist Paul Bohannan asks two questions in determining the success of a polygamous family: (1) Do the co-wives get along? and (2) How do the half siblings relate to each other? "The most successful instances are those in which the context of both sets of relationships is firmly structured and where only a minimum is left for the individuals playing the roles to work out on a personal basis. A satisfactory structural relationship to fall back on if the personal relationship fails seems to be vital."[17] Mormons did not have the advantage of an inherited and solidly tested structure since polygamy was practiced for such a short time in the Church. Individual personalities proved the most important variables. Yet most polygamous families learned to solve problems and control conflict because they believed what they were doing was required of God.

As this study has shown, members of the Church of Jesus Christ of Latter-day Saints decided to go into polygamy based on religious belief. They would not have considered living the principle if they had not felt that they would be blessed and receive rewards in an afterlife. The ability to overcome problems of husbands dealing with more than one wife, wives dealing with co-wives, and children dealing with an extended family was possible because of that same faith. Religious motivations enabled them to deal with or suppress expected jealousies and disagreements that would occur in any family, especially where there were more than one wife.

Although those practicing polygamy were religiously motivated, their beliefs did not tell them how to lead daily lives. Unlike African societies who have practiced polygyny for generations, the Mormons did not have set procedures on how the husband and wife, the wives, and the children should relate to each other. Although the families had no societal traditions to fall back on, they were able to adapt most of the Euro-American monogamous traditions to their new life-style. Relationships varied depending on the family. In some cases they were very close, and wives related to each other as sisters and children considered their fathers' other wives' children as brothers and sisters. In other cases where the wives were different ages, they were almost like mothers and daughters. And sometimes they did not interact at all. The relationships between husbands and wives usually determined how the children in the different polygamous families got along. With no rules, each family established its own, so there was not a "typical" Mormon polygamous family. While some were very unhappy, most seemed to have gotten along very well.

Stresses on family relationships sometimes resulted in divorce, although not often since during the Victorian period separation and divorce were not usually considered viable alternatives. Death often led to family disagreements, especially over inheritance, and these proved more problematic in polygamous than in monogamous families. The laws Congress passed against polygamy and the underground that the Mormons adapted to avoid arrest also reorganized families. Finally, the Church's Manifestoes also meant that plural families had to adjust their life-styles.

Although differences arose between monogamous and polygamous families in the LDS Church during the late nineteenth and early twentieth centuries, polygamous families were very much a reflection of the Victorian ideal. Husbands, who were quite often farmers, worked outside the home; wives were responsible for the home chores; sons learned their future roles from their fathers; and daughters learned from their mothers. These roles were modified when the family underwent change. Both monogamous and polygamous husbands served missions, and then the wives might have to work outside the home. However, as soon as possible, the wives returned to their role as homemaker. Husbands were often away because of work, but polygamous husbands were with their families even less because they had to divide their time amongst several. Monogamous and polygamous families were active in Church activities and had religious activities at home. Children did not have especially close relationships with their fathers.

While other studies have emphasized the negative aspects of Mormon polygamous life, pointing to jealousies between husbands and wives and between the wives themselves, husbands being absent and wives having to be self-sufficient, and families being divided, this study shows that while these experiences did occur, they were the exception rather than the norm. Because they believed they were obeying a higher commandment of God, Latter-day Saints practicing polygamy had fewer negative experiences than have generally been reported. While negative experiences happened on a day-to-day basis — and probably more than in monogamous families — Mormon polygamous family life was not a completely new life-style but an adaptation of the Victorian family pattern.

Notes

Introduction

1. Ora Packard Clyde interview, 11; Larry Troutman interview, 11.
2. Jonathan S. Cannon interview, 13.
3. Richard S. Van Wagoner, *Mormon Polygamy: A History*, 209–22.
4. James Edward Hulett Jr., "The Sociological and Social Psychological Aspects of the Mormon Polygamous Family"; Kimball Young, *Isn't One Wife Enough?*

1. The Practice of Polygamy

1. George Peter Murdock, *Ethnographic Atlas*, 1–2, col. 14; Melvin Ember, "Warfare, Sex Ratio, and Polygyny," 197.
2. Genesis 16:1–3; 21:9–16; 25:1–6, 20–23, 29–30; 25:5–6; Exodus 21:10; and Deuteronomy 25:5–9.
3. I Samuel 1:1–2; II Samuel 11; and I Kings 11:1–3.
4. John Cairncross, *After Polygamy Was Made a Sin: The Social History of Christian Polygamy*; I Corinthians 7.
5. Cairncross, 8, 47.
6. Ibid., 54–63; Joyce Westphal conversation. Joyce Westphal told me that one of her ancestors had married plural wives during this time period.
7. Cairncross, 69.
8. This brief chapter on the history of polygamy in the LDS Church cannot begin to list all the research that has been done on the subject. What follows is simply an overview of polygamy in the Church. Secondary sources, rather than the primary sources, were consulted, so published books are cited rather than manuscripts. For more information on Mormon polygamy, the reader should refer to those secondary works that will also provide more information on the primary sources available. *Mormon Polygamy: A History* is an overview of the history of polygamy. Van Wagoner comes to no new conclusions, but he does give a summary of

other research. Gustive D. Larson, "Government, Politics, and Conflict," and "The Crusade and the Manifesto," in *Utah's History*, Richard D. Poll et al., lists the laws passed against polygamy. D. Michael Quinn, "LDS Church Authority and New Plural Marriages, 1890–1904," is the most complete study of post-Manifesto marriages and cohabitation.

9. I Nephi 13:26–27, Book of Mormon.

10. Doctrine and Covenants 132:1–3, 61.

11. Daniel W. Bachman, "New Light on an Old Hypothesis: The Ohio Origins of the Revelation on Eternal Marriage," 19–32; Linda King Newell and Valeen Tippets Avery, *Mormon Enigma: Emma Hale Smith: Prophet's Wife, "Elect Lady," Polygamy Foe*, 152. Also see 95–105, 130–56, and 297–98.

12. Van Wagoner, 4, 6.

13. B. H. Roberts, *Comprehensive History of the Church of Jesus Christ of Latter-day Saints*, 2:96–101; Van Wagoner, 5–7.

14. Leonard J. Arrington, *Brigham Young: American Moses*, 100; Van Wagoner, 89.

15. Arrington, 100–103; Van Wagoner, 22–23, 65–69.

16. *Journal of Discourses*, 1:53–66. Hereinafter referred to as JD. Hosea Stout, Journal, 1.

17. Van Wagoner, 91, 115, 138.

18. Larson, "Government, Politics, and Conflict," 244.

19. Van Wagoner, 108; Larson, "Government, Politics, and Conflict," 250–51.

20. Larson, "Government, Politics, and Conflict," 251, 252.

21. Van Wagoner, 111; Larson, "Government, Politics, and Conflict," 254.

22. Larson, "The Crusade and the Manifesto," 259–60.

23. Ibid., 267.

24. Quinn, 29–30; Van Wagoner, 132.

25. Van Wagoner, 138.

26. Scott Kenney, ed., *Wilford Woodruff Journal, 1833–1898*, 113–14; Official Declaration 1, Doctrine and Covenants; and Van Wagoner, 147.

27. Andrew Jonus Hansen, Autobiography, 48.

28. Ibid., 48–49.

29. Annie Gardner interview, 4.

30. Quinn, 48–49.

31. Ibid., 49; Van Wagoner, 147.

32. Quinn, 49.

33. Thomas G. Alexander, *Mormonism in Transition*, 61; Van Wagoner, 153–54.

34. Hansen, 49.

35. Rose B. Hayes and Mrs. Clark interview, 1.

36. Elizabeth Ann Schurtz McDonald interview, 1.

37. Quinn, 51.

38. Conover Wright interview, 2.

39. Lorin "Dutch" Leavitt interview, 5.

40. Quinn, 81.

41. Jessie L. Embry, "Exiles for the Principle: LDS Polygamy in Canada,"

108–16; B. Carmon Hardy and Victor Jorgensen, "The Taylor-Cowley Affair and the Watershed of Mormon History," 18.

42. Van Wagoner, 161.

43. Ibid., 169.

44. Ibid, 174.

45. Ibid., 184; Alexander, 67–68.

2. The Impact of the Antipolygamy Laws

1. Jane Synder Richards, Reminiscences, 50–51; Joel Hills Johnson, Autobiography, 84–85.

2. Torrey L. Austin interview, 4; George W. Terry, Journal, 12.

3. William James Frazier McAllister interview, 6; Martha Geneva Day Larsen interview, 3.

4. Austin interview, 5.

5. Truman Call interview, 1–2.

6. Christopher Layton, Autobiography, 51–52; Merle W. Wells, *Anti-Mormonism in Idaho, 1872–92* discusses some of the laws passed in Idaho against polygamy. David Boone and Chad J. Flake, "The Prison Diary of William Jordan Flake" gives an overview of the reaction to polygamy in Arizona.

7. Ann Amelia Chamberlain Esplin interview, 26.

8. Emma Westerman Ashworth interview, 1; Evan B. Murray interview, 1.

9. Austin interview, 5.

10. Emma Hoth McNeil interview, 2–3.

11. Gardner interview, 4.

12. Georgina Bollette Critchlow Bickmore interview, 22; Layton, 53.

13. James L. Wyatt interview, 11.

14. Lula Roskelley Mortensen interview, Appendix, 3.

15. Bickmore interview, 1–2; Nevada Watson Driggs interview, 1.

16. Esplin interview, 18.

17. Alma Elizabeth Mineer Felt interview, 6; Manomus Lovina Gibson Andrus interview, 4.

18. Morgan Hinman, Journal.

19. Jonathan E. Layne, Autobiography, 26; Levi Savage, Journal, 7.

20. Bickmore interview, 23.

21. Mortensen interview, 13; Reuben L. Hill interview, 2.

22. Emma McNeil Scott interview, 5; Bickmore interview, 22.

23. In B. Carmon Hardy, "The Mormon Colonies in Mexico, 1885–1912," 72.

24. Nelle Spilsbury Hatch, *Colonia Juarez: An Intimate Account of a Mormon Village*, 1.

25. A. James Hudson, "Charles Ora Card: Pioneer and Colonizer," 80–81; Donald Godfrey Card and Melva R. Witbeck, "The Journal of Charles Ora Card, September 14, 1886–July 7, 1903," 4.

26. "Polygamy in Mexico," 2; Card and Witbeck, 19.

27. Charles W. Kindrick, "The Mormons in Mexico," 703.

28. Hardy, "The Mormon Colonies in Mexico, 1885–1912," 78–79; Hatch, 11.; B. Carmon Hardy, "Early Colonization of Mormon Polygamists in Mexico and Canada: A Legal and Historiographical Review," 9–13.

29. Lowry Nelson, "Settlement of the Mormons in Alberta," *Group Settlements: Ethnic Communities in Western Canada*, C. A. Dawson, ed., 203–4.

30. Hardy and Jorgensen, 17–18; Embry, "Exiles for the Principle," 109–110; and *Statutes of Canada*, 1890, 53 Vic, c. 37.

31. Eunice Stewart Harris, Life Story, 9; Layne, 26.

32. There is a great deal of confusion about these marriages in Mexico—who authorized them, when they were performed, etc. D. Michael Quinn has carefully traced these plural marriages as well as other post-Manifesto marriages in "LDS Church Authority and New Plural Marriages, 1890–1904"; Ivins, 5–6.

33. Henry Eyring, Journal, 65; Edward Christian Eyring, Autobiography, 14, 17; and Caroline Eyring Miner, *The Life Story of Edward Christian Eyring (1868–1957)*, 31.

34. Cardston Alberta Ward Minutes, 25 November 1888; Embry, "Exiles for the Principle," 110.

35. Mildred Newton Stutz interview, 9–10.

36. Embry, "Exiles for the Principle," 112.

3. Demographic Characteristics

1. Hulett, "Sociological and Social Psychological Aspects"; Young, *Isn't One Wife Enough?*; Stanley S. Ivins, "Notes on Mormon Polygamy"; and Vicky Burgess-Olson, "Family Structure and Dynamics in Early Utah Mormon Families—1847–1855."

2. Dean L. May, "A Demographic Portrait of the Mormons, 1830–1980," *After 150 Years: The Latter-day Saints in Sesquicentennial Perspective*, Thomas G. Alexander and Jessie L. Embry, eds., 82; D. Gene Pace, "Community Leadership on the Mormon Frontier: Mormon Bishops and the Political, Economic, and Social Development of Utah before Statehood," 82, 238.

3. Nels Anderson, *Deseret Saints: The Mormon Frontier in Utah*, 400.

4. Pace, 238.

5. Anderson, 400.

6. Ivins's article based on over a thousand cases, Burgess-Olson's study of 100 plural wives and this study of 170 men support the conclusion that the husband was in his early twenties and the wife was in her early teens at the time of the first marriage. Ivins said that a husband married his second wife 13 years after the first. Christa Marie Sophie Ranglade Nelson, "Mormon Polygamy in Mexico," 60, found that the second marriage was about ten years after the first.

7. Ivins set the average time lapse at four years, Nelson set it at seven. Nelson found the husband's average age to be 46 at the time of a fourth marriage. Ivins

and Nelson agreed the time between the third and fourth marriages was the same as between the second and third.

8. Doctrine and Covenants 132:61.

9. Pace, 230.

10. Burgess-Olson found polygamous wives averaged 8.5 children to the average monogamous wife's 9.8. Ivins found even a greater difference — an average of 5.9 per polygamous and 8 per monogamous. James E. Smith and Phillip R. Kunz, "Polygamy and Fertility in Nineteenth Century America" found a much smaller difference — 7.4 for polygamous wives and 7.8 for monogamous wives. According to Pace's study of bishops, polygamous wives averaged 7.9 children and monogamous wives 8.9. Ivins set the average of children per husband at 15, while Nelson said that the men she researched averaged 13.6.

11. Pace found that first wives had an average of 9.6 children, second wives 7, third wives 7.3, and fourth wives 4.8. Monogamous bishops' second wives (usually their first wives had died) averaged 6.5. Nelson found that the first wife averaged 8.1 children, the second 7.3, the third 6.6, and the fourth 5.8. Burgess-Olson also found a declining number, the first wife averaging 9.1, the middle wife 7.5, and the youngest wife 7.6.

12. Burgess-Olson found that the monogamous wives had their children 1.8 years apart while the intervals for polygamous wives averaged 1.9 for the first wife, 2 for the middle, and 2.3 for the youngest wife.

13. Wyatt interview, 4; John Horsecroft Wyatt Family Group Sheets.

14. Georgia Stowell Lillywhite interview, 14; Brigham Stowell Family Group Sheets.

15. Lowell "Ben" Bennion, "The Incidence of Mormon Polygamy in 1880: 'Dixie' versus Davis Stake," 30–31; 36–37; Lowell "Ben" Bennion, "The Geography of Polygamy Among the Mormons in 1880"; Larry Logue, "A Time of Marriage: Monogamy and Polygamy in a Utah Town," 10; and Nelson, 57.

16. Bennion, "The Incidence of Mormon Polygamy in 1880," 30–31.

17. Aseneth Smith Conklin interview, 6; Edith Smith Patrick interview, 13; Thomas G. Alexander and James B. Allen, *Mormons and Gentiles: A History of Salt Lake City*, 3.

18. Pace, 175.

4. Motivations for Practicing Polygamy

1. JD, 1:64–65.

2. Ross Bean to Fay Ollerton, 13 December 1935.

3. Orson Welcome Huntsman, Utah Historical Records Survey.

4. Annie Richardson Johnson, *Heartbeats of Colonia Diaz*, 294.

5. JD, 1:59; Judith E. Brown, "Polygyny and Family Planning in Sub-Saharan Africa," 323; Ester Boserup, *Women's Role in Economic Development*, 38; and Steven Faux and Harold L. Miller Jr., "Evolutionary Speculations of the Oligarchic Development of Mormon Polygyny," 15–16.

6. George W. Brimhall, Autobiography, 2; Price Nelson interview, 4.

7. Reuben L. Hill interview, 1; Walter Clark interview, 5–6; and Edward Barrett Clark Family Group Sheets.

8. JD, 1:58.

9. Ibid, 1:59–60.

10. Orson Rega Card interview, 14–15; Joseph Donal Earl interview, 13; Dorris Dale Hyer interview, 10; and Linnie Fillerup Monteirth interview, 5.

11. J. E. Hickman to C. M. Haynes, 18 December 1907.

12. JD, 1:60–62.

13. Young, 43; Ida Stewart Pacey interview, 2.

14. Ember, 197; Cairncross, 200.

15. Ellen P. Moffett Done interview, 13.

16. Richard Poll et al., *Utah's History*, 118–21.

17. Bernitta Bartley interview, 25.

18. Sarah Hendricks interview, 14; Charles Smith Merrill interview, 10.

19. Monteirth interview, 6; Charles Richard Fillerup Family Group Sheet.

20. Card and Witbeck, 129; Mercy Weston Gibbons interview, 1; and Jesse Barney interview, 40.

21. May, 61–63.

22. Luke William Gallup, Journal.

23. Rhoda Ann Knell Cannon interview, 6; Young, 104.

24. Burgess-Olson, 8; Ursula Rich Cole interview, 4.

25. Loraine Farrell Ralph interview, 3.

26. E. W. Wright interview, 5.

27. J. W. Wilson interview, 2–3.

28. Lawrence Foster, *Religion and Sexuality: Three American Communal Experiences of the Nineteenth Century*, 211.

29. Eunice Stewart Harris, Life Story, 6.

30. Young, 118–19.

5. Entering Plural Marriage

1. Doctrine and Covenants 132:64–65.

2. Stories about the Joseph C. Bentley, Charles Edmund Richardson, and John Theodore Brandley families are taken mainly from interviews with children and some autobigraphies. For information on Joseph C. Bentley and his three wives, Margaret, Gladys, and Maud, see Maud Taylor Bentley, Autobiography and the following interviews in the LDS Polygamy Project: Anthony Ivins Bentley (Embry, 1976), Harold Bentley, Lavinia Bentley Jackson, Richard Ivins Bentley, Rinda Bentley Sudweeks, and Israel Ivins Bentley. For information on Charles Edmund Richardson and his four wives, Sadie, Sarah, Becky, and Daisie, see Jessie L. Embry, *Richardson Family History* which includes a paper about the Richardson family and all of the oral histories with the children of the Richardson family. For information on John Theodore Brandley and his four wives, Marie,

Margaret, Eliza, and Emma, see Louis Brandley interview (Embry, 1983), and Louis Brandley interview (Ursenbach, 1976). Louis Brandley also donated copies of histories that he had written about his father and his wives to the Redd Center which are catalogued with his oral history interview in the Manuscript Division of the Harold B. Lee Library.

3. Burgess-Olson, 108; Felt interview, 9; and Agatha Walker McAllister interview, 4.

4. Andrew Jonus Hansen, Autobiography, 26; John Jacob Walser interview, 5.

5. Hortense Young Hammond interview, 8.

6. Kenneth L. Cannon III and Jessie L. Embry, "Seymour B. Young."

7. Mae Bingham Douglas interview, 2; E. W. Wright interview, 1.

8. Harriet Snarr Hutchings interview, 10; Daniel Hammer Snarr Family Group Sheets.

9. Douglas Cannon interview, 4.

10. LaVetta Cluff Lunt Taylor interview, 5; Heber Manasseh Cluff Family Group Sheets.

11. Gottlieb Ence, Life Sketch, 36.

12. Mary Elizabeth Woolley Chamberlain, Autobiography, 1936–1939, 106; Dorris Dale Hyer interview, 1.

13. Edna Clark Ericksen interview, 16–17.

14. Ida Walser Skousen interview, 1.

15. Farel Knudson Chamberlain Kimball interview, 2; Rosalia Tenney Payne interview, 4.

16. Annabell Wheeler Hart interview, 2.

17. Walter Barney interview, 4.

18. Miner, 31; Matilda Peterson, Autobiography, 3.

19. Chamberlain, 104–5.

20. George Lake, Autobiography, 9.

21. Arthur E. Snow interview, 1.

22. Quoted in Matthias Cowley, *Wilford Woodruff: Fourth President of the Church of Jesus Christ of Latter-day Saints: History of his Life and Labors as Recorded in his Daily Journals*, 560; David John, Journal, 419.

23. Quoted in Cowley, 490.

24. John, 421.

25. William Forman, Autobiography.

26. Merle Gilbert Hyer and Estelle Hyer Ririe interview, 7; Andrew Hyer Family Group Sheets.

27. Laura Andersen Watkins interview, 5; Mary Diantha Cox Sherratt interview, 10; and Austin interview, 3.

28. John C. Larsen interview, 2; Arabelle Parkinson Daines interview, 1; and Lucy Fryer Vance interview, 1.

29. Michael Gordon, "The Ideal Husband as Depicted in the Nineteenth-Century Marriage Manual," *The American Man*, Elizabeth H. Pleck and Joseph N. Pleck, eds.

30. Johnson, Autobiography, 52–53.

31. John Mack Faragher, *Women and Men on the Overland Trail*, 155.

32. Walter John Winsor, Story, 4–5.

33. Layton, Autobiography, 34; Warren Foote, Autobiography, 139.

34. Mary E. Croshaw Farrell interview, 2.

35. Laura Moffet Jones interview, 3.

36. Chamberlain, 105–6; Lydia Naegle Romney interview, 2.

37. Murlyn Lamar Brown interview, 11.

38. Claude E. Hawkes interview, 1; Anderson P. Anderson interview, 2.

39. Priddy Meeks, Journal, 15–16; Lawrence Leavitt interview, 9.

40. Emma Goddard interview, 3.

41. Daniel Skousen Family Group Sheets; Viva Skousen Bluth Brown interview, 9; and Hannah Skousen Call interview, 17.

42. Mary Lucile Clark Ellis interview, 19; George Albert Wilcox, 2.

43. Gibbons interview, 2.

44. Felt interview, 1; Rudgar H. Daines interview, 18.

45. Mary Jane Rigby Roskelley interview, 1; Marva Little interview, 1–2.

46. Clarence Allen interview, 22.

6. Living Arrangements and Visiting Patterns

1. Kimball Young, 153–54.

2. Murdock, col. 14; Beatrice B. Whiting, "Changing Life Styles in Kenya," 214; and Pamela A. R. Blakely, "Co-wives in Africa: A Discussion of Polygyny in Eastern Zaire."

3. Boserup, 47; Blakely.

4. Martin Ottenheimer and Harriet Ottenheimer, "Matrilocal Residence and Nonsororal Polygyny: A Case from the Comoro Islands," 332–33.

5. Caroline Eyring Miner and Edward L. Kimball, *Camilla: A Biography of Camilla Eyring Kimball*, 13; Severin N. Lee interview, 1.

6. Andrew W. Nash interview, 1.

7. Jennie Lowe Huff interview, 3.

8. Mary Elizabeth Tullidge Little, Autobiography, in *Our Pioneer Heritage*, Kate Carter, ed., 15:106–9.

9. George S. Pond interview, 11–12.

10. Isaiah Coombs, Journal, 2.

11. Laura Moffet Jones interview, 1.

12. Caroline Pederson Hansen, Autobiography, in *Our Pioneer Heritage*, Kate Carter, ed., 12:70–71.

13. Hayes and Clark interview, 1.

14. Ella Saunders Cardon interview, 2

15. Allen interview, 2–3.

16. Pond interview, 10.

17. Evan B. Murray interview (Hulett, 1937), 2.

18. Mary Ann Stowell Jackson interview, 4.

19. Joseph Hodges interview, 1–3; Morris Hodges interview, 9.

20. William and Mary Ann Leach Adams, Biography, 9; Bickmore interview, 7.

21. Ruth May Fox interview, 4; Rudgar H. Daines interview, 17.

22. Jessie L. Embry, "The Role of LDS Polygamous Families, Blanding: A Case Study."

23. Wilma Fillerup Turley interview, 16–17.

24. Mercelle Farr Atkinson interview, 9–10; Maybelle Farr Dickerson interview, 12.

25. Young, 178.

26. Karl Skousen interview, 5; Lorna Call Alder interview, 18; and Marva Whipple Cram Little interview, 4.

27. Douglas Cannon interview 1, 6; Esther Phelps Whatcott interview, 5.

28. Miner, 4.

29. Glenn Whetten interview, 14.

30. Eldon Payne interview, 17.

31. Bickmore, 9.

32. Marvin Ezra Clark interview, 5.

33. Amy Allen Pulsipher interview, 2.

34. Wallace Stowell interview, 4; Karma Parkinson Parkinson interview, 10.

35. Asenath Skousen Walser interview, 22; William Hodges interview, 4.

36. Maude Nuttal Haws interview, 9, 13.

37. Wasel Black Washburn interview, 8; Roxey Roskelley Rogers interview, 8.

38. Verda Spencer Adams interview, 4; Teresa Richardson Blau interview, 2.

39. Viva Skousen Bluth Brown interview, 5; Annie Richardson Johnson interview, 5.

40. Hannah Skousen Call interview, 12; Elizabeth Acord Beck interview, 5–6.

41. Maud Kearl Hodges interview, 4.

42. Little interview, 8.

43. Alder interview, 19.

44. Charles Durfee interview, 10.

45. Anthony Ivins Bentley interview, 11; Richard Ivins Bentley interview, 6.

46. Joseph Eyring interview, 19–20; LeRoy Eyring interview, 4.

47. Albert L. Payne interview, 4.

48. Elizabeth Telford Hyer interview, 3.

49. Anthony Ivins Bentley interview (Embry, 1976), 7: Lavinia Bentley Jackson interview, 27.

50. Elizabeth Ann Schurtz McDonald interview, 3.

51. Florence Jackson Payne interview, 2.

52. Washburn interview, 8; Katherine Cannon Thomas interview, 8.

53. Frederick W. Taylor interview, 3.

7. Daily Life and Family Roles

1. Genesis 3:19.

2. Young, 175.

3. Norman Juster, *So Sweet to Labor: Rural Women in America 1865–1985*, 13; Barbara Welter, "The Cult of True Womanhood, 1820–1860," *The American Family in Social Historical Perspective*, Michael Gordon, ed.

4. Remi Clignet, *Many Wives, Many Powers*, 356.

5. Young, 157; Burgess-Olson, 94.

6. Carl N. Degler, *Out of Our Past: The Forces that Shaped Modern America*, 452; George Heiner, Federal Writers Project.

7. Annie Marie Darius, Federal Writers Project; Peter B. Johnson, Federal Writers Project.

8. Zaides Walker Miles and Nan Walker Atkins interview, 1; Elwood Earl Larsen interview, 16.

9. Alma W. MacGregor interview, 1; George Black interview, 7.

10. Marjorie Cannon Pingree interview, 1; Edward Hunter Jefferies, 1.

11. Franklin Lyman Stout interview, 6; Vera Anderson Christensen interview, 8–10.

12. Andrew Jonus Hansen, Autobiography, 47, 30.

13. Embry, *Richardson Family History*. Except for specific quotes, all the information about the Charles Edmund Richardson family comes from this source. Hazel Richardson Taylor interview, 7.

14. Julie Roy Jeffrey, *Frontier Women: The Trans-Mississippi West*, 149; Joan Iversen, "Feminist Implications of Mormon Polygyny," 507.

15. Maureen Ursenbach Beecher, "Under the Sunbonnets: Mormon Women with Faces," 484; Maureen Ursenbach Beecher, "Women's Work on the Mormon Frontier," 290.

16. Kathleen Marquis, " 'Diamond Cut Diamond': Mormon Women and the Cult of Domesticity in the Nineteenth Century," 108.

17. Reuel Nephi Pomeroy interview, 1–5.

18. Brandley interview (Embry, 1982), 15.

19. Jonathan S. Cannon interview, 2; Walter Haws interview, 14.

20. Stephanie Smith Goodson, "Plural Wives," *Mormon Sisters*, Claudia Bushman, ed., 104.

21. Young, 175; Terrance Heaton interview, 3; and Bartley interview, 10.

22. Hill interview, 2.

23. Hutchings interview, 13–14; Ether Haynie interview, 6.

24. Zina Patterson Dunford interview, 8; Louis Cardon interview, 19.

25. Joseph Hodges interview, 1; Morris Hodges, 3.

26. Franklin Lyman Stout interview, 9; Mary Viola Allred Stout interview, 9.

27. Beck interview, 6.

28. JD, 9:188–89.

29. Eva C. Webb, "The Other Mother," *Heart Throbs of the West*, Kate Carter, ed., 1:285–86.

30. JD, 9:188–89.

31. Cannon interview, 2, 4–5.

32. Cecelia Peterson Bott Morris interview, 1; Joseph Eyring interview, 12.

33. Jeneveve Eyring Layton interview, 4.

34. Dunford interview, 6; Caroline Olsen, Federal Writers Project.

35. Lula A. Larsen interview, 4.

36. Laura Andersen Watkins interview, 5.

37. Henry M. Stark interview, 4.

38. Dunford interview, 14.

39. Embry, *Richardson Family History*; Jesse Barney interview, 4; and Orin Barney interview, 5.

40. Vearl Cluff interview, 2.

41. Glen Lowe interview, 4–5; Huff interview, 11.

42. A. John Clarke interview, 1–4.

43. Jeffrey, 25.

44. Carl N. Degler, *At Odds: Women and the Family in America from the Revolution to the Present*, 27; Carroll Smith-Rosenberg, "The Female World of Love and Ritual Relations Between Women in Nineteenth-Century America," *The American Family in Social-Historical Perspective*, Michael Gordon, ed., 339.

8. Church Positions and Religious Activity

1. Richard O. Cowan and Wilson K. Anderson, *The Living Church: The Unfolding of the Programs and Organization of the Church of Jesus Christ during the Twentieth Century*, 185; Jan Shipps, "In the Presence of the Past: Continuity and Change in Twentieth Century Mormonism," *After 150 Years: The Latter-day Saints in Sesquicentennial Perspective*, Thomas G. Alexander and Jessie L. Embry, eds., 23; and Gordon Irving, "The Church and Young Men in Union, Utah, 1875–1920."

2. Young, 105.

3. Reuel Pomeroy interview, 3.

4. Young, 105.

5. Leonard J. Arrington and Davis Bitton, *The Mormon Experience: A History of the Latter-day Saints*, 204.

6. Pace, 227–28.

7. Ibid., 96; Earl Chadwick interview, 3; and May Smith Morgan interview, 11.

8. Mrs. Will Corbett interview, 2; John C. Larsen interview, 2; and William Hodges interview, 3.

9. Bruce Gilchrist interview, 2; Roberta Allred interview, 3.

10. Don Kofford Hansen interview, 13, 15; Vivian Elizabeth Haines interview, 7; Elvera Colledge Miles interview, 14; Ruth Jorgensen Cox interview, 7; and George H. Mortimer interview, 9.

11. Evan B. Murray interview (Embry, 1976), 3; Walter Barney interview, 4; Elizabeth Acord Beck interview, 7; and Gladys Call Mallory interview, 6.

12. Janett Wright Humphreys interview, 11; Karl Skousen interview, 4; and Alexander, 86.

13. Alder interview, 24; Richard Ivins Bentley interview, 5; Pima, Arizona, Ward Minutes; John Murray Nicol interview, 5; and Xarissa Merkley Clarke interview, 12.

14. Rhoda Ann Knell Cannon interview, 15.

15. George S. Pond interview, 5; Melvin J. Taag, "The Life of Edward James Wood: Church Patriot," 128.

16. Chadwick interview, 3; Howard J. Engh interview, 15; and Vivian Elizabeth Haines interview, 7.

17. Reed W. Warnick interview, 7; Elizabeth Graham MacDonald, Archives, 39.

18. Wallace Wood interview, 4; Everett Mark Hamilton interview, 3; Grace Viola Jorgensen Hadfield interview, 6; and Mary Westover Carroll interview, 7.

19. Olive LeBaron Greenhalgh interview, 11; Lavinia Bentley Jackson interview, 27; and MacDonald, 39.

20. Hutchings interview, 11; Anthony Ivins Bentley interview (Embry, 1976), 11.

21. Ruth Cannon Thatcher interview, 13; Ollie Marie Allsop Schoepf interview, 12.

22. "Editors' Table," 733–34.

23. Anson B. Call Jr. interview, 5.

24. Joseph Eyring interview, 5.

25. Alberta Lyman O'Brien interview, 2; G. Alvin Carpenter interview, 12.

26. Glen Lowe interview, 6.

27. Alder interview, 17; Karl Skousen interview, 7; Marvin Ezra Clark interview, 4; and Asenath Smith Conklin interview, 6.

28. Karl Skousen interview, 7; Loretta Merrill Rigby interview, 12; and David S. Cannon interview, 12.

29. Alba Jones Anderson interview, 10–11; Naomi Selman Thatcher interview, 9–10.

30. Dickerson interview, 3; Goldburn L. Knudson interview, 7.

31. Thomas Cottom Romney interview, 5; Evan Murray interview (Hulett, 1937), 3; and Whatcott interview, 8.

9. Relationships of Wives and Husbands

1. Carroll Smith-Rosenberg, 339; Michael Gordon, 145.

2. Jesse Smith Decker interview, 6–7; Sarah Perkins interview, 8.

3. Johnson, Autobiography, 67.

4. Ibid., 54–55.

5. George Q. Payne, Fay Ollerton Symposium, 6.

6. Farrell interview, 9.

7. Brighamina Christensen Taylor letters.

8. David Candland, Autobiography, 26–27.

9. Anthony Ivins Bentley interview (Embry, 1976), 12; Anthony Ivins Bentley interview (Cushman, 1971), 7–8.

10. Lydia Daines interview, 1; Allen interview, 17.

11. Lydia Naegle Romney interview, 4.

12. Ether Haynie interview, 7–8; Arabelle Parkinson Daines interview, 1.

13. Rebecca Roskelley Lewis interview, 3.

14. Mortensen interview, Appendix, 8.

15. Keith Romney interview, 14.

16. Anthony Ivins Bentley interview (Embry, 1976), 8.

17. Viv Bentley interview, 1.

18. Mabel Amelia Porter Carroll interview, 12.

19. Hyer and Ririe interview, 12.

20. Wood interview, 11–12.

21. Eliza Bowen Boyle interview, 2.

22. Rudgar H. Daines interview, 2; Arabelle Parkinson Daines interview, 1; and Rosalia Tenney Payne interview, 6.

23. Mary Reiser Gallacher, "The Other Mother," *Heart Throbs of the West*, Kate B. Carter, ed., 1:274; Leah Rees Reeder and Margaret Rees White interview, 3; and Frederick W. Taylor interview, 4.

24. Ivin R. Jackson interview, 25; Taylor letters, 17 July 1893.

25. George S. Tanner interview, 4.

26. Gallup; Esther Anderson Huntsman interview, 2–3; and Derryfield N. Smith et al., *Silas Derryfield Smith*, 38.

27. Alice Louise Reynolds interview, 3.

28. MacDonald, 40–42.

29. Ida Walser Skousen interview, 2; Beulah Stout Limb interview, 6; and John C. Larsen interview, 3.

30. Ida Walser Skousen interview, 5; Edith Smith Bushman interview, 5.

31. Laura Moffet Jones interview, 5.

32. Rogers interview, 9.

33. Eyring, Autobiography, 17.

34. Joseph Eyring interview, 10.

35. David Guymon interview, 32; Wayne Carroll interview, 10.

36. Jesse Barney interview, 33; Orin Barney interview, 7.

37. Walter Haws interview, 18; Rhoda Ann Knell Cannon interview, 7.

38. Lawrence Leavitt interview, 8; Catherine Scott Brown interview, 2.

39. Martha Spence Heywood, Journal, 40.

40. Oara Cluff Pace interview, 10; Sarah Dearmon Pea Rich letter, 25 August 1853.

41. William Broomhead letter, 10 July 1897.

42. Taylor letters, 14 April 1894, 24 December 1895.

43. Pacey interview, 3; Benjamin Johnson, Journal, 24; Rich letters, 31 January 1861; and Robert Gardner, Journal, 27.

44. David Candland; Phineas Cook, Autobiography; and John Jacob Walser interview, 5.

45. Terry, Journal, 10; Arabelle Parkinson Daines interview, 2; and Benjamin Julius and Harriet Jane Hakes Johnson interview, 3.

46. Beck interview, 5; G. Milton Jameson interview, 8; and Maud Farnsworth interview, 5.

47. Thomas L. Lowe letters; Layton, 35–36; and Andrew Jonus Hansen, 42.

48. Josephine Spillsbury Vance interview, 12–13.

49. Alice Smith Kartchner interview, 5; Irene Larsen Whitehead interview, 15; Mabel Moody Whitmer interview, 17; and Elbert Hans Anderson interview, 9.

50. Henry Earl Day interview, 11; Fenton L. Williams interview, 13.

51. Ida Walser Jackson interview, 18; Anthony Ivins Bentley interview (Embry, 1976), 12.

10. Relationships between Wives

1. Watson and Smith interview, 3.

2. Charles White interview, 2; Kartchner interview, 9.

3. Rosalia Tenney Payne interview, 4–5.

4. Pacey interview, 6; Iona Tanner Jackson interview, 9.

5. Jane Flake Woods interview, 5; Hawkes interview, 3; and Robert Haynie interview, 9.

6. Edgar L. Cazier interview, 3; Isaac B. Ball, Radio Talk Show, 14 February 1932, p. 2; Florence Wilson Anderson interview; 2; and Louis Brandley, "Emma Biefer Brandley," 3.

7. Ida Walser Jackson interview, 8–9; Sherratt interview, 9; Kenneth W. Godfrey, Audrey M. Godfrey, and Jill Mulvay Derr, *Women's Voices: An Untold History of the Latter-day Saints, 1830–1860*, 286.

8. Young, 126; Remi Clignet and Joyce A. Sween, "For a Revisionist Theory of Human Polygyny," 452.

9. Mary Ann Stowell Jackson interview, 3.

10. Dunford interview, 9–10; Julie Dunfrey, "Living the Principle," Videotape.

11. Young, 447; Jessie L. Embry, "Sisters or Competitors"; and Rogers interview, 8.

12. Mortenson interview, Appendix 5; Embry, "Sisters or Competitors."

13. Helen Ware, "Polygyny: Women's Views in a Transitional Society, Nigeria, 1975," 190.

14. Joseph F. Smith, "A Mormon Polygamous Family as Viewed by One of its Third Generation," 16.

15. White interview, 2–3; Laura Moffet Jones interview, 2; and Caroline Pederson Hansen, 12 1969), 70.

16. Hutchings interview, 8–9; Robert Haynie interview, 8; and Bessie Jameson Judy interview, 18.

17. Benjamin LaSalle Farnsworth interview, 12; Juanita Brooks interview, 2; and Lestra Stewart Marison interview, 2.

18. William L. Wyatt interview, 2; Nilus Stowell Memmott interview, 11–12.

19. Keith Romney interview, 15; Dennison Romney interview, 13.

20. Dennison Romney interview, 13; Rulon Romney interview, 4.

21. Dennison Romney interview, 6–7.

22. Ibid., 7; Rulon Romney interview, 5, 7; and Celia Romney Geertson interview, 15.

23. Roskelley interview, 1, 3, 4; Emma Roskelley Hansen interview, 2.

24. Roskelley, 3–4.

25. Faragher, 138; Lucile Barlow Call interview, 9; Karl Skousen interview, 5; Harris interview, 1–2; and L. Oliver Skanchy interview, 2.

26. Bernal A. Harvey interview, 11; James Bartum Harvey interview, 15.

27. Eva C. Webb, 6–7.

28. Helen Tanner Watkins interview, 23, 31.

29. Laura Andersen Watkins interview, 13.

30. Eldon Payne interview, 28; Frank Romney interview, 4; Pace interview, 3; and Frances Grant Bennett interview, 6.

31. Harris, Life Story, 12.

11. The Children of Plural Families

1. Degler, *At Odds*, 461; Joe L. Dubbert, *A Man's Place: Masculinity in Transition*, 21, 23; and Donald H. Bell, "Up from Patriarchy: The Male Role in Historical Perspective," *Men in Difficult Times: Masculinity Today and Tomorrow*, Robert A. Lewis, ed., 317.

2. Julie Dunfrey, " 'Living the Principle' of Plural Marriage: Mormon Women, Utopia, and Female Sexuality in the Nineteenth Century," 533. Also see Joan Iversen, "Feminist Implications of Mormon Polygyny," 505–22; Michio Kitahara, "Living Quarter Arrangements in Polygyny and Circumcision and Segregation of Males at Puberty," 402; Annie Clark Tanner, *A Mormon Mother*, 269; Caroline Eyring Miner interview, 11; Archie L. Jenkins interview, 15; and Rigby interview, 8.

3. Washburn, 12–13; Howlett interview, 7.

4. Heywood, 71–72; Alder interview, 24.

5. Layton interview, 4; Rose Eyring Calder interview, 3; and Ara O. Call interview, 9.

6. Pond interview, 1; Albert L. Payne interview, 6; Anson B. Call Jr., 14; and Abraham Stout interview, 19.

7. Rita Skousen Johnson interview, 4; William Walser interview, 14; and Jonathan S. Cannon interview, 11.

8. Mary Ann Stowell Jackson interview, 4; Dunfrey, " 'Living the Principle' of Plural Marriage," 533.

9. Tanner, 172–73, 221, 269, 271, 312.

10. Ibid., 270; Jenkins interview, 15.

11. Fern Cluff Ingram interview, 9; Pingree interview, 2.

12. Robert Haynie interview, 1–2; Joseph T. Bentley interview, 24.

13. Pomeroy interview, 2, 4.

14. John Brown; Taylor letters, 9 July 1900.

15. Taylor letters, 9 May 1908; Lyman Andros Shurtliff, Letter, 1854; and Layton, 44.

16. Joseph W. Pratt interview, 4.

17. Elma Jane Jones Anderson interview, 10.

18. Esther Webb Pope interview, 3; Catherine Scott Brown interview, 15.

19. Dorothy Geneve Young Willey, "Childhood Experiences in Mormon Polygamous Families at the Turn of the Century," 90.

20. Alma Uriah Jones interview, 21; Annie Richardson Johnson interview, 6.

21. Howlett interview, 17.

22. Morris Hodges interview, 3.

23. Albert L. Payne interview, 3; Glen Lowe interview, 6.

24. Rinda Bentley Sudweeks interview, 10; LeRoy Eyring interview, 7; and Miner interview, 10.

25. Viva Skousen Bluth Brown interview, 20; Aseneth Skousen Walser interview, 20.

26. Judy interview, 5.

27. Dunford interview, 12.

28. Hannah Skousen Call interview, 13; Elizabeth Adams McFarland interview, 9.

29. Abalone Porter Hurst interview, 9.

30. Brandley interview (Embry, 1982), 15; Brandley, "Eliza Brandley," 1.

31. Pearl Jarvis Augustus interview, 3.

32. Viva Skousen Bluth Brown interview, 15.

33. Abraham Marion Bergeson interview, 8; Harry Moroni Whitmer interview, 8.

34. Hamilton interview, 38–39; Roberta Allred interview, 11–12.

35. Degler, *Out of Our Past,* 462.

36. Blau interview, 5; George E. Hancey interview, 18; Hazel Richardson Taylor interview, 5; Jefferies interview, 10; and Agnes Ford Johnson interview, 7.

37. Anthony Ivins Bentley interview (Embry, 1976), 33; Clark Hamblin interview, 9.

38. Ione Naegle Moss interview, 19; Seneth Hyer Thomson interview, 6.

39. Laura Andersen Watkins interview, 10–11; Lavina Bentley Jackson interview, 13; and Richard Ivins Bentley, 6.

40. Kenneth E. Weight interview, 14; Xarissa Merkley Clarke interview, 10; and Chadwick interview, 9.

41. Cazier interview, 6; Washburn interview, 12.

42. Franklin Lyman Stout interview, 11; Elma Jane Jones Anderson interview, 10.

43. Hazel Richardson Taylor interview, 5.

44. Frank Romney interview, 5; Rulon Romney interview, 2.

45. Mercelle Farr Atkinson interview, 5.

46. Ibid., 11; Viva Skousen Bluth Brown interview, 5.

47 Pope interview, 4; Douglas Cannon interview, 5; and Bickmore interview, 3.

48. Tanner interview, 3.

49. Rose Brown Hayes and Mrs. Clark interview, 4.

50. Rudgar H. Daines interview, 19; Ellis interview, 12, 20.

51. Washburn interview, 10; Thomson interview, 9; and Heaton interview, 10.

52. Ellis interview, 9; Hyer and Ririe interview, 12.

53. Augustus interview, 10.

54. Pope interview, 9; Rochelle Fairbourn, conversation with author, 1982.

12. *Divorce and Inheritance*

1. Carol Cornwall Madsen, "Marriage and Divorce in Territorial Utah," 4, 5, 8; Young, *Isn't One Wife Enough?* 229.

2. Eugene E. Campbell and Bruce L. Campbell, "Divorce Among Mormon Polygamists: Extent and Explanations," 5.

3. Ibid, 6.

4. Ibid.

5. Madsen, 6, 8.

6. Phillip R. Kunz, "One Wife or Several? A Comparative Study of Late Nineteenth-Century Marriage in Utah," *The Mormon People: Their Character and Traditions*, Thomas G. Alexander, ed., 69.

7. Campbell and Campbell, 8, 12, 15, 23; Madsen, 6, 7, 8.

8. Madsen, 10; Richards, 54; and Candland, 17.

9. Foote, 140, 266.

10. Ibid., 240.

11. Ibid., 265.

12. Edward William Payne Family Group Sheets; Eldon Payne interview, 26; and Rosalia Tenney Payne interview, 3.

13. Belle Harris Merrill Nelson Berry interview, 6; Price Nelson interview, 5, 8.

14. Arthur Day interview, 4.

15. Truman Call interview, 2, 11.

16. Clarence Turley interview, 13–15.

17. Joyce Richardson Heder interview, 7; Justin Richardson interview, 11.

18. Campbell and Campbell, 23; Keith Romney interview, 13.

19. Quoted in Martha Sonntag Bradley, " 'Hide and Seek': Children on the Underground," 139.

20. Quoted in Ibid., 138.

21. Young, 264.

22. Emma J. Rasmussen interview, 2; Hyrum S. Jensen interview, 4; and Farrell interview, 6.

23. John Pulsipher, Account.

24. Lavinia Bentley Jackson interview, 33.

25. Harold W. Bentley interview, 35–36.

26. Jenkins interview, 13–14; Francis Moulton, "Polygamy in Heber Valley," 3.

27. R. Collin Mangrum, "Furthering the Cause of Zion: An Overview of the Mormon Ecclesiastical Court System in Early Utah," 90.

28. Joseph Hodges interview, 3.

29. William Hodges interview, 4.

30. Morris Hodges interview, 5–6.

31. Rulon Romney interview, 9.

32. Miles and Atkins interview, 2–3.

33. Turley interview, 16.

13. Participant Evaluation

1. Felt interview, 4; Caroline Pederson Hansen, Autobiography, 70.

2. Mary Jane Done Jones interview, 2, 5.

3. Margaret McNeil Ballard, Autobiography, 26.

4. Elvera Manful, "L. W. Kimball," 8; Felt, 3.

5. Pomeroy interview, 8; Beck interview, 3.

6. Miner, 129; Memmott, 13; and Allen interview, 4.

7. Eyring, Autobiography, 19.

8. Esaias Edwards, Journal, 1; George Q. Payne, Fay Ollerton Symposium, 3.

9. John J. Esplin interview, 3; Benjamin Julius and Harriet Jane Hakes Johnson interview, 5.

10. Martin B. Bushman, Autobiography.

11. Conrad Keeler Naegle interview, in process; Hutchings interview, 2.

12. Ivan R. Richardson interview, 15–16.

13. Louis Brandley interview, 21; Winnifred Newton Thomas interview, 1.

14. Florence Jackson Payne, Fay Ollerton Symposium, 3; Mabel Amelia Porter Carroll interview, 15; and Whatcott interview, 4.

15. Huff interview, 17; Scott interview, 5; and Keith Romney interview, 14.

16. Steven F. Faux, "Evolutionary Speculations on the Oligraphic Development of Mormon Polygamy," preface.

17. Paul Bohannan, *Social Anthropology*, 110.

Bibliography

Two of the major sources of information for this study were the Kimball Young Collection and the Charles Redd Center for Western Studies Oral History Projects. The originals of the Kimball Young Collection are in the Garrett Theological Seminary at Northwestern University. The copies used in this study are at the Manuscript Division of the Harold B. Lee Library, Brigham Young University, Provo, Utah. In the bibliography, the Kimball Young Collection is identified as KYC. Mainly two oral history projects were used, the LDS Polygamy (LDSP) and LDS Family Life (LDSFL). Other projects cited include the Charles Redd Project, the LDS Afro-American Project, and Utah Politics Project. Transcripts and tapes are available at the Manuscript Division of the Harold B. Lee Library. Journals and autobiographies from Special Collections, Harold B. Lee Library, are listed as BYUSC; those in the Manuscript Division are listed as BYUM. Sources used from the LDS Church Archives, Historical Department, Church of Jesus Christ of Latter-day Saints, Salt Lake City, Utah, are listed as LDSCA. Special Collections at the Utah State University Library, Logan, Utah, are listed as USUSC. Family Group Sheets are in the Genealogical Library, Church of Jesus Christ of Latter-day Saints, Salt Lake City, Utah (LDSGL). Collections of the Utah State Historical Society, Salt Lake City, Utah, are USHS. The oral history program in the Archives at Weber State College, Ogden, Utah, is listed as WSC. Records were also used at the Bancroft Library, University of California-Berkeley, California, and are cited as Bancroft.

Adams, Verda Spencer. Interviewed by Marsha Martin, 1982. LDSP.

Adams, William, and Mary Ann Leach Adams. Biography. KYC.

Alder, Lorna Call. Interviewed by Jessie L. Embry, 1976. LDSP.

Alexander, Thomas G. *Mormonism in Transition: A History of the Latter-day Saints, 1890-1930*. Champaign: University of Illinois Press, 1986.

Alexander, Thomas G., and James B. Allen. *Mormons and Gentiles: A History of Salt Lake City*. Boulder: Pruett Publishing Co., 1984.

Allen, Clarence. Interviewed by James Comish, 1979. LDSP.

Allred, Roberta. Interviewed by Laurel Schmidt, 1982. LDSFL.

Anderson, Alba Jones. Interviewed by Marsha Martin, 1982. LDSFL.

Anderson, Anderson P. Interviewed by James Hulett, 1937. KYC.

Anderson, Elbert Hans. Interviewed by Marsha Martin, 1983. LDSFL.

Anderson, Elma Jane Jones. Interviewed by Rochelle Fairbourn, 1981. LDSP.

Anderson, Florence Wilson. Interviewed by Marsha Martin, 1983. LDSP.

Anderson, Nels. *Deseret Saints: The Mormon Frontier in Utah*. Chicago: University of Chicago Press, 1942.

Andrus, Manomus Lovina Gibson. Interviewed by James Hulett, 1935. KYC.

Arrington, Leonard J. *Brigham Young: American Moses*. New York: Alfred A. Knopf, 1985.

Arrington, Leonard J., and Davis Bitton. *The Mormon Experience: A History of the Latter-day Saints*. New York: Alfred A. Knopf, 1979.

Ashworth, Emma Westerman. Interviewed by James Hulett, 1935. KYC.

Atkinson, Mercelle Farr. Interviewed by Jessie L. Embry, 1980. LDSP.

Augustus, Pearl Jarvis. Interviewed by Jessie L. Embry, 1976. LDSP.

Austin, Edna Cowley. Interviewed by Leonard Grover, 1980. LDSP.

Austin, Torrey L. Interviewed by Jessie L. Embry, 1976. LDSP.

Bachman, Daniel W. "New Light on an Old Hypothesis: The Ohio Origins of the Revelation on Eternal Marriage," *Journal of Mormon History* 5 (1978): 19–32.

Ball, Isaac B. Radio Talk Show, 14 February 1932, San Francisco KTAB. LDSCA.

Ballard, Margaret McNeil. Autobiography. BYUSC.

Barney, Jesse. Interviewed by Stevan Martin Hales, 1982. LDSP.

Barney, Orin. Interviewed by Jessie L. Embry, 1982. LDSP.

Barney, Walter. Interviewed by Jessie L. Embry, 1981. LDSP.

Bartley, Bernitta. Interviewed by Stevan Martin Hales, 1982. LDSP.

Bean, Ross S., to Fay Ollerton, 13 December 1935. KYC.

Beck, Elizabeth Acord. Interviewed by James Hulett, 1935. KYC.

Beecher, Maureen Ursenbach. "Under the Sunbonnets: Mormon Women with Faces." *BYU Studies* 16 (Summer 1976): 471-84.

Beecher, Maureen Ursenbach. "Women's Work on the Mormon Frontier." *Utah Historical Quarterly* 49 (Summer 1981): 279-90.

Bell, Donald H. "Up From Patriarchy: The Male Role in Historical Perspective." *Men in Difficult Times: Masculinity Today and Tomorrow*. Robert A. Lewis, ed. Englewood Cliffs: Prentice-Hall, Inc., 1981.

Bennett, Frances Grant. Interviewed by Marlena Chipman Shanin, 1976. LDSCA.

Bennion, Lowell "Ben." "The Geography of Polygamy Among the Mormons in 1890." Paper presented at the Mormon History Association annual meeting, 11 May 1984, Provo, Utah.

Bennion, Lowell "Ben." "The Incidence of Mormon Polygamy in 1880: 'Dixie' versus Davis Stake." *Journal of Mormon History* 11(1984): 23-42.

Bentley, Anthony Ivins. Interviewed by Mike Cushman, 1971. WSC.

Bentley, Anthony Ivins. Interviewed by Jessie L. Embry, 1976. LDSP.

Bentley, Harold W. Interviewed by Tillman Boxell, 1978. LDSP.

Bentley, Israel Ivins. Interviewed by Leonard Grover, 1980. LDSP.

Bentley, Joseph T. Interviewed by Jessie L. Embry, 1980. LDSP.

Bentley, Maud Taylor. Autobiography, n.d. BYUSC.

Bentley, Richard Ivins. Interviewed by Leonard Grover, 1980. LDSP.

Bentley, Viv. Interviewed by James Hulett, 1935. KYC.

Bergeson, Abraham Marion. Interviewed by Amy Bentley, 1984. LDSFL.

Berry, Bell Harris Merrill Nelson. Interviewed by James Hulett, 1935. KYC.

Bickmore, Georgina Bollette Critchlow. Interviewed by Stevan Martin Hales, 1982. LDSP.

Black, George. Interviewed by Laurel Schmidt, 1981. LDSFL.

Blakely, Pamela A. R. "Co-wives in Africa: A Discussion of Polygyny in Eastern Zaire." Lecture presented for the Women's Research Institute, BYU, 23 January 1985.

Blau, Teresa Richardson. Interviewed by Leonard Grover, 1980. LDSP.

Bohanan, Paul. *Social Anthropology*. New York: Holt, Rinehart, Winston, Inc., 1963.

Book of Mormon.

Boone, David, and Chad J. Flake. "The Prison Diary of William Jordan Flake." *Journal of Arizona History* 24 (Summer 1983): 145-70.

Boserup, Ester. *Women's Role in Economic Development*. London: George Allen and Unwin Ltd., 1970.

Boyle, Eliza Bowen. Interviewed by James Hulett, 1935. KYC.

Bradley, Martha Sonntag. " 'Hide and Seek:' Children on the Underground." *Utah Historical Quarterly* 5 (Spring 1983): 133-53.

Brandley, Louis. "Eliza Brandley." LDSP.

Brandley, Louis. "Emma Biefer Brandley." LDSP.

Brandley, Louis. Interviewed by Charles Ursenbach, 1976. LDSCA.

Brandley, Louis. Interviewed by Jessie L. Embry, 1982. LDSP.

Brimhall, George W. Autobiography, n.d. KYC.

Brooks, Juanita. Interviewed by James Hulett, 1935. KYC.

Broomhead, William. Letter, 10 July 1897. LDSCA.

Brown, Catherine Scott. Interviewed by Jessie L. Embry, 1980. KYC.

Brown, Effie Hawkes. Interviewed by James Hulett, 1937. KYC.

Brown, John. Journal. LDSCA.

Brown, Judith E. "Polygyny and Family Planning in Sub-Saharan Africa." *Studies in Family Planning* 12 (1971): 322-26.

Brown, Murlyn Lamar. Interviewed by Amy Bentley, 1984. LDSFL.

Brown, Viva Skousen Bluth. Interviewed by Jessie L. Embry, 1976. LDSP.

Burgess-Olson, Vicky. "Family Structure and Dynamics in Early Utah Mormon Families — 1847-1885." Ph.D. diss., Northwestern University, 1975.

Bushman, Edith Smith. Interviewed by Steven J. Christiansen, 1979. LDSP.

Bushman, Martin B. Autobiography, n.d. LDSCA.

Cairncross, John. *After Polygamy Was Made a Sin: The Social History of Christian Polygamy*. London: Routledge and Kegan Paul, 1974.

Calder, Rose Eyring. Interviewed by Leonard Grover, 1980. LDSP.

Call, Anson B., Jr. Interviewed by Jessie L. Embry, 1976. LDSP.

Call, Ara O. Interviewed by Jessie L. Embry, 1976. LDSP.

Call, Hannah Skousen. Interviewed by Jessie L. Embry, 1981. LDSP.

Call, Lucile Barlow. Interviewed by Jessie L. Embry, 1980. LDSP.

Call, Truman. Interviewed by Laurel Schmidt, 1981. LDSP.

Campbell, Eugene E., and Bruce L. Campbell. "Divorce Among Mormon Polygamists: Extent and Explanations." *Utah Historical Quarterly* 46 (Winter 1978): 4-20.

Candland, David. Autobiography, n.d. LDSCA.

Cannon, David S. Interviewed by Laurel Schmidt, 1981. LDSP.

Cannon, Douglas. Interviewed by Leonard Grover, 1980. LDSP.

Cannon, Jonathan S. Interviewed by Leonard Grover, 1979. LDSP.

Cannon, Kenneth L., III, and Jessie L. Embry. "Seymour B. Young." Unpublished manuscript in possession of author.

Cannon, Rhoda Ann Knell. Interviewed by James Hulett, 1935. KYC.

Card, Donald Godfrey, and Melva R. Witbeck. "The Journal of Charles Ora Card, September 14, 1886-July 7, 1903." USUSC.

Card, Orson Rega. Interviewed by Jessie L. Embry, 1982. LDSP.

Cardon, Ella Saunders. Interviewed by James Hulett, 1936. KYC.

Cardon, Louis. Interviewed by Kimberly Jensen James, 1981. LDSP.

Cardston, Alberta, Ward Minutes. LDSCA.

Carpenter, G. Alvin. Interviewed by Marsha Martin, 1981. LDSFL.

Carroll, Mabel Amelia Porter. Interviewed by Gary L. Shumway, 1984. LDSP.

Carroll, Mary Westover. Interviewed by Marsha Martin, 1982. LDSFL.

Carroll, Wayne. Interviewed by Chris Nelson, 1982. LDSP.

Cazier, Edgar L. Interviewed by Laurel Schmidt, 1982. LDSP.

Chadwick, Earl. Interviewed by Laurel Schmidt, 1981. LDSFL.

Chamberlain, Mary Elizabeth Woolley. Autobiography, 1936-1939. BYUSC.

Christensen, Vera Anderson. Interviewed by Stevan Martin Hales, 1982. LDSFL.

Clark, Edward Barrett. Family Group Sheets. LDSGL.

Clark, Marvin Ezra. Interviewed by Leonard Grover, 1981. LDSP.

Clark, Walter. Interviewed by Leonard Grover, 1979. LDSP.

Clarke, A. John. Interviewed by Marsha Martin, 1982. LDSFL.

Clarke, Xarissa Merkley. Interviewed by Marsha Martin, 1982. LDSFL.

Clignet, Remi. *Many Wives, Many Powers*. Evanston: Northwestern University Press, 1970.

Clignet, Remi, and Joyce A. Sween. "For a Revisionist Theory of Human Polygyny." *Signs* 6 (Spring 1981): 445-68.

Cluff, Heber Manasseh. Family Group Sheets. LDSGL.

Cluff, Vearl. Interviewed by Jessie L. Embry, 1982. LDSP.

Clyde, Ora Packard. Interviewed by J. Keith Melville, 1979. Utah Politics.

Cole, Ursula Rich. Interviewed by James Hulett, 1937. KYC.

Conklin, Aseneth Smith. Interviewed by Leonard Grover, 1979. LDSP.

Cook, Phineas. Autobiography, n.d. LDSCA.

Coombs, Isaiah. Journal. KYC.

Corbett, Mrs. Will. Interviewed by James Hulett, 1937. KYC.

Cowan, Richard O., and Wilson K. Anderson. *The Living Church: The Unfolding of the Programs and Organizations of the Church of Jesus Christ During the Twentieth Century*. Provo, Utah: Brigham Young University Printing Services, 1974.

Cowley, Matthias. *Wilford Woodruff: Fourth President of the Church of Jesus Christ of Latter-day Saints; History of His Life and Labors as Recorded in His Daily Journals*. Salt Lake City: Deseret News, 1916.

Cox, Ruth Jorgensen. Interviewed by Jessie L. Embry, 1982 LDSFL.

Daines, Arabelle Parkinson. Interviewed by James Hulett, 1938. KYC.

Daines, Lydia. Interviewed by James Hulett, 1937. KYC.

Daines, Rudger H. Interviewed by Jessie L. Embry, 1976. LDSP.

Darius, Annie Maria. Federal Writers Project. Bancroft.

Day, Arthur. Interviewed by Leonard Grover, 1980. LDSP.

Day, Henry Earl. Interviewed by Amy Bentley, 1983. LDSFL.

Decker, Jesse Smith. Interviewed by Stevan Martin Hales, 1982. LDSFL.

Degler, Carl N. *At Odds: Women and the Family in America from the Revolution to the Present*. New York: Oxford University Press, 1980.

Degler, Carl N. *Out of Our Past: The Forces that Shaped Modern America*. New York: Harper & Row, 1984.

Dickerson, Maybelle Farr. Interviewed by Leonard Grover, 1980. LDSP.

Doctrine and Covenants.

Done, Ellen P. Moffett. Interviewed by Mike Cushman, 1971. WSC.

Douglas, Mae Bingham. Interviewed by James Hulett, 1938. KYC.

Driggs, Nevada Watson. Interviewed by A. Hamer Reiser, 1975. LDSCA.

Dubbert, Joe L. *A Man's Place: Masculinity in Transition*. Englewood Cliffs: Prentice-Hall, 1979.

Dunford, Zina Patterson. Interviewed by Jessie L. Embry, 1980. LDSP.

Dunfrey, Julie. " 'Living the Principle' of Plural Marriage: Mormon Women, Utopia, and Female Sexuality in the Nineteenth Century." *Feminist Studies* 10 (Fall 1984): 523-36.

Dunfrey, Julie. "Living the Principle." Videotape Production. Utah Endowment for the Humanities Media Center. Salt Lake City.

Durfee, Charles. Interviewed by Dean L. May, 1979. LDSP.

Earl, Joseph Donal. Interviewed by Stevan Martin Hales, 1982. LDSP.

"Editors' Table." *Improvement Era* 18 (June 1915): 733-34.

Edwards, Esais. Journal. KYC.

Ellis, Mary Lucile Clark. Interviewed by Stevan Martin Hales, 1982. LDSP.

Ember, Melvin. "Warfare, Sex Ratio, and Polygyny." *Ethnology* 13 (April 1974): 197-206.

Embry, Jessie L. "Exiles for the Principle: LDS Polygamy in Canada." *Dialogue: A Journal of Mormon Thought* 18 (Fall 1985): 108-16.

Embry, Jessie L. *Richardson Family History*. Provo, Utah: Charles Redd Center for Western Studies, 1982.

Embry, Jessie L. "The Role of LDS Polygamous Families, Blanding: A Case Study." Unpublished manuscript in possession of author.

Embry, Jessie L. "Sisters or Competitors." Copy in possession of author.

Ence, Gottlieb. Life Sketch, n.d. LDSCA.

Engh, Howard J. Interviewed by Marsha Martin, 1983. LDSFL.

Ericksen, Edna Clark. Interviewed by Leonard Grover, 1980. LDSP.

Esplin, Ann Amelia Chamberlain. Interviewed by Ronald K. Esplin, 1973. LDSCA.

Esplin, John J. Interviewed by James Hulett, 1935. KYC.

Eyring, Edward Christian. Autobiography, 1931. BYUSC.

Eyring, Henry. Journal. BYUSC.

Eyring, Joseph. Interviewed by Jessie L. Embry, 1976. LDSP.

Eyring, LeRoy. Interviewed by Leonard Grover, 1980. LDSP.

Fairbourn, Rochelle. Conversation with author, 1982.

Faragher, John Mack. *Women and Men on the Overland Trail*. New Haven: Yale University Press, 1979.

Farnsworth, Benjamin LaSalle. Interviewed by Amy Bentley, 1984. LDSP.

Farnsworth, Maud. Interviewed by Stevan Martin Hales, 1982. LDSP.

Farrell, Mary E. Croshaw. Interviewed by James Hulett, 1937. KYC.

Faux, Steven F. "Evolutionary Speculations on the Oligraphic Development of Mormon Polygamy." Unpublished manuscript in possession of author.

Faux, Steven F., and Harold L. Miller Jr. "Evolutionary Speculations of the Oligraphic Development of Mormon Polygyny." *Ethnology and Sociobiology* 5 (1984): 15-31.

Felt, Alma Elizabeth Mineer. Interviewed by James Hulett, 1935. KYC.

Fillerup, Charles Richard. Family Group Sheets. LDSGL.

Foote, Warren. Autobiography. LDSCA.

Forman, William. Journal. USHS.

Foster, Lawrence. *Religion and Sexuality: Three American Communal Experiences of the Nineteenth Century.* New York: Oxford University Press, 1981.

Fox, Ruth May. Interviewed by James Hulett, 1935. KYC.

Gallacher, Mary Reiser. "The Other Mother." *Heart Throbs of the West*, Kate B. Carter, ed. 12 vols. Salt Lake City: Daughters of the Utah Pioneers, 1939. 1:281-99.

Gallup, Luke William. Journal. LDSCA.

Gardner, Annie. Interviewed by James Hulett, n.d. KYC.

Gardner, Robert. Journal. KYC.

Geertson, Celica Romney. Interviewed by Jessie L. Embry, 1976. LDSP.

Gibbons, Mercy Weston. Interviewed by James Hulett, 1937, 1938. KYC.

Gilchrist, Bruce. Interviewed by Marsha Martin, 1983. LDSFL.

Goddard, Emma. Interviewed by James Hulett, 1935. KYC.

Godfrey, Kenneth W., Audrey M. Godfrey, and Jill Mulvay Derr. *Women's Voices: An Untold History of the Latter-day Saints, 1930-1950.* Salt Lake City: Deseret Book Co., 1982.

Goodson, Stephanie Smith. "Plural Wives." *Mormon Sisters.* Claudia Bushman, ed. Salt Lake City: Olympus Publishing Co., 1976.

Gordon, Michael. "The Ideal Husband as Depicted in the Nineteenth-Century Marriage Manual." *The American Man.* Elizabeth H. Pleck and Joseph N. Pleck, eds. Englewood Cliffs: Prentice-Hall, 1980.

Greenhalgh, Olive LaBaron. Interviewed by Amy Bentley, 1984. LDSFL.

Guymon, David. Interviewed by Gary L. Shumway, 1981. LDSP.

Hadfield, Grace Viola Jorgensen. Interviewed by Marsha Martin, 1983. LDSFL.

Haines, Vivian Elizabeth. Interviewed by Stevan Martin Hales, 1981. LDSFL.

Hamblin, Clark. Interviewed by Jessie L. Embry, 1982. LDSFL.

Hamilton, Everett Mark. Interviewed by Stevan Martin Hales, 1981. LDSFL.

Hammond, Hortense Young. Interviewed by Leonard Grover, 1980. LDSP.

Hancey, George E. Interviewed by Leonard Grover, 1979. LDSP.

Hansen, Andrew Jonus. Autobiography, n.d. LDSCA.

Hansen, Caroline Pederson. Autobiography. *Our Pioneer Heritage*, Kate Carter, ed. Salt Lake City: Utah Daughters of the Pioneers, 1969. 12:66-76.

Hansen, Don Kofford. Interviewed by Marsha Martin, 1983. LDSFL.

Hansen, Emma Roskelley. Interviewed by James Hulett, 1938. KYC.

Hardy, B. Carmon. "The Mormon Colonies in Mexico, 1885-1912." Ph.D. diss., Wayne State University, 1963.

Hardy, B. Carmon. "Early Colonization of Mormon Polygamists in Mexico and Canada: A Legal and Historiographical Review." Unpublished manuscript in the possession of author.

Hardy, B. Carmon, and Victor Jorgenson. "The Taylor-Cowley Affair and the Watershed of Mormon History." *Utah Historical Quarterly* 48 (Winter 1980): 4-36.

Harris, Eunice Stewart. Interviewed by James Hulett, 1935. KYC.

Harris, Eunice Stewart. Life Story, n.d. KYC.

Hart, Annabell Wheeler. Interviewed by Amy Bentley, 1984. LDSFL.

Harvey, Bernal A. Interviewed by Jessie L. Embry, 1976. LDSP.

Harvey, James Bartum. Interviewed by Leonard Grover, 1979. LDSP.

Hatch, Nelle Spilsbury. *Colonia Juarez: An Intimate Account of a Mormon Village*. Salt Lake City: Deseret Book, 1954.

Hawkes, Claude E. Interviewed by James Hulett, 1937. KYC.

Haws, Maude Nuttal. Interviewed by Rochelle Fairbourn, 1982. LDSP.

Haws, Walter. Interviewed by Jessie L. Embry, 1982. LDSP.

Hayes, Rose B., and Mrs. Clark. Interviewed by James Hulett, 1936. KYC.

Haynie, Ether. Interviewed by Leonard Grover, 1980. LDSP.

Haynie, Robert. Interviewed by Jessie L. Embry, 1982. LDSP.

Heaton, Terrance. Interviewed by Marsha Martin, 1982. LDSP.

Heder, Joyce Richardson. Interviewed by Leonard Grover. LDSP.

Heiner, George. Federal Writers Project, Bancroft.

Hendricks, Sarah. Interviewed by James Comish, n.d. LDSP.

Heywood, Martha Spence. Journal. KYC.

Hickman, J. E., to C. M. Haynes, 18 December 1907. Charles Redd Center.

Hill, Reuben L. Interviewed by James Hulett, 1937. KYC.

Hinman, Morgan. Journal. LDSCA.

Hodges, Joseph. Interviewed by James Hulett, 1937. KYC.

Hodges, Maud Kearl. Interviewed by James Hulett, 1937. KYC.

Hodges, Morris. Interviewed by Jessie L. Embry. LDSP.

Hodges, William. Interviewed by James Hulett, 1938. LDSP.

Howlett, Ada S. Interviewed by Stevan Martin Hales, 1982. LDSFL.

Hudson, A. James. "Charles Ora Card: Pioneer and Colonizer." Master's thesis. Brigham Young University, 1961.

Huff, Jennie Lowe. Interviewed by Jessie L. Embry, 1976. LDSP.

Hulett, James Edward, Jr. "The Sociological and Social Psychological Aspects of the Mormon Polygamous Family." Ph.D. diss., University of Wisconsin, 1939.

Humphreys, Janett Wright. Interviewed by James Hulett, 1937. KYC.

Huntsman, Esther Anderson. Interviewed by James Hulett, 1937. KYC.

Huntsman, Orson Welcome. Utah Historical Records Survey. KYC.

Hurst, Abalone Porter. Interviewed by Gary L. Shumway, 1981. LDSP.

Hutchings, Harriett Snarr. Interviewed by Amy Bentley, 1984. LDSP.

Hyer, Andrew Larse. Family Group Sheets. LDSGL.

Hyer, Dorris Dale. Interviewed by Tillman Boxell, 1978. LDSP.

Hyer, Elizabeth Telford. Interviewed by James Hulett, 1938. KYC.

Hyer, Merle Gilbert, and Estelle Hyer Ririe. Interviewed by Tillman Boxell, 1978. LDSP.

Ingram, Fern Cluff. Interviewed by Leonard Grover, 1980. LDSP.

Irving, Gordon. "The Church and Young Men in Union, Utah, 1875-1920." Paper presented at the Mormon History Association annual meeting, Salt Lake City, 1986.

Iversen, Joan. "Feminist Implications of Mormon Polygyny." *Feminist Studies* 10 (1984): 502-22.

Ivins, Heber Grant. "Polygamy in Mexico." Unpublished manuscript in possession of author. A copy is also in Special Collections, University of Utah, Salt Lake City.

Ivins, Stanley S. "Notes on Mormon Polygamy." *Utah Historical Quarterly* 35 (Fall 1967): 309-21.

Jackson, Ida Walser. Interviewed by Jessie L. Embry, 1976. LDSP.

Jackson, Iona Tanner. Interviewed by Jessie L. Embry, 1982. LDSP.

Jackson, Ivin R. Interviewed by Tillman Boxell, 1978. LDSP.

Jackson, Lavinia Bentley. Interviewed by Jessie L. Embry, 1982. LDSP.

Jackson, Mary Ann Stowell. Interviewed by James Hulett, 1935. KYC.

Jameson, G. Milton. Interviewed by Gregory Maynard, 1973. Charles Redd.

Jefferies, Edward Hunter. Interviewed by Marsha Martin, 1983. LDSFL.

Jeffrey, Julie Roy. *Frontier Women: The Trans-Mississippi West, 1840-1880.* New York: Hill and Wang, 1979.

Jenkins, Archie L. Interviewed by Leonard Grover, 1980. LDSP.

Jensen, Hyrum S. Interviewed by James Hulett, 1938. KYC.

John, David. Journal. BYUM.

Johnson, Agnes Ford. Interviewed by Jessie L. Embry, 1982. LDSFL.

Johnson, Annie Richardson. *Heartbeats of Colonia Diaz*. Mesa, n.p., 1972.

Johnson, Annie Richardson. Interviewed by Leonard Grover, 1980. LDSP.

Johnson, Benjamin F. Journal. KYC.

Johnson, Benjamin Julius, and Harriet Jane Hakes Johnson. Interviewed by James Hulett, 1936. KYC.

Johnson, Joel Hills. Autobiography, n.d. Bancroft.

Johnson, Peter B. Federal Writers Project. Bancroft.

Johnson, Rita Skousen. Interviewed by Chris Nelson, 1981. LDSP.

Jones, Alma Uriah. Interviewed by Gary L. Shumway, 1981. LDSP.

Jones, Laura Moffet. Interviewed by James Hulett, 1935. KYC.

Jones, Mary Jane Done. Interviewed by James Hulett, n.d. KYC.

Journal of Discourses. 26 vols. Liverpool and London: Latter-day Saint Book Depot, 1854-86.

Judy, Bessie Jameson. Interviewed by Marsha Martin, 1982. LDSP.

Juster, Norton. *So Sweet to Labor: Rural Women in America 1865-1895*. New York: Viking Press, 1979.

Kartchner, Alice Smith. Interviewed by Steven J. Christiansen, 1979. LDSP.

Kenny, Scott, ed. *Wilford Woodruff Journal, 1833-1898*. Midvale, Utah: Signature Books, 1983-84.

Kimball, Farel Knudson Chamberlain. Interviewed by Jessie L. Embry, 1979. LDSP.

Kindrick, Charles W. "The Mormons in Mexico." *The American Monthly Review of Reviews* 19 (June 1899): 702-5.

Kitahara, Michio. "Living Quarter Arrangements in Polygyny and Circumcision and Segregation of Males at Puberty." *Ethnology* 13 (October 1974): 401-13

Knudson, Goldburn L. Interviewed by Leonard Grover, 1979. LDSP.

Kunz, Phillip R. "One Wife or Several? A Comparative Study of Late Nineteenth-Century Marriage in Utah." *The Mormon People: Their Character and Traditions*. Thomas G. Alexander, ed. Provo, Utah: Brigham Young University Press, 1980.

Lake, George. Autobiography, n.d. LDSCA.

Larsen, Elwood Earl. Interviewed by Stevan Martin Hales, 1982. LDSFL.

Larsen, John C. Interviewed by James Hulett, 1938. KYC.

Larsen, Lula. Interviewed by Rochelle Fairbourn, 1982. LDSP.

Larsen, Martha Geneva Day. Interviewed by James Hulett, 1935. KYC.

Larson, Gustive D. "Government, Politics and Conflict," and "The Crusade and the Manifesto." *Utah's History*. Richard D. Poll, ed., et al. Provo, Utah: Brigham Young University Press, 1978.

Layne, Jonathan E. Autobiography, n.d. BYUSC.

Layton, Christopher. Autobiography, n.d. LDSCA.

Layton, Jeneveve Eyring. Interviewed by Rochelle Fairbourn, 1982. LDSP.

Leavitt, Lawrence. Interviewed by Jessie L. Embry, 1980. LDSP.

Leavitt, Lorin "Dutch." Interviewed by Leonard Grover, 1980. LDSP.

Lee, Severin N. Interviewed by James Hulett, 1937. KYC.

Lewis, Rebecca Roskelley. Interviewed by Leonard Grover, 1980. LDSP.

Lillywhite, Georgiana Stowell. Interviewed by Jessie L. Embry, 1982. LDSP.

Limb, Buelah Stout. Interviewed by Leonard Grover, 1980. LDSP.

Little, Marva Whipple Cram. Interviewed by Rochelle Fairbourn, 1982. LDSP.

Little, Mary Elizabeth Tullidge. Autobiography. *Our Pioneer Heritage*. Kate Carter, ed. Salt Lake City: Daughters of Utah Pioneers, 1972. 15:99-109.

Logue, Larry. "A Time of Marriage: Monogamy and Polygamy in a Utah Town." *Journal of Mormon History* 11 (1984): 3-26.

Lowe, Glen. Interviewed by Jessie L. Embry, 1976. LDSP.

Lowe, Thomas. Letters. LDSCA.

McAllister, Agnes Walker. Interviewed by James Hulett, 1935. KYC.

McAllister, William James Frazier. Interviewed by James Hulett, 1935. KYC.

McDonald, Elizabeth Ann Schurtz. Interviewed by James Hulett, 1936. KYC.

MacDonald, Elizabeth Graham. Archives, 1875. LDSCA.

McFarland, Elizabeth Adams. Interviewed by James Hulett, 1936. KYC.

MacGregor, Alma W. Interviewed by James Hulett, 1935. KYC.

McNeil, Emma Hoth. Interviewed by James Hulett, 1938. KYC.

Madsen, Carol Cornwall. "Marriage and Divorce in Territorial Utah." Unpublished manuscript in possession of author.

Mallory, Gladys Call. Interviewed by Gary L. Shumway, 1981. LDSP.

Manful, Elvera. "L. W. Kimball." Federal Writers Project. KYC.

Mangrum, R. Collin. "Furthering the Cause of Zion: An Overview of the Mormon Ecclesiastical Court System in Early Utah." *Journal of Mormon History* 10 (1983): 79-90.

Marison, Lestra Stewart. Interviewed by James Hulett, 1936. KYC.

Marquis, Kathleen. " 'Diamond Cut Diamond:' Mormon Women and the Cult of Domesticity in the Nineteenth Century." *Papers in Women's Studies*, University of Michigan 2 (1974): 105-23.

May, Dean L. "A Demographic Portrait of the Mormons, 1830-1980." *After 150 Years: The Latter-day Saints in Sesquicentennial Perspective*. Thomas G. Alexander and Jessie L. Embry, eds. Provo, Utah: Charles Redd Center for Western Studies, 1983.

Meeks, Priddy. Journal. KYC.

Memmott, Nilus Stowell. Interviewed by Gary L. Shumway, 1982. LDSP.

Merrill, Charles Smith. Interviewed by Amy Bentley, 1984. LDSFL.

Miles, Elvera Colledge. Interviewed by Amy Bentley, 1984. LDSFL.

Miles, Zaides, and Nan Walker Atkins. Interviewed by James Hulett, n.d. KYC.

Miner, Caroline Eyring. Interviewed by Leonard Grover, 1980. LDSP.

Miner, Caroline Eyring. *The Life Story of Edward Christian Eyring (1868-1957)*. Salt Lake City: Publisher's Press, 1966.

Miner, Caroline Eyring, and Edward L. Kimball. *Camilla: A Biography of Camilla Eyring Kimball*. Salt Lake City: Deseret Book Co., 1980.

Monteirth, Linnie Fillerup. Interviewed by Amy Bentley, 1984. LDSP.

Morgan, May Smith. Interviewed by Amy Bentley, 1983. LDSP.

Morris, Cecelia Peterson Bott. Interviewed by Jessie L. Embry, 1976. LDSP.

Mortensen, Lula Roskelley. Interviewed by Jessie L. Embry, 1976. LDSP.

Mortimer, George H. Interviewed by Amy Bentley, 1983. LDSFL.

Moss, Iona Neagle. Interviewed by Gary L. Shumway, 1981. LDSFL.

Moulton, Francis. "Polygamy in Heber Valley," n.d. LDSCA.

Murdock, George Peter. *Ethnographic Atlas*. Pittsburgh: University of Pittsburgh Press, 1967.

Murray, Evan B. Interviewed by James Hulett, 1937. KYC.

Murray, Evan B. Interviewed by Jessie L. Embry, 1976. LDSP.

Naegle, Conrad Keeler. Interviewed by Jessie L. Embry, 1981. LDSP.

Nash, Andrew W. Interviewed by James Hulett, 1937. KYC.

Nelson, Christa Marie Sophie Ranglade. "Mormon Polygamy in Mexico." Master's Thesis, University of Utah, 1983.

Nelson, Lowry. "Settlement of the Mormons in Alberta." *Group Settlements: Ethnic Communities in Western Canada*. C. A. Dawson, ed. Toronto: Macmillan Co., 1936.

Nelson, Price. Interviewed by James Hulett, 1935. KYC.

Newell, Linda King, and Valeen Tippetts Avery. *Mormon Enigma: Emma Hale Smith: Prophet's Wife, "Elect Lady," Polygamy Foe*. New York: Doubleday and Company, Inc., 1984.

Nicol, John Murray. Interviewed by Amy Bentley, 1983. LDSFL.

O'Brien, Alberta Lyman. Interviewed by Stevan Martin Hales, 1981. LDSFL.

Old Testament, King James Version.

Olsen, Caroline. Federal Writers Project. Bancroft.

Ottenheimer, Martin, and Harriet Ottenheimer. "Matrilocal Residence and Nonsororal Polygyny: A Case from the Comoro Islands." *Journal of Anthropological Research* 35 (1979): 329-35.

Pace, D. Gene. "Community Leadership on the Mormon Frontier: Mormon Bishops and the Political, Economic, and Social Development of Utah Before Statehood." Ph.D. diss., Ohio State University, 1983.

Pace, Oara Cluff. Interviewed by Amy Bentley, 1984. LDSP.

Pacey, Ida Stewart. Interviewed by James Hulett, 1937. KYC.

Parkinson, Karma Parkinson. Interviewed by Tillman Boxell, 1978. LDSP.

Patrick, Edith Smith. Interviewed by Leonard Grover, 1980. LDSP.

Payne, Albert L. Interviewed by Jessie L. Embry, 1976. LDSP.

Payne, Edward William. Family Group Sheets. LDSGL.

Payne, Eldon. Interviewed by Jessie L. Embry, 1976. LDSP.

Payne, Florence Jackson. Fay Ollerton Symposium, 1935. KYC.

Payne, George Q. Fay Ollerton Symposium, 1935. KYC.

Payne, Rosalia Tenney. Interviewed by James Hulett, 1936. KYC.

Perkins, Sarah. Interviewed by James Hulett, 1937. KYC.

Peterson, Matilda. Autobiography, n.d. KYC.

Pima, Arizona, Ward Minutes, 1920-30. LDSCA.

Pingree, Marjorie Cannon. Interviewed by Amy Bentley, 1983. LDSP.

Poll, Richard et al. *Utah's History.* Provo, Utah: Brigham Young University Press, 1978.

"Polygamy in Mexico." Anthony W. Ivins Collection. USHS.

Pomeroy, Reuel Nephi. Interviewed by Jessie L. Embry, 1980. LDSP.

Pond, George S. Interviewed by Leonard Grover, 1980. LDSP.

Pope, Esther Webb. Interviewed by Leonard Grover, 1980. LDSP.

Pratt, Joseph W. Interviewed by Marsha Martin, 1982. LDSP.

Pulsipher, Amy Allen. Interviewed by Tillman Boxell, 1978. LDSP.

Pulsipher, John. Account, n.d. KYC.

Quinn, D. Michael. "LDS Church Authority and New Plural Marriages, 1890-1904." *Dialogue: A Journal of Mormon Thought* 18 (Spring 1985): 9-105

Ralph, Lorraine Farrell. Interviewed by James Hulett, 1938. KYC.

Rasmussen, Emma J. Interviewed by James Hulett, 1937. KYC.

Reeder, Leah Rees, and Margaret Rees White. Interviewed by James Hulett, 1937. KYC.

Reynolds, Alice Louise. Interviewed by James Hulett, 1937. KYC.

Rich, Charles C. Letters. Bancroft.

Richards, Jane Synder. Reminiscences. Bancroft.

Richardson, Ivan R. Interviewed by Leonard Grover, 1979. LDSP.

Richardson, Justin. Interviewed by Leonard Grover, 1981. LDSP.

Rigby, Loretta Merrill. Interviewed by Katherine Cook, 1981. LDSP.

Roberts, Brigham H. *Comprehensive History of the Church of Jesus Christ of Latter-day Saints.* Salt Lake City: Deseret News Press, 1930.

Rogers, Roxey Roskelley. Interviewed by Jessie L. Embry, 1979. LDSP.

Romney, Dennison. Interviewed by Chris Nelson, 1981. LDSP.

Romney, Frank. Interviewed by Jessie L. Embry, 1976. LDSP.

Romney, Keith. Interviewed by Jessie L. Embry, 1981. LDSP.

Romney, Lydia Naegle. Interviewed by James Hulett, 1937. KYC.

Romney, Rulon. Interviewed by Chris Nelson, 1981. LDSP.

Romney, Thomas Cottom. Interviewed by James Hulett, 1937. KYC.

Roskelley, Mary Jane Rigby. Interviewed by James Hulett, 1938. KYC.

Savage, Levi. Journal. Bancroft.

Schoepf, Ollie Marie Allsop. Interviewed by Amy Bentley, 1984. LDSFL.

Scott, Emma McNeil. Interviewed by James Hulett, 1938. KYC.

Sherratt, Mary Diantha Cox. Interviewed by Stevan Martin Hales, 1982. LDSP.

Shipps, Jan. "In the Presence of the Past: Continuity and Change in Twentieth Century Mormonism." *After 150 Years: The Latter-day Saints in Sesquicentennial Perspective.* Thomas G. Alexander and Jessie L. Embry, eds. Provo, Utah: Charles Redd Center for Western Studies, 1983.

Shumway, Phyllis Fillerup. Interviewed by Gary L. Shumway, 1982. LDSP.

Shurtliff, Lyman Andros. Letter. LDSCA.

Simmons, Mary Culmer. Interviewed by James Hulett, 1935. KYC.

Skanchy, L. Oliver. Interviewed by James Hulett, 1937. KYC.

Skousen, Daniel. Family Group Sheets. LDSGL.

Skousen, Ida Walser. Interviewed by Leonard Grover, 1979. LDSP.

Skousen, Karl. Interviewed by Leonard Grover, 1979. LDSP.

Smith, Derryfield N., et al. *Silas Derryfield Smith.* Mesa: n.p., 1970.

Smith, James E., and Phillip R. Kunz. "Polygamy and Fertility in Nineteentl Century America." *Population Studies* 30 (1976): 465-79.

Smith, Joseph F. "A Mormon Polygamous Family as Viewed by One of its Thirc Generation." BYU Psychology 297, n.d. KYC.

Smith-Rosenberg, Carroll. "The Female World of Love and Ritual Relations Between Women in Nineteenth-Century America." *The American Family in Social-Historical Perspective.* Michael Gordon, ed. New York: St. Martin's Press, 1978.

Snarr, Daniel Hammer. Family Group Sheets. LDSGL.

Snow, Arthur E. Interviewed by James Hulett, 1937. KYC.

Stark, Henry. Interviewed by Amy Bentley, 1983. LDSP.

Statutes of Canada, 1890, 53 Vic., c. 37.

Stout, Abraham. Interviewed by Tillman Boxell, 1978. LDSP.

Stout, Franklin Lyman. Interviewed by Stevan Martin Hales, 1982. LDSP.

Stout, Hosea. Journal. KYC.

Stout, Mary Viola Allred. Interviewed by Amy Bentley, 1983. LDSP.

Stowell, Brigham. Family Group Sheets. LDSGL.

Stowell, Wallace. Interviewed by Jessie L. Embry, 1982. LDSP.

Stutz, Mildred Newton. Interviewed by Jessie L. Embry, 1982. LDSP

Sudweeks, Rinda Bentley. Interviewed by Jessie L. Embry, 1976. LDSP.

Taag, Melvin J. "The Life of Edward James Wood: Church Patriot," Master's Thesis, Brigham Young University, 1959.

Tanner, Annie Clark. *A Mormon Mother.* Salt Lake City: University of Utah Library Tanner Trust Fund, 1976.

Tanner, George S. Interviewed by Jessie L. Embry, 1976. LDSP.

Taylor, Brighamina Christensen. Letters. LDSCA.

Taylor, Frederick W. Interviewed by James Hulett, 1937. KYC.

Taylor, Hazel Richardson. Interviewed by Ivan Carbine, 1957. LDSP.

Taylor, LaVetta Cluff Lunt. Interviewed by Stevan Martin Hales, 1982. LDSP.

Terry, George W. Journal. LDSCA.

Thatcher, Naomi Selman. Interviewed by Marsha Martin, 1983. LDSFL.

Thatcher, Ruth Cannon. Interviewed by Leonard Grover, 1980. LDSP.

Thomas, Katherine Cannon. Interviewed by Leonard Grover, 1980. LDSP.

Thomas, Winnifred Newton. Interviewed by Jessie L. Embry, 1982. LDSP.

Thomson, Seneth Hyer. Interviewed by Leonard Grover, 1980. LDSP.

Troutman, Larry. Interviewed by Alan Cherry, 1985. LDS Afro-American.

Turley, Clarence. Interviewed by Gary L. Shumway, 1981. LDSP.

Turley, Wilma Fillerup. Interviewed by Rochelle Fairbourn, 1982. LDSP.

Vance, Josephine Spillsbury. Interviewed by Fay Ollerton, 1935. KYC.

Vance, Lucy Fryer. Interviewed by Jessie L. Embry, 1982. LDSP.

Van Wagoner, Richard S. *Mormon Polygamy: A History.* Salt Lake City: Signature Books, 1986.

Walser, Asenath Skousen. Interviewed by Jessie L. Embry, 1976. LDSP.

Walser, John Jacob. Interviewed by James Hulett, 1935. LDSP.

Walser, William. Interviewed by Jessie L. Embry, 1976. LDSP.

Ware, Helen. "Polygyny: Women's Views in a Transitional Society, Nigeria, 1975." *Journal of Marriage and the Family* 41 (1979): 185-95.

Warnick, Reed W. Interviewed by Marsha Martin, 1983. LDSFL.

Washburn, Wasel Black. Interviewed by Amy Bentley, 1983. LDSP.

Watkins, Helen Tanner. Interviewed by Stevan Martin Hales, 1982. LDSP.

Watkins, Laura Andersen. Interviewed by Leonard Grover, 1980. LDSP.

Watson, William, and Mrs. Orson Smith. Interviewed by James Hulett, 1937. KYC.

Webb, Eva C. "The Other Mother." *Heart Throbs of the West.* Kate B. Carter, ed. 12 vols. Salt Lake City: Daughters of the Utah Pioneers, 1947. 1:281-99.

Weight, Kenneth E. Interviewed by Marsha Martin, 1983. LDSFL.

Wells, Merle W. *Anti-Mormonism in Idaho, 1872-92*. Provo, Utah: Brigham Young University, 1978.

Welter, Barbara. "The Cult of True Womanhood, 1820-1860." *The American Family in Socio-Historical Perspective*. Michael Gordon, ed. New York: St. Martin's Press, 1978.

Westphal, Joyce. Conversation with author, 1986.

Whatcott, Esther Phelps. Interviewed by Rochelle Fairbourn, 1982. LDSP.

Whetten, Glen. Interviewed by Jessie L. Embry, 1981. LDSP.

White, Charles. Observations by an unidentified researcher, 1935. KYC.

Whitehead, Irene Larsen. Interviewed by Marsha Martin, 1983. LDSFL.

Whiting, Beatrice B. "Changing Life Styles in Kenya." *Daedalus* 106 (Spring 1977): 208-25.

Whitmer, Henry Moroni. Interviewed by Jessie L. Embry, 1982. LDSFL.

Whitmer, Mabel Moody. Interviewed by Jessie L. Embry, 1980. LDSFL.

Wilcox, George Albert. Interviewed by James Hulett, 1937. KYC.

Willey, Dorothy Geneve Young. "Childhood Experiences in Mormon Polygamous Families at the Turn of the Century." Master's Thesis, Utah State University, 1983.

Williams, Fenton L. Interviewed by Stevan Martin Hales, 1981. LDSFL.

Wilson, J. W. Interviewed by Fay Ollerton, 1935. KYC.

Winsor, Walter John. Life Story. KYC.

Wood, Wallace. Interviewed by Jessie L. Embry, 1980. LDSP.

Woods, Jane Flake. Interviewed by James Hulett, n.d. KYC.

Wright, Conover. Interviewed by James Hulett, 1938. KYC.

Wright, E. W. Interviewed by James Hulett, 1937. KYC.

Wyatt, James L. Interviewed by Jessie L. Embry, 1976. LDSP.

Wyatt, John Horsecroft. Family Group Sheets. LDSGL.

Wyatt, William L. Interviewed by Jessie L. Embry, 1976. LDSP.

Young, Kimball. *Isn't One Wife Enough?* New York: Henry Holt and Co., 1954.

Index